T0318204

Strategic Management of Diversity in the Workplace

Strategic Management of Diversity in the Workplace discusses the strategic management of ethnic and cultural diversity by taking particular examples from Australia, Canada, the United Kingdom and the United States of America, in order to determine the salient benefits that organisations could derive when ethnic and cultural differences are seen as opportunities, not as problems, and are viewed as benefits rather than threats.

Strategic Management of Diversity in the Workplace provides a clear demonstration of the benefits, conflicts and challenges faced by organisations. The renewed interest in multiculturalism in academic and policy circles revives the debate about issues related to the management of ethnic diversity in society at large and in specific settings, such as corporate Australia. This book specifically focuses on this problematic area by aiming to explore the practice of management and application of multiculturalism in the workplace. This book seeks to examine post-multiculturalism in Australia and explore whether it has affected the ways in which corporate Australia deals with issues of diversity and the lessons learned here are ones that apply across the business world.

Strategic Management of Diversity in the Workplace would be of interest for researchers, academics, undergraduate and postgraduate business degrees students in the fields of Strategic Human Resources Management, Cross-Cultural Management, Managing Workplace Training and Managing and Leading People.

Emile Chidiac is Adjunct Associate Professor at Edith Cowan University in Western Australia. His research focuses on strengths and weaknesses of organisations, immigration, diversity, diversity management, multiculturalism, citizenship and Australian Constitutional Law. He is currently doing his PhD in Law at Macquarie University.

Routledge Research in Employment Relations

Series editors:
Rick Delbridge and Edmund Heery
Cardiff Business School, UK

Aspects of the employment relationship are central to numerous courses at both undergraduate and postgraduate level.

Drawing from insights from industrial relations, human resource management and industrial sociology, this series provides an alternative source of research-based materials and texts, reviewing key developments in employment research.

Books published in this series are works of high academic merit, drawn from a wide range of academic studies in the social sciences.

Employment Relations under Coalition Government
The UK Experience, 2010–2015
Edited by Steve Williams and Peter Scott

Work-Life Balance in Times of Recession, Austerity and Beyond
Edited by Suzan Lewis, Deirdre Anderson, Clare Lyonette, Nicola Payne and Stephen Wood

Trade Unions and Arab Revolutions
The Tunisian Case of UGTT
Hèla Yousfi

A New Theory of Industrial Relations
People, Markets and Organizations after Neoliberalism
Conor Cradden

Strategic Management of Diversity in the Workplace
A Comparative Study of the United States, Canada, United Kingdom and Australia
Emile Chidiac

For a full list of titles in this series, please visit www.routledge.com

Strategic Management of Diversity in the Workplace

A Comparative Study of the United States, Canada, United Kingdom and Australia

Emile Chidiac

Routledge
Taylor & Francis Group

LONDON AND NEW YORK

First published 2018 by Routledge

2 Park Square, Milton Park, Abingdon, Oxon, OX14 4RN

605 Third Avenue, New York, NY 10017

Routledge is an imprint of the Taylor & Francis Group, an informa business

First issued in paperback 2020

Library of Congress Cataloging-in-Publication Data
A catalog record for this book has been requested

ISBN: 978-1-138-72047-3 (hbk)
ISBN: 978-0-367-73424-4 (pbk)

Typeset in Sabon
by Apex CoVantage, LLC

Contents

List of Tables   vii
List of Figures   viii
List of Abbreviations   ix
Author's Biography   x
Introduction   xi

1   Multiculturalism   1
    Multiculturalism(s): A Short Introduction 1
    Multiculturalism in the US 6
    Multiculturalism in Canada 11
    Multiculturalism in the UK 18
    Multiculturalism in Australia 24
    References 34

2   Diversity in the Workforce: Facts and Figures   40
    Diversity in the US Workforce 40
    Diversity in the Canadian Workforce 44
    Diversity in the UK Workforce 48
    Diversity in the Australian Workforce 49
    References 51

3   Strategic Management of Diversity: Benefits
    and Challenges   54
    Strategic Management of Diversity 54
    Benefits of Strategic Management of Diversity 63
    Challenges of Strategic Management of Diversity 68
    Implementation of Diversity Programs 72
    References 75

4   **Diversity Management in the US, Canada, the UK
      and Australia: Legal and Political Analysis**   80
      *Diversity Management in the US: Political
          and Legal Analysis 80*
      *Diversity Management in Canada: Political
          and Legal Analysis 94*
      *Diversity Management in the UK: Political
          and Legal Analysis 100*
      *Diversity Management in Australia: Political
          and Legal Analysis 105*
      References 117

5   **Diversity Management in Practice**   123
      *The Practice of Strategic Management of Diversity
          in the US: A Review of Case Studies 123*
      *The Practice of Strategic Management of Diversity
          in Canada 131*
      *The Practice of Strategic Management of Diversity
          in the UK 134*
      *The Practice of Strategic Management of Diversity
          in Australia 136*
      References 149

     Conclusion   153

     Index   167

Tables

1.1	Foreign-born Population as a Proportion of the Total Population in G8 Countries and Australia	3
1.2	US Population by Race and Ethnicity (%)	7
1.3	Sources of Immigration to the US by Era	9
1.4	Population by Ethnic Origin in Canada, 2016	14
1.5	Immigrant Population by Place of Birth and Period of Immigration, 2006	14
1.6	Visible Minority Population in Canada, 2011	15
1.7	Generation Status of Visible Minority Population in Canada, 2016	15
1.8	Historical Population Statistics in the UK	19
1.9	Ethnicity of the Non-UK-born Population by Period of Arrival, England and Wales, 2011	20
1.10	Australian Historical Population Statistics	25
1.11	Statistics of a Culturally and Linguistically Diverse Australia	26
2.1	Occupation Distribution of Recently Arrived Immigrants in the US	41
2.2	Employment Status of the US Civilian Non-institutional Population by Age and Race, 2016	43
2.3	Participation, Employment and Unemployment Rates by Racialised Groups in Canada, 2006	45
2.4	Diversity and Inclusion Staff Size by Employer Size	47
3.1	Differences between Principles of Equal Opportunity and Diversity Management	61
4.1	Major US Legislation Related to Workplace Discrimination	82
4.2	Major Canadian Legislation Related to Workplace Discrimination	96
4.3	Major UK Legislation Related to Workplace Discrimination	103
4.4	Major Australian Legislation Related to Workplace Discrimination	108
5.1	2017 Top 50 Companies for Diversity	129
5.2	Benefits of Diversity Management in Australia	141
C.1	Major Legislative Responses to the Changing Identifications of Diversity in the US, Canada, the UK and Australia	161

Figures

1.1   SWOT Analysis of Multiculturalism   4
1.2   Changing Identifications of Diversity in Australia   29

Abbreviations

AA	Affirmative Action
AAA	*Affirmative Action Act*
ABS	Australian Bureau of Statistics
ADEA	*Age Discrimination in Employment Act*
APS	Australian Public Service
BAME	Black, Asian and Minority Ethnic
BME	Black and Minority Ethnic
CALD	Culturally and Linguistically Diverse
CCRF	*Canadian Charter of Rights and Freedoms*
CEO	Chief Executive Officer
CSR	Corporate Social Responsibility
EEA	*Employment Equity Act*
EEO	Equal Employment Opportunity
EEOC	Equal Employment Opportunity Commission
EOWWA	*Equal Opportunity for Women in the Workplace Act*
EU	European Union
FA	Framework for Action
HRM	Human Resource Management
LGBT	Lesbian, Gay, Bisexual and Transgender
NHS	National Health Service
OPS	Ontario Public Service
OPSDO	Ontario Public Service Diversity Office
RBC	Royal Bank of Canada
SWOT	Strengths, Weaknesses, Opportunities and Threats
UK	United Kingdom
UN	United Nations
UNESCO	United Nations Educational, Scientific and Cultural Organization
US	United States
WERS	Workplace Employment Relations Survey
WGEA	*Workplace Gender Equality Act*

Author's Biography

Emile Chidiac is Adjunct Associate Professor at Edith Cowan University in Western Australia. His research focuses on cultural diversity, multiculturalism, strategic management of diversity in the workplace, strengths and weaknesses of organisations. He carried out intensive research on acquisition, revocation and protection of citizenship and Australian Constitutional Law. He has contributed to the Australian Legal Dictionary published by Butterworths.

Dr Chidiac is a Qualified Accountant, Certified Internal Auditor, a Chartered Secretary, an Accredited Interpreter and Translator, a Chartered Linguist and a Justice of the Peace. He practised accountancy, immigration law, interpreting and translation, and worked as a journalist and broadcaster. He is active in the community promoting cultural awareness, diversity and multiculturalism. Music and poetry are his two passions. He is a classically trained Lutenist and writes poetry in Arabic, English and French.

Emile Chidiac holds a Doctorate in Business Administration (DBA) from Southern Cross University, a Master of Arts (MA) (Honours) in Linguistics from the University of Western Sydney, a Diploma in Company Directors from the University of New England, a Graduate Certificate in Australian Migration Law and Practice from Victoria University, Graduate Diploma in Interpreting and Translation, Final Diploma in Interpreting and Translation, from the Chartered Institute of Linguists in London, and Graduate Diploma in Accountancy from International College. He is currently doing his PhD in Law at Macquarie University.

Dr Chidiac's professional association memberships include:

- Foundation Fellow of the Australian Institute of Company Directors
- Fellow of the Australian Taxation and Management Accountants in Australia
- Associate Fellow of the Institute of Managers and Leaders
- Associate Member of the Australian Institute of Credit Management
- Member of the Governance Institute of Australia
- Member of the Australian Human Resources Institute
- Chartered Member of the Chartered Institute of Linguists in London
- Member of the Institute of Internal Auditors in Australia

Introduction

This book offers a comparative view of the diversity management concerns facing certain nations, as well as the various dimensions of diversity, by illustrating a comparative study of multiculturalism and diversity management in four English-speaking countries: Australia, Canada, the United Kingdom (UK) and the United States (US). It describes the levels of segregation in each country, and the various ethnic minority groups. The various types of diversity management highlight the benefits of a diverse workforce and indicate how to gain advantage from the various skills of people from different ethnic and cultural backgrounds. Diversity management as a concept has been subject to a heated discussion, being called 'just another HR [human resources] fad' and 'just another name for EEO' (Nankervis et al. 2011, 193). This book focuses on globalisation and the benefits of having skilled immigrants in the workplace, which facilitate entry to new markets and customer bases. The various skills brought by the diverse workforce, especially in terms of language, prove to be of great competitive advantage to organisations seeking business expansion.

Many workers have experienced discrimination in the workplace. Some individuals have missed opportunities, promotions and challenges, or have experienced racism because of being members of particular ethnic minority groups. This discrimination derives from fear of the so-called 'others' who join the workforce with cultural differences, which creates a gap between 'us' and 'them', irrespective of the advantages of their differences. Individuals must endeavour to learn from each other and be aware of the richness of other cultures and the benefits they have to offer. These cultural differences can be converted into advantages, while challenges can become opportunities, if members of the dominant and mainstream group are willing to learn and accept others. The unknown will remain surrounded by ambiguity and fear until it is revealed to people who are genuinely willing to accept the explanation and reality. However, 'one cannot get change without changing' (Myers 2011, 13), and some people fear change, even though it may be for the best. It is worth remembering the motto of the French Revolution: '*liberté, égalité, fraternité*'—liberty, equality, fraternity. These three simple words denote deep meanings of sociological, logical and philosophical symbols awaiting realisation to embrace all human beings who are willing to participate in establishing a better world for harmony and peace.

In accordance with international law, the concept of minority was used in many international treaties between the seventeenth and nineteenth centuries. In the seventeenth century, the minority referred to in such treaties was that of 'religious minorities'. Under the mandate of the League of Nations, the formula of 'racial, linguistic and religious minorities' (League of Nations 1929) was stated in official documents such as the Treaty of Versailles (Housden 2014) to incorporate all possible references. After World War II, the word 'racial' was substituted by 'ethnic', and the United Nations (UN) subsequently commenced using the formula of 'ethnic, linguistic and religious minorities' (Ruiz Vieytez 2014, 196). Additionally, the concept of 'national minority' was introduced in the European Convention on Human Rights in 1950, and the UN Assembly adopted a *Declaration on the Rights of Persons Belonging to National or Ethnic, Religious and Linguistic Minorities* on 18 December 1992 (Ruiz Vieytez 2014).

In the twenty-first century, the increasing movement of people across borders as refugees, migrants and job seekers has indeed made the world a global village. Multiculturalism has become incorporated as a social policy by countries such as Australia, Canada, the UK and the US, which has led to inevitable cultural and ethnic diversity in the populations of these countries. This has led to a culturally diverse workforce, caused by the influx of immigrants of different cultural backgrounds seeking employment in their adopted countries. These newcomers include skilled individuals who can contribute to their employing organisations if used to their full potential and managed well. In addition, organisations that implement diversity policies to appreciate this diverse workforce can see a wide range of benefits for the organisation and its customers.

Immigration has undoubtedly had a great effect on the workforce because of the influx of immigrants seeking employment in various organisations. Skilled immigrants are more successful in finding work than unskilled immigrants, yet, with appropriate training and guidance by management, even unskilled immigrants are able to increase productivity. Skills, experiences and prior learning brought into the workforce by immigrants are human assets from which organisations can benefit if employees are used to their full potential and managed well (Chidiac 2015).

International migration has increased recently, and is now a normal feature of contemporary societies. A central concern for policy makers and government agents is to investigate the extent to which migrants have assimilated into the culture to which they have relocated. Migrants were expected to assimilate to the new culture, but they became minorities and outsiders (O'Reilly 2016). In this context, one of the key issues is the concept of multiculturalism. All nations and societies are multicultural to some degree. Importantly, multiculturalism is not just about culture, but about civic aspiration. In his essay on identity, philosopher Charles Taylor stated that the novelty of multiculturalism lies in its demand of two different ideas of equality. The first idea is of equal dignity, which demonstrates that every citizen should enjoy the same rights and immunities. The second idea is of equal recognition, which calls for recognition of 'the unique identity of this individual or group, their distinctiveness from everyone else' (Soutphommasane 2012, 49–50).

Until recently, Australia, Canada and the US were considered countries dominated by white men. However, in seeking continent-wide domination, the three countries' governments decided to import immigrants to build their dominated nations. These three nations experienced labour shortages because indigenous people were few in number and further reduced because of the violence they experienced through colonial contact and because of disease. These settler societies eventually attracted more immigrants, became self-sustaining colonies and ultimately formed federations. Unlike Australia, Canada and the US were driven by a 'whites-only' nationalism. However, non-British immigrants managed to assimilate, and British North America gradually became English Canada. Eventually, both Canada and the US became cultural melting pots, but their governments followed an Anglo-conformism policy, rather than multiculturalism (Vickers and Isaac 2012).

Many societies are considered multicultural because they have people from diverse cultural backgrounds who have been accepted and approved within a single society, and gained public recognition and support. Multicultural policies started in the 1970s in democratic countries, such as Australia, Canada, the US and parts of Western Europe, including the UK and the Netherlands. However, the new waves of immigrants were perceived to be too 'different' to easily assimilate, which became a major problem for some policy makers, while others welcomed it. The British Home Secretary, Roy Jenkins, stated in 1966:

> Integration is perhaps rather a loose word. I do not regard as meaning the loss, by immigrants, of their own national characteristics and culture. I do not think that we need in this country a 'melting pot', which will turn everybody out in a common mould, as one of a series of carbon copies of someone's misplaced vision of the stereotypical Englishman. I . . . define integration, therefore, not as a flattening process of elimination, but as equal opportunity, accompanied by cultural diversity, in an atmosphere of mutual tolerance.
>
> (Cantle 2015, 83)

Multiculturalism as a policy focuses on the measures taken to broaden the national identity to ensure that it encompasses broad cultural differences. If all societies are multicultural to some degree, then the reverse is also correct—that all nations require a unifying principle that is distinct and applicable to the specific nation, and the choice of conforming to this principle is a measure of inclusion or exclusion. This unifying principle must be a means to distinguish the nation and all its members as having a common part of their identity, which can be cultural characteristics, including a common language or religious tradition. The degree to which a nation is deemed to be multicultural depends on the inclusiveness of this unifying principle. It seems that the more open the unifying principles of a nation, the more inclusive and multicultural the nation will be (Asari, Halikiopoulou and Mock 2008).

The various waves of immigration in Australia, Canada, the UK and the US had a significant effect on the workforce, bringing both skilled and unskilled immigrants. The shortage of labour and need for the newcomers to seek employment in their newly adopted countries to support their families and improve their living conditions increasingly affected the workforce in the migration countries. Many organisations realised that immigrants brought with them skills such as languages, experience and knowledge of foreign markets. Organisations soon recognised that immigrants, if given the opportunities and managed well, would increase productivity and contribute greatly to the organisation. Thus, a diverse workforce is a positive business approach that maximises the talent pool in the workplace, and improves the corporate image by making organisations more attractive to job seekers. Further, diversity decreases absenteeism and turnover, and enhances organisational reputation (Ohemeng and McGrandle 2015).

The increase in workforce diversity is attributable to various factors, including globalisation, anti-discrimination legislation and changes in demographics. Despite its constant presence, diversity remains difficult to define because it deals with both visible and invisible characteristics, and is subjective because it is created by individuals who view others either as similar or dissimilar to themselves. The terms 'diversity' and 'multiculturalism' are used interchangeably, yet there are differences between them. Diversity is defined as the differences between two people, such as differences in race, gender, sexual orientation, religion, background and socio-economic status. From a human resource management (HRM) perspective, diversity refers to policies designed to meet government compliance standards. Multiculturalism goes beyond diversity to concentrate on inclusiveness, understanding and respect. Diversity focuses on the 'otherness' of differences between individuals, with the aim of ensuring that, through policies, everyone is treated the same. However, while this is legally the proper way to act, multiculturalism deals with a system of advantages on the basis of race, gender and sexual orientation. Given this background, diversity management has many aims:

(1) understanding cultural differences, (2) recognizing the importance of diversity, (3) preventing discrimination against disadvantaged groups (i.e., women and minorities), (4) encouraging cultural interactions across gender and race, and (5) enhancing cultural development and leadership practices in the organisation.

(Kim and Park 2017, 2)

Organisations that recognise employees' skills and talents and give them the opportunity to perform to their potential will be rich in human capital and benefit from the differences that these employees bring to the workforce. Employees are the best assets to organisations, and, if properly managed, can produce numerous benefits for both employees and the workplace. The onus is on management to implement a diversity management program that is capable of attracting individuals from different cultural backgrounds, using their skills and talents to improve the bottom-line figure, and expanding their businesses by gaining access to global markets. It is essential to create awareness in the workplace that enables employees to learn from one another, thereby uniting all employees under the umbrella of fair treatment and justice, without fear or favour.

Strategic management of ethnic and cultural diversity in the workplace has received little attention in academic research, despite growing interest in the professional world in this complex and critical aspect of managing human capital, which reveals the importance and controversy of the solutions proposed to manage diversity (Dass and Parker 1999). The term 'diversity management' is described as being multifaceted and fluid, and has been challenged and criticised by scholars for its wide and inconsistent meaning (Baker and Kelan 2015). 'Management of diversity' conveys conscious strategies of social control, and a technical or administrative 'problem' to be 'solved' by organising the diverse workforce. However, diversity is not a problem, but an asset of significant value. The term 'celebration' of diversity is inadequate to denote the reaction of societies towards social diversity. 'Cultural competence' is more desirable as a concept of individuals and of organisations, yet loses its focus when applied to large heterogeneous groups, including companies, communities and societies. Other terms such as 'immigrant settlement', 'multiculturalism' and 'anti-racism' are not useful definitions, which leaves 'management of diversity' as the term to understand (Andrew 2007).

Multicultural policies form part of diversity management strategies in Australia and Canada, while they are considered part of 'bottom-up' anti-racism coalition building in the US. In the 1960s, the racist immigration policies were abolished by these three governments because of pressure imposed by the UN. Nevertheless, despite the non-racist immigration policies, the white descendants of Europeans and British settlers in Australia remained in charge of immigration policy. While Australia and Canada had a high level of authorised immigrants, the number was much lower in the US, notwithstanding the high rates in the previous century. Both Australia and Canada have experienced boatloads of unauthorised immigrants attempting to gain entry by landing on their shores (Vickers and Isaac 2012). When the overtly racist policies in Australia and Canada were ended to avoid international sanctions (Vickers and Isaac 2012), immigration became important following the failure of policies of assimilation and exclusion such as White Australia immigration policy. International pressure had little influence on the US because of its status as a superpower (Vickers and Isaac 2012).

While corporate policies related to diversity have been largely driven by legislation, the changing demographics of immigration in countries such as Australia and Canada, alongside the promotion of globalisation, have taken diversity to a level that requires a response involving more than just legislative compliance. Today, corporations are employing people from various ethnic backgrounds to represent the diversity of society and cater to the needs of their ethnically diverse customer base (Chidiac 2015). In terms of the challenges and benefits of diversity management, management of organisations appreciates a diverse workforce and sees a wide range of benefits for the organisation and its customers. Diversity management policies enable organisations to benefit from the diverse workforce, which has the potential to increase productivity, open up business networks and facilitate access to overseas markets. By maximising the productivity and efficiency of the diverse workforce, and recognising the skills and talents of employees, organisations can benefit from cultural diversity. Employees are the most valuable asset of any organisation, and diversity enables employees of various backgrounds to offer their skills and human resources, which can be used to enter the global marketplace. Thus, a diverse workforce is viewed as a competitive advantage to broaden the business scope of an organisation. According to Trudeau (2015), diversity is not a challenge to be overcome or a difficulty to be tolerated, but a tremendous source of strength recognised by Canadians.

This book considers multiculturalism and management of diversity in the workplace in the US, the UK, Canada and Australia, with some case studies to reflect on the outcomes and shared experiences in various settings. Recognising the full potential of employees from diverse backgrounds may enhance equity in the workplace and encourage employees to contribute more to different dimensions of work. The significance of this book lies in the fact that the countries examined—Australia, Canada, the UK and the US—are ethnically and culturally diverse countries. By examining the policies and practices of organisations in these countries to identify diversity issues related to race and ethnicity, a better understanding will be obtained to enable better strategic management of ethnic diversity in the workplace. Highlighting the importance of this issue, Jackson and Ruderman (1999) claimed that interactions with members of other cultures lead to the development of a variety of skills, including learning the foreign languages used by the different groups. At the organisational level, most companies expect their workers with diverse backgrounds to conform to the policies and principles of the majority in the workplace. Therefore, it is essential to investigate the process of acculturation, how organisations manage a multicultural workplace and how managers turn rhetoric into reality through management practices.

While this book has essentially been written for students, academics and research scholars, diversity practitioners may also benefit from considering the various issues and challenges faced by organisations when managing diversity in the workplace. It is essential for students and academics to learn about management of diversity in other countries, and how diversity is viewed by various organisations. Multiculturalism is reflected in many facets, depending on the diversity of the workforce (which has been greatly affected by waves of migration) and the degree of acceptance by the mainstream group. Globalisation and migration have played a key role in the change that led to diverse workforces in organisations. However, this change has not occurred without fear, rejection and suspicion—fear of the unknown, rejection of any change to existing policies and suspicion of anything new. Changing policies in the workplace requires knowledge, conviction and good management by the organisational hierarchy to recognise the benefits of immigrants and their skills and experiences. Management should know how to convert challenges into opportunities that will yield benefits to the organisation and its customers, especially via the entrance of new markets. Organisations have acknowledged that employees are the most valuable assets in the workplace, and any attempt to deviate from this notion represents a lost opportunity (Chidiac 2015).

Further, after implementing a diversity policy, it is important for organisations to remain vigilant because they must invest great effort to adopt, implement and monitor such policies. Great improvements in productivity have been experienced by some organisations after introducing a diversity policy in the workplace. Employees' interactions are imperative at work because of the beneficial outcomes arising from interactions between employees and management, and among employees themselves (Chidiac 2015).

There are many terms defining diversity in various countries, as used in different contexts and viewed by many organisations. This book presents the state of cultural diversity in four English-speaking countries: Australia, Canada, the UK and the US. Diversity in these countries is reviewed, with different results in the management of diversity in the workplace. This study focuses on the challenges and benefits arising from a diverse workforce, and considers how to convert the challenges into opportunities and to overcome fear of change when implementing diversity policies. It is believed that all four countries would benefit from effective management of diversity in the workplace, based on the understanding that diversity goes beyond skin colour and ethnicity. However, with respect to diversity management, I argue that most organisations do little more than comply with government diversity-related legislation, rather than implementing their own appropriate diversity policy.

Additionally, diversity includes various differences in the workplace that must be considered when managing diversity. While equal employment opportunity (EEO) deals with eliminating discrimination from the workplace, managing diversity views differences as a source of strength and competition. Diversity encompasses visible and non-visible differences that lead to productivity, and where employees feel valued and have their skills appropriately used (Kandola and Fullerton 1998). Diversity management involves managing differences in the workplace, which can improve performance in the organisation. Diversity management is also referred to as a management philosophy that recognises and values heterogeneity in the organisation, with the intention to enhance performance (Groutsis, Ng and Ozturk 2014).

The increase in international migration has led Australia, Canada, the UK and the US to manage and accommodate immigrants and their conflicting cultural differences. Immigrants come with cultural differences and skills, and seek employment in various organisations in accordance with their levels of education, languages, experiences and talents. These newcomers tend to fill the demand of labour shortages in the receiving country by offering their human resources to organisations. However, most immigrants face discrimination in the workplace because of fear, ignorance or unawareness of different cultures by the dominant mainstream group. Thus, the onus is on the management of organisations to implement a diversity policy to manage the diverse workforce effectively, and to ensure that employees are valued and recognised to reap the benefits of the diverse workforce.

Overview of Chapters

Each chapter in this book addresses a core topic and reflects relevant issues pertaining to the various topics discussed in this book.

Chapter 1, titled 'Multiculturalism', explains the establishment of British imperial policy, and the influence of the 'White Australia' policy that encouraged newcomers to Australia to assimilate. This chapter discusses Australia's influx of immigration and how this influx is attributed to the replacement of the White Australia policy, the introduction of multiculturalism in Australia in 1973, and the change of Australia from an Anglo-Celtic to multicultural nation. Further, this chapter discusses immigrants and their effect on Australia, and, how, according to Clyne (2008), social inclusion became relevant to migrants and refugees. This chapter considers Australia's waves of immigrants since 1788 and how Australia developed into a multicultural society—with a focus on how social, cultural and demographic changes in Australia continue to affect the workforce. Multiculturalism has been subject to criticisms worldwide, and Australia is not immune. The focus in this chapter is on the diverse opinions of the opponents and proponents of multiculturalism, and the effect of multiculturalism on organisational practices related to the management of diversity. Eventually, this chapter also considers the focus on immigration that had an impact on diverse workforce.

Multiculturalism became the official policy in Canada in 1971, and consequently became popular in the UK and the US. Chapter 1 also discusses the different legal definitions of multiculturalism, and how they are governed in Australia, Canada, the UK and the US, with a common factor based on the increasing foreign-born population in these countries. In the UK, the rise of Islamist extremism and the race riots in 1958 were attributed to multiculturalism, while Muslim people were not as much disturbed in the US until the terrorist attacks on 11 September 2001. Additionally, the UK was the first country to reject the 'assimilation' of immigrants, claiming that multiculturalism is leading to social divisions, with some blame on international terrorism. Among the other countries, multiculturalism remains the strongest in Canada, where the most ethnically diverse government exists.

Chapter 2, titled 'Diversity in the Workforce—Facts and Figures', explores the effect of globalisation, migration and social justice on the diverse workforce, and how implemented policies help the underrepresented groups. It discusses the effect of globalisation, migration and social justice on the representation of diverse groups in organisations. Canada was the pioneering country to adopt a multicultural policy and promote cultural heritage, rather than assimilation. While there is no legislative obligation for Australian organisations to adopt a diversity policy, Canadian organisations tend to have strong commitment to diversity, with only a minority of organisations implementing a compliance culture. Canada is made strong through diversity, inclusion and understanding that economic growth depends on newcomers to maintain a certain standard of living. In the UK, organisations are giving diversity some consideration to ensure the fair representation of ethnic minorities in both the public and private sectors. In addition, the diverse labour market in the UK is a result of ethnic minorities' participation. While equality legislation is enforced in the public sector, it is voluntary in the private sector. Australia, as a multicultural nation, has developed a diverse workforce and raises the question of whether the increasing diversity in the workplace is managed well. The need for diversity management is becoming an issue that must be addressed because of globalisation and its importance in relation to global markets. While immigration has an effect on the workforce, its experiences are yet to be investigated in Australian organisations. In the US, immigrants brought their cultures to the country, thereby increasing the ethnic diversity. This chapter explores the extent to which the implemented policies seem to have helped the underrepresentation of certain groups in the workforce because of the natural reflection of diversity in the US workforce. This chapter explores the claim that organisations can benefit from demographic diversity in the US workplace.

Chapter 3, titled 'Strategic Management of Diversity—Benefits and Challenges', deals with the strategic management of diversity in the workplace, and how to take advantage of employees' skills and abilities in organisations by focusing on the need to implement training to improve awareness of diversity and management. Further, the strategic management of diversity should focus on taking full advantage of employees' skills and abilities in the organisation, emphasising employee differences and ignoring similarities, as well as the 'hearable difference'—one of the issues upon which the researcher focuses. Benefits and challenges emanate from diversity management in the workplace, the implementation of diversity policy, and the ways different cultural values and beliefs are managed by organisations and attract the best employees. Different cultural values, beliefs and views create a competitive advantage in a diverse workforce by enabling employees to contribute to their full potential and subsequently benefit both employers and employees. Management has realised that employees' cultural differences constitute strength for the organisation, which is a great benefit that can improve business. Organisations with a diverse workforce tend to have communication-related problems caused by issues such as language barriers, prejudice and derogatory comments. Additionally, a challenge lies in the type of diversity climate provided in organisations.

Chapter 4, titled 'Diversity Management in the US, Canada, the UK and Australia—Legal and Political Analysis', evaluates the development of legislations related to employment, and the ability of employees to sue if they experience discrimination in the workplace. The focus is on equality and diversity in larger private organisations, and the way affirmative action (AA)/EEO policies focused on underrepresented groups and newcomers in the US, Canadian, British and Australian workforces. This chapter discusses the differences in equity legislation in the public and private sectors of these countries, together with diversity, how adaptation of diversity is taken in organisations, the challenges arising out of the cultural differences and demographic changes in their workforces. AA and EEO were introduced in the 1970s in the US to prevent discrimination in employment, while the Equal Employment Opportunity Commission (EEOC) was established to deal with claims and minor compliance. In Canada, legally speaking, the federal *Employment Equity Act (EEA)*, which is similar to AA in the US, was passed in 1986 to improve labour force diversity. Diversity management in Canada considers the shortage of skilled labour and ways to enter ethnic markets. In the UK, the *Equal Pay Act 1970* was introduced to ensure equal pay and working conditions between men and women, which was superseded by the *Equality Act 2010*. While there was no legislation passed in Australia between 1945 and 1970, legislative responses to diversity-related issues started to emerge with the enactment of the *Racial Discrimination Act* in 1975. The landmark legislative development in Australia was the establishment of the Equal Opportunity Commission and enactment of the *Affirmative Action Act* in 1986. Currently, the Australian Acts that deal with diversity-related issues encompass racial, age, sex and disability discrimination, as well as fair work and gender equality in the workplace.

Chapter 5, titled 'Diversity Management in Practice', focuses on the way that public and private organisations manage diverse workforces in Australia, Canada, the UK and the US. It discusses how diversity improves productivity and increases profits when multiculturalism is promoted in an organisation. Creating an environment where people are appreciated and valued for their differences, strengths and talents, as well as including women and minorities, can advance business opportunities. Moreover, cultural diversity is needed in business to improve communication among employees in the workplace. Employees are the greatest asset in an organisation, and effective management of diversity in the workplace helps organisations use their human resources and compete effectively. This chapter highlights the evidence of strong commitment to diversity by various organisations, as well as equality legislation and the developments that have occurred in the legal framework.

References

Andrew, Caroline. 2007. 'City and Cityscapes in Canada: The Politics and Culture of Canadian Urban Diversity'. In *Managing Diversity: Practices of Citizenship*, edited by Nicholas Brown and Linda Cardinal, 115–36. Ottawa: The University of Ottawa Press.

Asari, Eva-Maria, Daphne Halikiopoulou and Steven Mock. 2008. 'British National Identity and the Dilemmas of Multiculturalism'. *Nationalism and Ethnic Politics* 14 (1): 1–28.

Baker, Darren T. and Elisabeth K. Kelan. 2015. 'Policy and Practice of Diversity Management in the Workplace'. In *Managing Diversity and Inclusion: An International Perspective*, edited by J. Syed and M. F. Ozbilgin, 76–106. London: SAGE Publications.

Cantle, Ted. 2005. *Community Cohesion: A New Framework for Race and Diversity*. New York: Palgrave Macmillan.

Chidiac, Emile. 2015. 'A Study of the Strategic Management of Ethnic and Cultural Diversity in Australian Settings: A Multiple Case Study' (PhD thesis, Southern Cross University).

Clyne, M. 2008. 'A Linguist's Vision for Multicultural Australia'. Eureka Street. Accessed 1 December 2008. www.eurekastreet.com.au/article.aspx?aeid=9919.

Dass, P. and B. Parker. 1999. 'Strategies for Managing Human Resource Diversity: From Resistance to Learning'. *Academy of Management Executive* 13 (2): 68–80.

Groutsis, D., Eddy S. Ng and Mustafa Bilgehan Ozturk. 2014. 'Cross-Cultural and Diversity Management Intersections: Lessons for Attracting and Retaining International Assignees'. In *International Human Resource Management*, edited by M. F. Ozbilgin, D. Groutsis and W. S. Harvey, 23–46. New York: Cambridge University Press.

Housden, M. 2014. *The League of Nations and the Organisation of Peace*. New York: The Cromwell Press.

Jackson, S. E. and M. Ruderman. 1999. *Diversity in the Workplace: Human Resources Initiatives*. New York: The Guildford Press.

Jenkins, R. 1966. 'Speech to the Meeting of Voluntary Liaison Committees'. 23 May.

Kandola, R. and J. Fullerton. 1998. *The Diversity Mosaic in Action: Managing the Mosaic*. 2nd ed. Trowbridge: The Cromwell Press.

Kim, Sungchan and Soyoung Park. 2017. 'Diversity Management and Fairness in Public Organizations'. *A Global Journal* 17 (2): 179–93.

League of Nations. 1929. 'Protection of Linguistic, Racial or Religious Minorities by the League of Nations'. Accessed 11 November 2017. http://biblio-archive.unog.ch/Dateien/CouncilMSD/C-24-M-18-1929-I_EN.pdf.

Myers, Verna. 2011. *Moving Diversity Forward: How to Go From Well-Meaning to Well-Doing*. Chicago: ABA Book Publishing.

Nankervis, A., R. Compton, M. Baird and J. Coffey. 2011. *Human Resource Management: Strategy and Practice*. South Melbourne: Cengage Learning Australia.

Ohemeng, Frank and Jocelyn McGrandle. 2015. 'The Prospects for Managing Diversity in the Public Sector: The Case of the Ontario Public Service'. *A Global Journal* 15 (4): 487–507.

O'Reilly, Karen. 2016. 'Migration Theories: A Critical Overview'. In *Routledge Handbook of Immigration and Refugee Studies*, edited by Anna Triandafyllidou, 25–33. New York: Routledge.

Ruiz Vieytez, Eduardo. 2014. 'Definitional Trends in the Legal Management of National and Religious Minorities (Diversity)'. In *Found in Multiculturalism: Acceptance or Challenge*, edited by Izabela Handzlik and Łukasz Sorokowski, 195–214. Frankfurt am Main: Peter Lang Edition.

Soutphommasane, Tim. 2012. *Don't Go back to Where You Came from: Why Multiculturalism Works*. Sydney: New South Publishing.

Trudeau, Justin. 2015. 'Diversity is Canada's Strength'. Accessed 12 December 2017. http://pm.gc.ca/eng/news/2015/11/26/diversity-canadas-strength.

Vickers, Jill and Annette Isaac. 2012. *The Politics of Race: Canada, the United States and Australia*. 2nd ed. Toronto: University of Toronto Press.

1 Multiculturalism

Multiculturalism(s): A Short Introduction

The concept of multiculturalism emerged from the civil rights movements of the 1960s and 1970s. Ethnic minorities and women's equality groups were dissatisfied because of the lack to progress to end inequality through civil rights legislation. Many immigrants and racioethnic groups living in multi-ethnic societies felt that their dreams had not been realised (Nkomo and Hoobler 2014). The advance and retreat of multiculturalism has been present in various countries, except Canada, where multiculturalism has been the most prominent worldwide. To start with the advance of multiculturalism, reference must be made to the increased migration starting in the 1960s, which led to the formation of multiculturalist policies in developing countries and the developed societies of North America, Western Europe and Australasia. A change of attitude occurred in the host countries with the new wave of migration, whereby the previous policies of assimilation that expected immigrants to adopt the majority culture became neither necessary nor desirable (Crowder 2013).

The term 'multiculturalism' was coined in Canada and became the nation's official policy in 1971. It gained some popularity in the 1980s and 1990s in other migrant-receiving countries, such as the US, the UK and Australia. There are varied definitions of multiculturalism, yet, overall, multicultural ideologies tend to encourage and appreciate different cultural groups, including their experiences and contributions. Multiculturalism encourages these groups to maintain their culture and cultural identities, and emphasises the notion that no group is superior or privileged (Nkomo and Hoobler 2014). The United Nations Educational, Scientific and Cultural Organization (UNESCO) (2006, 17) stated that 'the term multicultural describes the culturally diverse nature of human society. It not only refers to elements of ethnic or national nature, but also includes linguistic, religious and socio-economic diversity'. A distinction is generally made between two different meanings of multiculturalism: an empirical concept that refers to cultural and moral diversity, and a normative concept that celebrates cultural plurality (Jahanbegloo and Parekh 2011). A multicultural society is distinguished by cultural diversity, and multiculturalism is considered a normative doctrine because it represents a specific approach to that diversity (Jahanbegloo and Parekh 2011). In other words, multiculturalism has three core dimensions:

> (a) a reflection of a country's ethnocultural demographic diversity, (b) a political philosophy aimed at recognising and accommodating the differences that achieve objectives based on the above political philosophy, and (c) a public policy instrument to help achieve objectives based on the above political philosophy.
>
> (Ng and Bloemraad 2015, 620)

However, multiculturalism does not have a straightforward definition, and depicts multiple meanings. Interestingly, to complicate matters further, America's multiculturalism is not the same as that of Europe—the histories, origins, intentions and present practices are not the same, and the future will not be the same either. Therefore, the meaning of multiculturalism, both in theory and practice, can vary from one place to another, especially when comparing attitudes towards multiculturalism in countries in Western and Eastern Europe; North, Central and South America; Australasia; Africa and Asia. For example, in Canada and Australasia, multiculturalism does not encompass indigenous peoples, and indigenous groups refuse to have their claims covered by multiculturalism because of the question of legitimacy of the state concerning indigenous peoples. In contrast, in other parts of the world, such as Latin America, indigenous peoples use the term 'multiculturalism' to refer to their claims, as opposed to immigrant groups (Ivison 2010).

European approaches to multiculturalism operate on different principles and subsequently produce different outcomes. The European approach tends to be more accommodating of differences. Europe's politically involved Christian communities—in accordance with the dominant European multiculturalism—have made more criticisms of Islam than their American counterparts to educate 'acceptable' Muslim partners who might enhance social stability, rather than serve as allies against secularism. Although there are striking differences in how multiculturalism is legally defined and politically governed in the US, Canada, the UK and Australia, they share in common the fact that they all have large foreign-born populations, as shown in Table 1.1. Additionally, the share of the foreign-born population in the total population is increasing in these four countries.

As a result of the increasing levels of human mobility across borders, the world is no longer perceived as a system of separate communities, but viewed as a mixture of many interacting relations. Therefore, 'the other' could be any person, regardless of the country in which the individual lives (Jawor 2014). Sociology has also strengthened the feeling that the social environment belongs to 'our' people, and that we feel safe 'among us', while

Table 1.1 Foreign-born Population as a Proportion of the Total Population in G8 Countries and Australia

Country of residence	Census year	Foreign-born population (%)
Japan	2000	1.0
Italy	2009	8.0
Russian Federation	2002	8.2
France	2008	8.6
UK	2010	11.5
US	2010	12.9
Germany	2010	13.0
Canada	2011	20.6
Australia	2010	26.8

Source: Statistics Canada (2011).

anything 'strange' or 'other' is viewed as a threat. From this point of view, xenophobia and homophobia can be considered natural. It is human nature to fear anything unknown and unfamiliar. According to Jawor (2014, 135), the cure is not to exclude 'the other' or to include the other into 'mainstream' culture, but to exclude the other by eliminating the division between majority and minorities, thereby making the other one of us: 'We are all different and we are all equal, just like the colours of the rainbow palette: everyone is different, but they are all parallel'.

After the US attacks on 11 September 2001, there has been a shift in global and economic structures, which led to a focus on immigration, not only in the US, but also in Western Europe. This focus seems to have replaced the questions of identity that ruled the debate of multiculturalism in the 1970s and 1980s, where identities were distinguished by phrases such as 'Asian American', 'Native American', 'Black German', 'German Turkish' and 'British Asian' (Lauter 2009). However, multiculturalism focuses on the issue of legitimisation—whether one is and is perceived as a legal, legitimate, full citizen (Lauter 2009). Having accepted so many immigrants, liberal states must tolerate the multicultural transformation of their societies, simply because they are dubious about imposing cultural ways upon their members. Further, multiculturalism is not a description of culturally diverse societies, but a claim to recognise cultural difference; thus, it becomes the responsibility of the state (Joppke 1996).

Three 'logics' of multiculturalism have been identified to represent three models to help understand the essence of multiculturalism. The first logic is protective or communitarian multiculturalism, which aims to publicly recognise ethno-cultural groups and preserve the cultural integrity and authenticity related to their life. The second logic is liberal multiculturalism, which can be regarded the most prominent political theory, where multiculturalism is protected because of its promotion of liberal values, including equality, autonomy, toleration and equal respect. Protecting the human rights of minority groups is an essential element of democracy, as shown through national legislation and international practice (Ivison 2010). A liberal state can be accused of illiberalism if multiculturalism is not adopted (Guiora 2014). The third logic is imperial, which is neither protective nor liberal, and questions how 'minorities' and 'majorities' are defined (Ivison 2010). The strengths, weaknesses, opportunities and threats (SWOT) analysis of multiculturalism in Figure 1.1 provided by Ng and Bloemraad (2015) highlights the current discussions and challenges of multiculturalism.

The debate over immigration in the US and the West has shifted to where the immigrants come from, and the focus on domestic multiculturalism has shifted to a globalised 'migrant' culture. Western secular democracies were built on compromises that enabled the various religions introduced by immigrants to flourish. However, the form of religious expression known as 'deism' constituted the core belief system of many people in the eighteenth century. In various parts of the developing world, especially in the Middle East, people have been attracted to extreme religious fundamentalism as a choice against Western domination. It seems that the attacks in the US on 11 September 2001, in Madrid in 2004, and in London in 2005 created a conflict between radical Islam and democracy. One of the leading advocates of European multiculturalism, British sociologist, Modood (2007, 14), expressed anxiety about multiculturalism after 11 September 2001, and questioned the appropriateness of multiculturalism in the twenty-first century by arguing that 'it is the form of integration that best meets the normative implications of equal citizenship'.

In the late 1990s in Australia, politician Pauline Hanson was very popular in leading her One Nation Party's crusade against Asian immigration and multiculturalism in Australia. In October 2010, German Chancellor Angela Merkel declared that 'Multiculturalism is dead' (The Guardian 2010), when

Strengths	Opportunities
Multiculturalism enhances cultural tolerance and helps in the inclusion of cultural minorities	Multiculturalism creates 'fault lines' among cultural and religious groups, may promote divided and parallel lives, and may produce a challenge to equality in liberal societies
Weaknesses	**Threats**
Multiculturalism can be used as a means to attract talents, become a competitive advantage for nations and become a tool for politicians to use for their political benefit	Multiculturalism may seem to be incompatible with Western liberal values, a burden on the welfare of the state and a challenge to existing national identities

Figure 1.1 SWOT Analysis of Multiculturalism

Source: Ng and Bloemraad (2015).

Germany had never adopted a multicultural policy in the first place, or endorsed an official public policy recognising cultural differences. Moreover, some German politicians called for a halt to immigration from Turkey and the Middle East (Soutphommasane 2012). Especially after 11 September 2001, multiculturalism has been criticised by many, with the numbers of critics increasing over the years in response to some sensational cases raised by the media. Examples include the threats made against the novelist Salman Rushdie, the author of *Satanic Verses*, the murder of the Dutch film-maker Theo van Gogh, the 'Danish cartoons' controversy as well as the London bombings of 7 July 2005 (Crowder 2013). Critics claim that these cases manifest a failure of multiculturalism, when it is actually doubtful whether these instances had anything to do with multiculturalism, or were endorsed or encouraged by multiculturalist policies. Critics have also claimed that multiculturalist policies have been created by policy elites, not by popular demand. Thus, ordinary people view such programs as being imposed on them by elitists who have made their lives more difficult (Crowder 2013).

Undoubtedly, the events of 11 September 2001 and the al-Qaeda-inspired attacks in Madrid and London have caused anxiety and concerns about immigration, social cohesion and multicultural permissiveness resulting in so-called home-grown terrorism (Soutphommasane 2012). Majority and minority populations are becoming increasingly multicultural because of immigration. However, multiculturalism has become one of the major fatalities—alongside procedural justice and civil liberties—in Western democracies in the era following the 11 September 2001 attacks (Wegner 2009). The so-called corporate multiculturalism continues until the present time as a form of an administrative instrument (Wegner 2009). Yet, after the incident on 11 September, President George W. Bush called for increased tolerance of Muslims and their culture.

It is argued that 11 September 2001 was an event that led to a new period in diversity management, now known as the 'post-9/11' era. Multiculturalism gained a new factor referred to as 'anti- and/or post-multiculturalism discourse', which was first used in the UK with the intention to enhance cohesion, assimilation and a common identity (Garcea, Kirova and Wong 2008). The predominant claim in this emerging discourse is that the emphasis on cultural diversity and individual identities by those supporting multiculturalism undermines the cohesion and common identity that is necessary in any society. For example, in Australia, multiculturalism has been blamed of being 'used to hollow out what it means to be and to become an Australian citizen, depriving citizenship of its cultural base in a distinctive Australian nationality' (Crowder 2013, 3). The former British Prime Minister David Cameron inferred that the weakening of collective British identity and the rise of Islamist extremism in the UK are attributed to multiculturalism (Crowder 2013). Guiora (2014) argued that Western Europe's governments have allowed immigrants to form self-segregating parallel societies, instead of allowing them integrate to become part of their new societies.

The concern is based on the conviction that the nation-state is dedicating resources, time and protection to those who are assumed to be 'attacking' their country's immigrants. This failed state is grounds for intervention, and a failure to protect people in the immigrant community constitutes a failure of the government to perform its required obligation (Guiora 2014). With respect to multiculturalism, it is stated that:

> No society has ever succeeded in implementing a system of multicultur-alism without sooner or later seeing it deteriorate into hostility or con-flict. Medieval Spain and the Balkans illustrate that it is impossible to preserve harmony if the different groups maintain their differences from one generation to the next. On the other hand, many societies have been able to integrate disparate groups and meld them into a new society. All modern nations, including France and England, are the product of such a mixing of cultures. Accommodations, where they have remained within the bounds of common sense, have not tended to hinder this process.
>
> (St-Onge 2015, 25–6)

In addition, performance can be affected and give wider results if minority cultures feel threatened in the environments. While multiculturalism is con-sidered an asset, diversity in itself does not have benefits (Appelbaum et al. 2015). To benefit from multiculturalism, the best way to handle diversity is to recognise the shortcomings of a group so they can be managed (Appel-baum et al. 2015). Therefore, the onus is on management to identify the cul-tural differences and backgrounds of a group, and to value and support all employees. The performance of a diverse group depends on good manage-ment. However, for a diverse group to be managed well, existing stereotypes must be removed and channels of communication enhanced. Appelbaum et al. (2015) claimed that problems occur when different cultures intersect and members of groups present themselves as superior, while members of other groups feel inferior. Thus, managing diversity requires people to be adaptable and have the communication skills to respond to situations that value diversity, with positive expectations.

Multiculturalism in the US

It is necessary to distinguish between the issues of 'melting pot' versus 'mosaic'. America is described as a 'melting pot' of races and ethnic groups that are dissolving and reforming. The *Naturalisation Act of 1790* was the first law in the US stipulating the conditions for obtaining citizenship, in which aliens had to be of good character, have lived in the country for two years, take an oath of support for the constitution, and be a free white per-son. Indentured servants, slaves, free black people and American Indians were excluded. Women were able to obtain citizenship through their white fathers, but without the right to own property or vote (Carter 2016). Americans believed that the whole continent belonged to them, even though they had taken control of American Indians' land—and then denied American Indians citizenship. American Indians finally managed to gain US citizenship in the twentieth century through the *Indian Citizenship Act of 1924*, yet still without the right to vote (Carter 2016). The *Civil Rights Act of 1866* granted citizenship to all people born in the US, while the *Citizenship Clause* recognised that an individual had both state and national citizenship, but no state was able to interfere with the privileges of the latter (Carter 2016).

Most immigrants to the US had expected to become Americans—they were running away from difficult pasts to assimilate into a better future. Nevertheless, while the 'melting pot' does not work socially, it has succeeded in education. However, it took decades of political, judicial and legislative pressure to include a few minorities in the 'melting pot'. It seems that economic hardship may be the contributing factor to the rising ethnic tensions in terms of earnings among working-class groups, such as white, black and Latino, and multiculturalism. In addition, there was a gap between the rising income of the 'haves' and the declining income of the 'have-nots' (Price 1992).

Based on the history of demographic change in the US, newcomers have always changed the social fabric of the country. The new influx of immigrants in the 1830s—especially German and Irish peasants—changed the face of the US working-class population. Between the 1880s and mid-1920s, more than 25 million 'new immigrants' arrived in the US. During World War I, this wave started to diminish, and internal migration led to the arrival of millions of African American and Mexican workers and their families to join the industrial communities, thereby forming the modern American working-class population. The interaction of diverse ethnic groups and integration of women created the nation's powerful industrial union movement in this era (Barrett 2016). As shown in Table 1.2, the level of ethnic diversity in the US has been steadily increasing since the 1960s. While the share of the white population was 84% in 1960, it had decreased to 62% in 2015. In the same period, all other ethnicities increased their share in the US population.

Table 1.2 US Population by Race and Ethnicity (%)

Race	1960	1970	1980	1990	2000	2005	2010	2015
White	84.7	82.6	79.0	74.4	68.9	66.3	63.9	61.8
Black	10.3	10.7	11.4	11.8	12.1	12.2	12.3	12.5
Hispanic	3.6	4.8	6.8	9.6	13.2	14.9	16.5	17.6
Asian	0.6	0.8	1.6	2.7	4.0	4.6	5.1	5.6
Indian/Native	0.2	0.3	0.4	0.5	0.5	0.6	0.6	0.6
Two or more races	0.6	0.8	0.8	1.0	1.3	1.4	1.6	1.9
Total	100	100	100	100	100	100	100	100

Source: Data compiled from Pew Research Center (2015, 92).

In addition to Hispanics, the share of Asian individuals in the US population has substantially increased since the 1960s. According to Hsu (2016), the *Immigration Act of 1965* (also known as the *Hart-Celler Act*) is responsible for the growth in the Asian population and diversity from 1 million in 1960 to about 16 million in 2009 because of the liberalisation of the immigration law, which once only allowed white Anglo-Saxon Protestant individuals. Under the 'Asiatic Exclusion' policy and the national origins quota systems, few Asian immigrants were able to enter the US, and those few were men seeking employment or business opportunities, leaving behind their families and communities. However, nationalist China's role as America's main friend in Asia led to the repeal of the Chinese exclusion laws in 1943, after which the Chinese became the first Asians to obtain entry quotas and naturalisation rights, followed by Filipinos and Indians in 1946 (Hsu 2016).

In the nineteenth and early twentieth centuries, religion-based discrimination also existed in America. Catholic and Jewish people faced ferocious prejudice and discrimination during that period. Racism was so bad that Catholic Irish were portrayed by the mainstream as apes, and depicted as subhuman and beastlike. In the 1920s, immigration restrictions were successfully driven by the resurrection of the Ku Klux Klan movement, which was anti-Catholic, anti-Jewish and anti-black people. During the 1950s and 1960s, the hostility against the Catholics and Jews faded, as they were socially ascendant and appeared as peers of Protestants. By the 1970s, Catholic groups experienced improved social standing on a large scale, and intermarried with people from the mainstream group, while Jewish people were accepted into elite colleges, and anti-Semitism disappeared with the revelation of the Holocaust (Alba 2016).

After World War II, there were cultural and social moves towards a more multicultural and multiracial American society. While this dramatic transformation was occurring, a generation of American-born Asians played an active role in the national upheaval of the civil rights movement. America's anti-communist projects in the Southeast Asian peninsula caused a new influx of migration of Vietnamese, Cambodian and Laotian people, whose homes were destroyed. America's bitter loss in Vietnam must have caused some issues of 'guilt, obligation, ambivalence, hostility, and amnesia' (Hsu 2016, p. 59) behind the influx of 1 million refugees in many waves, caused by American intervention. Countries such as Australia, Canada and the US (Table 1.3) received their share of this outflow and provided permanent homes for some of these refugees. There are now many Asians living in the US as undocumented immigrants, who initially overstayed their tourist, student or temporary work visas, and the Philippines is considered one of 10 countries sending illegal immigrants to the US. Since the 1980s, the largest Asian communities in the US comprise ethnic Chinese, Filipino, South Asian, Korean, Vietnamese and Japanese people (Hsu 2016).

Table 1.3 Sources of Immigration to the US by Era

		Total	Share (%)
Modern era (1965–2015)		**58,525,000**	**100**
Regions	Latin America	29,750,000	51
	South/East Asia	14,700,00	25
	Europe	6,900,000	12
	Africa/Middle East	4,550,000	8
	Canada	1,150,000	2
	All other	1,450,000	2
Southern/Eastern Europe wave (1890–1919)		**18,244,000**	**100**
Regions	South/East Europe	11,377,000	62
	North/West Europe	4,757,000	26
	Canada	835,000	5
	Latin America	551,000	3
	Africa/Middle East	332,000	2
	South/East Asia	315,000	2
	Other/not specified	77,000	< 0.5
Northern Europe wave (1840–1889)		**14,314,000**	**100**
Regions	North/West Europe	11,700,000	82
	South/East Europe	1,058,000	7
	Canada	1,034,000	7
	South/East Asia	293,000	2
	Latin America	101,000	1
	Africa/Middle East	5,000	< 0.5
	Other/not specified	124,000	1

Source: Data compiled from Pew Research Center (2015, 11).

Economics is still a driving force behind immigrants fleeing war and religious persecution in their native lands—a desire to improve their lives, even by migrating illegally. Religion is a major feature in American life, as witnessed by the arrival of Muslims, Buddhists and Hindus, which complicated the issue of the usual acceptance of the Protestant, Catholic and Jewish religious identification of Americans. Additionally, the terrorism threat has led to increased non-acceptance of Muslims, as evidenced by the opposition to building mosques and the attacks on Sikhs because they look like Muslims (Bayor 2016). Waves of immigrants have flooded the US, attracted by economic opportunity and personal freedom, and are transforming the country into an ethnically heterogeneous and increasingly changing population. It is not wrong to think that immigration will change people—because it does—but it is wrong to fear that change. The American identity is constantly changing and being reinvented through the cross-cultural 'negotiations' that differentiate a multicultural society (Hackney 1997). Bayor (2016) argued that non-white immigrant groups have faced a denial of citizenship status and discrimination beyond what they can endure. Even today,

American-born US citizens of Asian and Mexican descent are considered by some white people as foreigners in their native land (Bayor 2016).

Chester Finn, who served in the US Department of Education under President Ronald Reagan, advocated teaching patriotism in American schools. He expressed his view as follows:

> Respect for diversity is a necessary ingredient. But so is love of freedom—and the act that it has enemies who loathe it. So is the fragility of a free and diverse society, and the central obligation of that society to defend itself against aggressors. So, too, is respect for heroes, including those who froze at Valley Forge, who stormed the beaches of Normandy, and who perished while trying to rescue terrorist victims in lower Manhattan. This more martial strand of patriotism makes some educators nervous. So does the sense of pride in America that accompanies it. They'd rather emphasize our failings and our differences.
>
> (Hutchins-Viroux 2009, 135)

The various stakeholders in the US seem to agree that schools should teach 'respect for diversity', yet this expression may be misinterpreted. Respecting diversity requires minorities' viewpoints to be legitimised and incorporated into the official national narrative. Students should be informed that truth is subjective and that they should consider other people's viewpoints. Respecting diversity signifies that America consists of many different ethnic groups. However, avoiding conflict, discrimination and inequality is important for fear of causing antagonism. Thus, teaching about a great part of minorities' experiences is not taught in American history. However, in general, books are committed to showing a multicultural image of America and its history by including photographs of contemporary Americans who are members of ethnic groups that are rarely mentioned in historical events. Despite multiculturalists' proposals, most books do not portray Muslim Americans, who migrated to America in four waves—the first of which was between 1875 and 1912 from Lebanon, Syria, Jordan, Palestine and Israel (Handzlik 2014). The only exception seems to be the 2003 book titled *Our Nation* published by McGraw-Hill that includes such photographs and presents an exercise teaching about Muslims in the US (Hutchins-Viroux 2009).

The story of immigrants to the US reflects a process of adaptation, acculturation and assimilation. The driving force of immigration to the US is in search of freedom and opportunities, yet both domestic and foreign developments remain a challenge to immigration and ethnicity. The public policy changed from Americanisation, assimilation and Anglo-conformity of the so-called 'melting pot' into a general tolerance of ethnic difference within the framework of American citizenship, loyalty and patriotism, which accepted the proposition that the hyphens between two words could show a link or a division. (Bukowczyk 2016). While the term 'multiculturalism' was used as a synonym for 'diversity', it acknowledged the existence of oppressed racial minorities who happened to be different from white ethnic groups and were subjected to racial inequality (Bukowczyk 2016, 492). Americans must come to terms with 'difference' to cooperate across racial and ethnic lines. The areas of commonality between members of diverse groups and American citizens should be identified to help remove the threat that human beings fear when they encounter 'the other'. Common values and commitments would give people joy and stimulation from the cultural enrichment that derives from diversity (Hackney 1997).

Multiculturalists have had more success about discrimination, which can now be discussed openly against black, Chinese and Mexican people. Notably, the government policies and civil rights movement of the 1950s and 1960s were successful in eliminating discrimination (Hutchins-Viroux 2009). The ongoing fight against discrimination in an attempt to generate social justice is the core of progressive multiculturalism (Hutchins-Viroux 2009). Due to successive waves of migration over 200 years, each immigrant group brought its own culture, language and institutions, and competed with each other over the best model to fit their experiences and needs. This led to the formation of working-class cultures based on ethno-cultural identity, with unions and fraternal and educational groups, as well as radical political ethnic lines. This 'making' occurred in every community of migrants in the US, leading to working-class cultures and movements that were threatened by division in terms of race, religion, ethnicity, gender and skill. The challenge of working-class organisers was to bridge these divisions to establish a strong movement of diverse people (Barrett 2016).

Multiculturalism in Canada

Pierre Elliott Trudeau served as Prime Minister of Canada from 1968 to 1984, and gave Canada the vision of multiculturalism. Historian Michael Bliss (1994, 246) labelled Trudeau 'the father of bilingual, multicultural Canada'. In the Canadian context, multiculturalism involves recognition of others of similar or different cultural experiences, imbued with tolerance and acceptance (Wood and Gilbert 2005). Diversity in Canada was legally acknowledged in 1971. In 1988, by virtue of Bill C-93, the *Canadian Multiculturalism Act* was passed, and diversity consequently became a reference to a multi-ethnic population (Xu 2013). The *Canadian Multiculturalism Act* affirmed the value of cultural pluralism, with the Canadians' intention to honour the richness of cultural diversity. A closer examination of the legislative process with regard to multiculturalism reveals that the policy of multiculturalism declared in 1971 focused on two issues: (i) maintaining cultural communities (the cultural component) and (ii) enhancing intercultural contact and minimising any obstacles that prevent such participation (the intercultural component) (Berry 2013). The multiculturalism policy implemented by the Government of Canada in 1971 stated that:

A policy of multiculturalism within a bilingual framework . . . (is) the most suitable means of assuring the cultural freedom of all Canadians. Such a policy should help to break down discriminatory attitudes and cultural jealousies. National unity, if it is to mean anything in the deeply personal sense, must be founded on confidence in one's own individual identity; out of this can grow respect for that of others, and a willingness to share ideas, attitudes and assumptions. . . . The Government will support and encourage the various cultural and ethnic groups that give structure and vitality to our society. They will be encouraged to share their cultural expression and values with other Canadians and so contribute to a richer life for all.

(Government of Canada 1971, quoted in Berry 2013, 664)

Management of diversity was first used in public policy in the Canadian *Policy of Multiculturalism with a Bilingual Framework*. The *Multiculturalism Act 1988* declared that the policy of the Government of Canada was to:

recognize and promote the understanding that multiculturalism reflects the cultural and racial diversity of Canadian society and acknowledges the freedom of all members of Canadian society to preserve, enhance and share their cultural heritage.

(Berry 2013, 664)

The Act also recognised that 'multiculturalism is a fundamental characteristic of the Canadian heritage and identity and that it provides an invaluable resource in the shaping of Canada's future' (Berry 2013, 664). At the same time, the Act sought:

to promote the full and equitable participation of individuals and communities of all origins in the continuing evolution and shaping of all aspects of Canadian society and assist them in the elimination of any barrier to that participation.

(Berry 2013, 664)

Moreover, it sought to 'ensure that all individuals receive equal treatment and equal protection under the law, while respecting and valuing their diversity' (Berry 2013, 664).

The two features of multiculturalism—diversity and equity—have remained pivotal to Canadian policy since the day of its inception. Interestingly, the recent inclusion of everyone into a Canadian civic society has become a focal point with an emphasis on a common citizenship for all. This shift is a considered a move from ethnicity multiculturalism focusing on cultural diversity towards equity multiculturalism focusing on equitable participation. The increasing diversity of the population in Canada is second only to Australia, and is concentrated in Canada's largest cities. The majority of people who arrived between 1991 and 2001 settled in Toronto, Vancouver or Montreal, where there is an increasing concentration of employment, while many areas outside the largest cities are experiencing a population decline. With the exception of the indigenous peoples, the non-white character of immigration is another significant change in Canada, giving rise to what is called officially 'visible minorities'. While recent immigration occupies Canada's largest cities, Ottawa is diversifying rapidly and is now considered third after Toronto and Vancouver in terms of the influx of recent immigration. There have been attempts by both federal and provincial governments to regionalise immigration to encourage newcomers to settle in smaller communities; however, the programs have been unsuccessful (Andrew 2007).

Canada was a culturally diverse domain even before the arrival of European settlers. It has 50 distinct Aboriginal cultures, with more than a dozen different languages in the Aboriginal population. As for immigration, Canada has the fifth-largest foreign-born population in the world (International Organization for Migration 2010). In Canada, the Aboriginal or cultural minority heritage constitutes just under one-quarter of the population (Marshall et al. 2013). Cultural acceptance seems to be a necessary component in Canada, embedded in the 'four R's' needed in the Aboriginal context: respect, reciprocity, relevance and responsibility (Marshall et al. 2013). Demonstrating respect is viewed by some scholars as an important issue, and people who experienced racism and discrimination indicated that acceptance remains a challenge in the dominant Canadian culture (Abdullah 2013). Tables 1.4 and 1.5 indicate the ethnic diversity in the Canadian population (Table 1.4) and the immigrant population by place of birth and period of immigration in Canada (Table 1.5).

Further, the concept of 'diversity' not only refers to demographic cultural differences, but to:

> a workforce made . . . distinct by the presence of many regions, cultures or skin colors, both sexes (in non-stereotypical roles), differing sexual orientations, varying styles of behaviour, differing capabilities, and usually, unlike backgrounds.
>
> (Hiranandani 2012, 1)

In its early days, the Canadian policy of multiculturalism insisted on providing services in languages other than English and French; 'celebrating' diversity; and challenging the dominant norms, such as dress code, habits, accents and prejudice. Eventually, the policy of multiculturalism in Canada has come to recognise other cultures, with racial/ethnic minorities entitled to retain their cultural heritage, thereby resulting in organisations hiring visible

Table 1.4 Population by Ethnic Origin in Canada, 2016

	Country total	*Percentage*
Ethnic origin	34,460,065	100
North American Aboriginal origins	2,130,520	6
Other North American origins	11,628,535	34
European origins	19,683,320	57
British Isles origins	11,211,850	33
French origins	4,680,820	14
Western European origins (except French origins)	4,600,855	13
Northern European origins (except British Isles origins)	1,201,320	3
Eastern European origins	3,431,245	10
Southern European origins	3,012,375	9
Caribbean origins	749,155	2
Latin, Central and South American origins	674,640	2
African origins	1,067,930	3
North African origins	355,045	1
Asian origins	6,095,235	18
West Central Asian and Middle Eastern origins	1,011,145	3
South Asian origins	1,963,330	6
East and Southeast Asian origins	3,163,360	9
Other Asian origins	22,740	0
Oceania origins	85,470	0

Source: Statistics Canada (2016a).

Table 1.5 Immigrant Population by Place of Birth and Period of Immigration, 2006

Total immigrant population		Period of immigration			
Place of birth	Total	*Before 1991*	*1991 to 1995*	*1996 to 2000*	*2001 to 2006*
Total immigrants	6,186,950	3,408,415	823,925	844,625	1,109,980
UK	579,620	515,135	20,630	18,200	25,655
US	250,535	168,840	18,770	24,155	38,770
Germany	171,405	149,020	6,155	8,595	7,635
Poland	170,490	123,435	32,655	7,905	6,495
France	79,550	44,685	7,815	9,860	17,185
Europe	976,160	640,140	68,375	72,135	86,520
Asia	2,164,205	759,850	403,715	440,340	560,275
Middle East	243,810	92,080	45,445	46,050	60,235
Latin	180,435	78,955	27,430	21,645	52,400
Africa	192,605	81,545	31,800	32,905	46,370
Others	1,178,135	754,730	161,135	162,835	208,440

Source: Statistics Canada (2006).

minorities who speak the language of a particular community (Hiranandani 2012). This particular change in the context of multiculturalism in Canada can be seen as a natural outcome of the increasing shares of a foreign-born and mixed-race population. However, Hiranandani (2012) argued that visible minorities remain subject to discrimination in the workplace. Tables 1.6 and 1.7 provide core statistics on the visible minority population in Canada.

Table 1.6 Visible Minority Population in Canada, 2011

	Total population number	Visible minority population number	%	Top three visible minority groups
Canada	32,852,325	6,264,755	19.1	South Asian, Chinese, black
Toronto	5,521,235	2,596,420	47.0	South Asian, Chinese, black
Montreal	3,752,475	762,325	20.3	Black, Arab, Latin American
Vancouver	2,280,695	1,030,335	45.2	Chinese, South Asian, Filipino
Ottawa—Gatineau	1,215,735	234,015	19.2	Black, Arab, Chinese
Calgary	1,199,125	337,420	28.1	South Asian, Chinese, Filipino
Edmonton	1,139,585	254,990	22.4	South Asian, Chinese, Filipino
Winnipeg	714,635	140,770	19.7	Filipino, South Asian, black
Hamilton	708,175	101,600	14.3	South Asian, black, Chinese

Source: Statistics Canada (2011).

Table 1.7 Generation Status of Visible Minority Population in Canada, 2016

Generation status

Visible minority	Total generation status		First generation		Second generation		Third generation or more	
	Total	%	Total	%	Total	%	Total	%
Total	34,460,065	100	8,219,555	100	6,100,720	100	20,139,790	1
Total visible minority population	7,674,580	22	5,280,880	64	2,123,115	35	270,665	1
Not a visible minority	26,785,485	78	2,938,750	36	3,977,605	65	19,869,125	99

Source: Statistics Canada (2016b).

Multiculturalism will remain an important issue in Canada because of declining birth rates and an ageing population, which leads to greater demand for skilled employees. Educating Canadians about the benefits of immigration to Canada will create more support for diversity and foster acceptance of newcomers. Settling immigrants in highly populated areas with rapid growth rates might generate negative attitudes towards newcomers, whereas directing immigrants to areas where their skills are in demand could promote settlement in wider Canadian communities (Mulder and Krahn 2005). Against this background, there has been a heated debate regarding whether multiculturalism in Canada has failed or succeeded. For those who argue that Canadian multiculturalism has failed, the failure is a worldwide phenomenon affected by rising global anxieties and backlash. Thus, there has been a shift from multiculturalism to social cohesion and integration in Western democracies.

Multiculturalism has been tried and has failed in Europe with serious social consequences, which has revealed to Canada—as a multicultural country—the inherent flaws of multiculturalism. Although multiculturalism has failed in Europe, it remains strong in Canada and major political parties have no aspiration of abolishing or retreating from multiculturalism. Indeed, the Canadian model of immigrant integration in Canada has succeeded, and it only requires minor changes. However, there has been a shift in relation to immigrant integration in Western democracies from multiculturalism and heading towards social cohesion and integration. While the failure of multiculturalism in Europe has led to more segregation, stereotyping and prejudice, Canada has not followed this European trajectory, although Canadians have not been immune to the influence of the European problems (Banting and Kymlicka 2010). Canada's immigrants have more skills than immigrants in other countries; thus, they bring human capital that enables them to move into the labour market. However, the presence of a multiculturalism policy has not contributed to the success of immigrants' integration in Canada—rather, it may impede it (Goodhart 2008). Palmer (2002) argued that Canada—like the US, Australia and New Zealand—had an assimilationist approach to immigration. Immigrants were expected to assimilate and eventually melt into the existing mainstream culture. Any group that was incapable of assimilating was not allowed to immigrate to Canada or become citizens (Banting and Kymlicka 2010). Findings from survey research indicated that Canadians, while favourable to immigration, are of the opinion that immigrants should change and assimilate into Canadian society, not the other way around (Andrew 2007). However, ethnocultural diversity has changed the lives of Canadians, especially those living in the largest cities. Thus, integration of 'new Canadians' has not been one-sided—as Canadian society has also wanted Canada and individuals to undergo more change (Andrew 2007).

Those who argue that Canadian multiculturalism has been a success story use the example of the refugee policy of the Canadian Government headed by Justin Trudeau. They claim that, unlike the US and most European Union (EU) countries, Canada supported multiculturalism by presenting the most ethnically diverse government in Canada, and subsequently accepted 25,000 government-sponsored refugees from Iraq and Syria. This move was supported by the public, and, in March 2016, the government approved the applications of 10,000 privately sponsored Syrian refugees to be completed by the end of 2016 or early 2017 (Mudde 2016). In an address, titled 'Diversity is Canada's Strength', given at Canada House in November 2015 in England, Justin Trudeau (2015), Prime Minister of Canada, spoke of Canada's diversity:

> Our commitment and inclusion isn't about Canadians being nice and polite—though of course we are. In fact, this commitment is a powerful and ambitious approach to making Canada, and the world, a better, and safer, place. It's easy, in a country like Canada, to take diversity for granted. In so many ways, it's the air we breathe. We've raised generation after generation of children who think nothing of hearing five or six languages spoken on the playground. Because it's 2015, people around the world are noticing the diversity of our Cabinet, and our Parliament. But the diversity of our country is not news. One-fifth of Canadians were born elsewhere, and chose to immigrate to Canada. In our largest city, more than half were born outside Canada. Against that backdrop, the importance of diversity can sometimes be taken for granted. But there is no doubt that we're a better country—a stronger, more successful country—because of it. Just consider the words that people use to describe Canada: We're open, accepting, progressive and prosperous. There is a direct line between each of those attributes and Canada's success in building a more diverse and inclusive society. We're not the only nation that's tried to do it. But what's made it work so well in Canada is the understanding that our diversity isn't a challenge to be overcome or a difficulty to be tolerated. Rather, it's a tremendous source of strength. Canadians understand that diversity is our strength. We know that Canada has succeeded—culturally, politically, economically—because of our diversity, not in spite of it.

Ryan (2010) argued that this action taken by the new Trudeau government confirms the adoption of multiculturalism, and that the lack of far-right politics in Canada is a result of its unique multiculturalism policy. While there has been backlash against multiculturalism and the intake of refugees in most Western democracies, Canada remains the only Western democratic country that still upholds multiculturalism. Canada demonstrates that a large intake of immigrants does not necessarily cause a negative response among the denizens of the country. Western democracies are under no obligation to replicate the policy of Canada's multiculturalism, but can learn from it. Canada demonstrates that a pro-multiculturalism policy can succeed in a multicultural country, and any adversary to immigration and multiculturalism can be surmounted on the condition that the political hierarchy is prepared to proactively support and explain their policies.

Multiculturalism in the UK

Historically, significant migration to Britain occurred in the post-World War II period. Approximately 800,000 people from New Commonwealth countries, most of whom were non-white, entered Britain between 1948 and 1962. Under the *British Nationality Act 1948*, these migrants entered Britain as British subjects, not foreign immigrants. Under this Act, Commonwealth subjects were entitled to enter Britain as citizens of the UK and colonies (Kim 2011). This Act presumed that any person who was a British subject, irrespective of race or colour, was eligible to enter and settle in Britain. As Kim (2011) stated, this Act seems to have been the formal instrument that validated the transformation of the UK into a multiracial society. Immigration from the New Commonwealth did not constitute a problem, but rather proof of the diversity of the empire, and recognition of the model of *Civis Britannicus Sum* (actually he was a British Subject). The term denotes an ancient concept of limited democracy from the Greek city states and the Roman Republic. It was used by republicans in the eighteenth century, and acquired by Palmerston for the British Monarchy. The equality extended to immigrants in the UK without recognising the difference was challenged, especially following the 1958 Nottingham race riots. These race riots were largely perpetrated by white residents against West Indians. In 1958, the city of Nottingham had an ethnic community totalling approximately 4,000, which comprised 1.2% of the population. Approximately 4,500 people were involved in the race riots (Kim 2011). The riots were partly motivated by deteriorating working conditions and unemployment in Nottingham and areas of west London. Thus, the strained race relations were exposed, which prompted policy makers in the 1940s to change their position. For example, this led to the introduction of the *Commonwealth Immigration Act 1962* (Kim 2011).

As seen in Table 1.8, the population statistics between 1991 and 2011, the diversity in the UK population has increased significantly. While the change in white population was 1.6% and 1% in the periods of 1991–2011 and 2001–2011, respectively, the change in all other than white population was 137% and 70.5% in the same respective periods. Table 1.9 further illustrates the increase in ethnic diversity in the UK by showing the changes the ethnicity of non-UK-born population.

Previous studies indicate that, in the post-imperial period after World War II, Britain changed from a 'civic' to an 'ethnic' nation, where membership was defined by birth and ancestry. Tom Nairn (quoted in Joppke 1996, 477) even observed that 'in the obscene form of racism, English nationalism has been re-born'. In the post-imperial period, 800,000 people born overseas

Table 1.8 Historical Population Statistics in the UK

Ethnic group	1991	2001	2011	1991–2011	2001–2011
	%	%	%	% Change	% Change
White British	—	87.3%	80.5%	—	−1.3%
White Irish	—	1.2%	0.9%	—	−17.9%
White other	—	2.6%	4.4%	—	80.2%
White Roma or Irish traveller	—	—	0.1%	—	
All white	93.5%	91.2%	86.0%	1.6%	1.0%
Mixed white-Caribbean	—	0.5%	0.8%	—	77.5%
Mixed white-African	—	0.2%	0.3%	—	105.7%
Mixed white-Asian	—	0.4%	0.6%	—	77.8%
Mixed other	—	0.3%	0.5%	—	82.9%
All mixed	—	1.3%	2.2%	—	82.2%
Indian	1.8%	2.0%	2.5%	58.4%	34.1%
Pakistani	1.0%	1.4%	2.0%	127.2%	54.5%
Bangladeshi	0.3%	0.5%	0.8%	152.8%	56.0%
Chinese	0.3%	0.4%	0.7%	127.0%	68.5%
Other Asian	0.4%	0.5%	1.5%	295.7%	238.1%
All Asian	3.8%	4.9%	7.5%	116.3%	65.4%
Caribbean	594,825	1.1%	1.1%	4.4%	4.0%
African	989,628	0.9%	1.8%	287.6%	100.1%
Other black	280,437	0.2%	0.5%	26.9%	186.0%
All black	1,864,890	2.2%	3.3%	78.3%	60.1%
Arab	—	—	0.4%	—	—
Other	0.6%	0.4%	0.6%	2.5%	46.4%
All other than white	6.5%	8.8%	14.0%	137.0%	70.5%
All other than white British	—	12.7%	19.5%	—	64.8%
Total population	100.0%	100.0%	100.0%	10.5%	7.1%

Source: Office for National Statistics (2011).

became British subjects with the right to settle in the UK. This led to a shift from the principle of 'allegiance to the crown' to the national principle of territorial of citizenship, and unfortunately, in the British coloured and a white nation, it was difficult to accomplish without the racial division of the *ins* and the *outs* in society. A conservative minister at Westminster stated the Commonwealth ideal that was commonly accepted among the British elite:

In a world in which restrictions on personal movement and immigra-tion have increased we can still take pride in the fact that a man can

Table 1.9 Ethnicity of the Non-UK-born Population by Period of Arrival, England and Wales, 2011

Ethnic group	Before 1981	1981–2000	2001–2006	2007–2011
White	%	%	%	%
British	52	27	11	9
Irish	63	22	7	9
Roma or Irish traveller	12	24	24	40
Other white	10	19	34	37
Mixed/multiple ethnic group				
White and black Caribbean	36	24	20	20
White and black African	7	32	36	25
White and Asian	22	25	25	27
Other mixed	17	28	28	27
Asian/Asian British				
Indian	38	20	21	21
Pakistani	28	32	22	18
Bangladeshi	19	47	19	16
Chinese	18	23	21	38
Other Asian	12	27	32	29
Black/African/Caribbean/ black British				
African	5	35	39	21
Caribbean	61	20	13	6
Other black	15	30	36	19
Other ethnic group				
Arab	8	32	24	37
Any other ethnic group	16	32	29	23
All	24	25	26	24

Source: Office for National Statistics (2011).

say *civis Britannicus sum* and whatever his colour may be, and we take pride in the fact that he wants and can come to the Mother Country.

(Joppke 1996, 478)

However, the 1958 riots were enough to persuade the elites in the UK to impose restrictions on New Commonwealth immigration reinstated what was described by Gary Freeman (quoted in Joppke 1996, 478) as 'fundamental congruence between public attitudes and public policy'. The *Commonwealth Immigrants Act 1962* curtailed entry to work permit holders and close family members of residents and permit holders. In 1968, British Asians facing expulsion from Kenya were refused entry to the UK, which was a violation of an earlier promise of protection. The *Immigration Act*

1971 introduced the 'patrial' clause, which associated right of residency with the existence of at least one grandparent in the UK, which was a clear way of saying that 'Britain preferred white immigrants', as stated in *The Economist* in 1982 (Joppke 1996, 478). Finally, the *British Nationality Act 1981* amended nationality law in the immigration regime already in operation, thereby forming a three-tier system of British dependent territory and overseas citizenship, and giving the right of entry and residence to 'British citizens' only (Joppke 1996). The idea of 'assimilating' immigrants was rejected by the UK before any other immigrant-receiving country in the West, including the US. The UK never attempted to 'assimilate' its colonial subjects (Joppke 1996).

Following the flux into the UK of British subjects from its colonies, defining race or colour became a challenge for UK policy makers, especially when designing census studies. For example, the memorandum submitted by the Home Office to the Select Committee on Race Relations and Immigration on 23 April 1969 confirmed:

> No doubt many people could be identified by inspection as broadly falling within the definition of white or coloured, but this is a different matter from providing precise guidance on how any doubts should be resolved (persons of mixed blood would be an obvious example) and it would be necessary to rely on subjective judgments which would obviously vary.
>
> (Thompson 2012, 1413)

Multiraciality remained a problem for the UK census designers throughout the 1980s. During the proposed census question between 1985 and 1989, the Office of Population, Census and Surveys did not attempt to classify mixed-race people, since the methods used in 1970 were unsuccessful. However, in the final version of the ethnic question of the 1991 census, people were asked to choose the group to which they belonged, or to tick the 'any other ethnic group' category. Since 2001, the UK has officially become a multi-ethnic, multicultural society, as government policy acknowledges religion as a means to recognise and work with minorities. Thus, the structure combining difference and diversity in the UK shifted in the 1950s and 1960s from 'race' to incorporate 'ethnicity', to 'culture', and then to 'faith' (Grillo 2010). Since the 1960s, there has been controversy about hijabs and turbans in the UK, which tend to have positive responses, yet when hijabs are extended to include niqabs and burqas, this may have negative effects. In addition, freedom of speech is well received; however, when speech relates to inciting racial or religious hatred, it is not favourable in society, thereby leaving discussions with no apparent solution (Grillo 2010).

Opposition seems to be interpreted as xenophobia, while, in others, it is a clash with principles of democracy and secular values. The 1997 British Labour Government tried to introduce a model known as 'cosmopolitan citizenship' to replace 'loyalty' and commitment to communities, with an emphasis on 'dialogue between groups and across boundaries'. Having inflexible multiculturalism would not align with such ideals at a time of tension, especially post-11 September (Grillo 2010). On 20 April 1968, Enoch Powell, a British Conservative Party politician, addressed the General Meeting of the West Midlands Area Conservative Political Centre. He warned in his speech of a cultural backlash and its impact on society if unrestricted immigration continued in the UK. He stated that it was unfeasible for people from other cultures ever to become British or English, even if they were born and raised in the UK. Additionally, between 1960 and 2000, policies initiated by two ministers (from the Home Office and Education) attempted to monitor immigration, acting on the belief that most immigrants intended to settle in the UK. The then Labour Home Secretary, David Blunkett (quoted in Grillo 2010, 53), declared in 2002 that:

> Respect for cultural difference has limits, marked out by fundamental human rights and duties. Some of these boundaries are very clear. [Some] practices are clearly incompatible with our basic values.

In 2001, northern cities in the UK experienced some disturbances that erupted in Bradford as British Asians and white extremists clashed with police. This event raised questions about the alienation of minorities, particularly young Muslims, following the attack in the US on 11 September. In relation to the shift from 'race' to 'faith', former British Prime Minister Tony Blair (quoted in Grillo 2010, 57) stated in 2001 that:

> our major faith traditions—all of them more historic and deeply rooted than any political party or ideology—play a fundamental role in supporting and propagating values which bind us together as a nation.

The reoccurring social tensions evidenced by the 1958 Nottingham and 1981 Brixton riots and the disturbances following the 11 September 2001 and 7 July 2005 terrorist attacks have resulted in heated tension regarding the success or failure of multiculturalism in the UK. In his reflection on the 11 September attacks, Blair (quoted in Guiora 2014, 42) declared: '[w]e celebrate the diversity in our country, we get strength from the culture and races that go to make up Britain today'. Blair's statement was well received by the British public, whereby:

> a Mori poll for the BBC in August 2005, following the London July bombings, showed that, although 32% of the population thought that multiculturalism 'threatens the British way of life', 62% believed that 'multiculturalism makes Britain a better place to live'.
>
> (Guiora 2014, 42)

However, when former British Prime Minister David Cameron (quoted in Howarth and Andreouli 2016, 2) addressed the 2011 Munich Security Conference, he declared that multiculturalism has not succeeded in the UK (Modood and Meer 2012):

> Under the doctrine of state multiculturalism, we have encouraged different cultures to live separate lives, apart from each other and apart from the mainstream. We've failed to provide a vision of society to which they feel they want to belong. We've even tolerated these segregated communities behaving in ways that run completely counter to our values.

In the UK, it seems that, while multiculturalist policies remained unchanged, they are politically in disarray. There are various reasons for the anti-multicultural turn, including claims that multiculturalism has paved the way for fragmentation and divisions. Multiculturalism has made 'native' populations hesitant in their moral stance on socio-economic disparities to the extent that some even blame it for international terrorism (Modood and Meer 2012).

The London bombings on 7 July 2005 demonstrated the problems that have occurred because of the lack of a civic British identity. Unlike the terrorist attacks in the US on 11 September 2001, the London bombings were undertaken by British citizens whose loyalties lay with their ethnic and religious identities, rather than with the British state. Thus, the absence of civic British identity is considered a cause of divisions in the UK that can lead to friction and conflict (Asari, Halikiopoulou and Mock 2008). Phillips (quoted in Asari, Halikiopoulou and Mock 2008, p. 5) added that multiculturalism should be scrapped because it may have come from a 'desire to recognize that diversity is a good thing and to appreciate the many qualities newcomers brought to Britain', yet has led to alienation, isolation and distance between communities (Asari, Halikiopoulou and Mock 2008, 5). In support of this argument, the conservative think-tank Civitas claimed that 'failure to establish unity in Britain has been largely due to the implementation of multiculturalism' (Asari, Halikiopoulou and Mock 2008, 5).

Those who claim that multiculturalism has been working effectively in the UK argue that multiculturalism has successfully replaced assimilation and integration. Taylor-Gooby and Waite (2014) stated that assimilation encourages minorities to adopt mainstream values and to integrate with little focus on cultural differences, and endeavours to remove the problems of social cohesion resulting from disadvantage and discrimination. Multiculturalism tends to respect cultural differences. According to Taylor-Gooby and Waite (2014), the UK still supports multiculturalism, despite its challenges and criticisms.

British multiculturalism was complicated by the postcolonial influx of immigrants, and the UK became culturally diverse in the twentieth century after World War II and the establishment of the Commonwealth after decolonisation. Most of Britain's new arrivals were from Commonwealth nations, with similar cultural ties to the empire; since most of the immigrants were from the Caribbean. Unlike Britain, Australian multiculturalism, as examined next, has been a response to immigration associated with settlement policies and services (Soutphommasane 2012).

Multiculturalism in Australia

Multiculturalism is defined as a system in which people with different backgrounds can interact, coexist and subsequently learn the culture of others by transcending the borders caused by racial, gender and generational differences (Hughes 1993). A multicultural society is essentially a multi-ethnic society. Australia is, and has always been, a multicultural society, and a short history of multiculturalism in Australia will help relate past developments to current issues. The establishment of the Australian Federation was based on a phase of lenient British imperial policy, which provided better employment opportunities to British subjects in the workplace, especially in the public sector. Between Federation and World War I, politicians supported legislation restricting non-British immigration, and favoured adherence to 'racial purity' and 'racial superiority' and the protection of Australian jobs (Cooper 2012). In today's terms, the workplace environment in the early days of Australian federation involved systematic discrimination against non-British subjects.

From the introduction of the *Commonwealth Immigration Restriction Act 1901* until 1966, the approach to immigration in Australia was influenced by the 'White Australia' policy, which encouraged the assimilation of new arrivals into the dominant Anglo-Australian culture. Thus, it was up to 'them' to like 'us' (Lever-Tracey and Quinlan 1988). This is particularly important because the White Australia policy has had a long influence on Australia's social development. This policy resulted in the construction of a populist national identity, which led to the exclusion and marginalisation of groups (Dunn et al. 2004).

After World War II, the ethnic mix of immigrants contributed to both the replacement of the White Australia policy and the introduction of a policy of multiculturalism by the Australian Labor Government in 1973. Multiculturalism in Australia as an official policy emerged in 1973 to ease the restrictions of the assimilation policies of the 1940s and 1950s. This new policy expected new settlers to learn English, acquire Australian cultural practices and become as one with Australian-born people (Koleth 2010). However, in the 1970s, there was acknowledgement that Australian society had changed in the previous two decades. There was a shift from a policy of assimilation aimed at maintaining a single cultural identity, while nominally acknowledging the language of multiculturalism and self-determination (Markus 2011).

Table 1.10 Australian Historical Population Statistics

	1954	1961	1971	1981	1991	2001	2011	2016
Australian born (000)	7,700	8,729	10,176	11,389	12,718	13,629	15,018	15,615
Overseas born (000)	1,286	1,779	2,579	3,128	4,053	5,140	6,490	7,786
Percentage born overseas	14.3	16.9	20.2	21.5	24.2	27.4	30.2	33.3
Total population (000)	8,986	10,508	12,755	14,517	16,771	18,769	21,508	23,401

Source: Data compiled from the ABS (2014, 2016) historical population statistics and census results.

The most significant cultural driver in Australia since World War II has been the overwhelming transformation of Australia from an Anglo-Celtic society to one of the world's most culturally diverse nations. Table 1.10 illustrates the influx of migrants and the extent of change in both the Australian population and workforce. The 2011 census revealed that over 30% of Australia's population was born overseas, and a further 20% had at least one parent born overseas (Australian Bureau of Statistics [ABS] 2012). In the 2016 census, the share of Australian population born overseas had increased to 33% (ABS 2016). Thus, the effect of multiculturalism was so great that multicultural policy put an end to the concept that other cultures were inferior to the 'mainstream' culture of white British Australia. Multiculturalism became an official policy in Australia in 1973, thereby easing the restrictions of the assimilation policies of the 1940s and 1950s.

The results of the latest national census detailed in Table 1.11 show that Australia is changing rapidly as a culturally diverse nation. The 2016 census revealed that two-thirds of the Australian population (67%) were born in Australia, while about half of Australians (49%) were either born overseas or had one or both parents born overseas. England and New Zealand remain the next most common countries of birth after Australia. However, the current census showed there has been an increase since the 2011 census in the number of people born in China and India. The statistics given for those born in China increased from 6.0% to 8.3%, and those born in India increased from 5.6% to 7.4% in the 2016 census. The clear majority of Australians recorded a religion in the 2016 census; however, the 'no religion' count increased to almost one-third of the Australian population, from 22% to 30% between 2011 and 2016. Australian statistician David W Kalisch (2016, 2) stated:

The independent Assurance Panel I established to provide extra Assurance and transparency of Census data quality concluded that the 2016 Census data can be used with confidence. The 2016 Census had a response rate of 95.1 per cent and a net undercount of 1.0 per cent. This

Table 1.11 Statistics of a Culturally and Linguistically Diverse Australia

	2016	2011
Language spoken at home (top five)		
1	English only—72.7%	English only—76.8%
2	Mandarin—2.5%	Mandarin—1.6%
3	Arabic—1.4%	Italian—1.4%
4	Cantonese—1.2%	Arabic—1.3%
5	Vietnamese—1.2%	Cantonese—1.2%
Country of birth (top five)		
1	Australia—66.7%	Australia—69.8%
2	England—3.9%	England—4.2%
3	New Zealand—2.2%	New Zealand—2.2%
4	China—2.2%	China—1.5%
5	India—1.9%	India—1.4%
Religion (top five)		
1	No religion—30.1%	Catholic—25.3%
2	Catholic—22.6%	No religion—22.3%
3	Anglican—13.3%	Anglican—17.1%
4	Uniting Church—3.7%	Uniting Church—5.0%
5	Christian, nfd—2.6%	Presbyterian—2.8%

Source: ABS (2016).

is a quality result, comparable to both previous Australian Censuses and Censuses in other countries, such as New Zealand, Canada, and the United Kingdom. Furthermore, 63 per cent of people completed the Census online, embracing the digital-first approach and contributing to faster data processing and data quality improvements. 2016 Census data provides a detailed, accurate and fascinating picture of Australia, which will be used to inform critical policy, planning and service delivery decisions for our communities over the coming years.

As a result of the waves of immigration since 1788, Australia has developed into a multicultural society. Thus, the influx of migration has increased migrant participation in the workforce, leading to the current Australian policy and legislative framework. Nareen Young, CEO of the Diversity Council Australia (2011), claimed that Australia is stable and successful because it is embracing cultural diversity, and stated a firm belief that diversity is an enduring strength. The President of Multicultural Development Australia, Jose Zepeda (2002), also emphasised the importance of inclusiveness in a multicultural workplace as a part of multicultural development. However, it seems there is not enough evidence supporting the claims by Young and Zepeda, given the limited amount of research on diversity management in Australia.

Previous research indicates that multiculturalism is valued in Australia and makes people more open to other cultures, and more open to changing and learning from others (Ang et al. 2006). Changes in attitude can arise from new generations, and the benefits of multiculturalism along with interactive cultural diversity appear to be increasing and more accepted as part of mainstream culture. Hence, the diversity-related problems occurring today may decrease when today's youngsters become tomorrow's adults. However, the current literature does not indicate whether organisations use their diverse employees' multicultural skills. This book specifically addresses this issue and analyses to what extent organisations use the rich skillsets of their multicultural workforces, and promote diversity to take precedence over assimilation.

Immigrants bring many benefits to their newly adopted country. Collins (2008) explained the economic benefits of immigration as similar to those of international trade. Immigration affects the receiving country, and Collins (2008) proposed three levels of these effects in Australia. The first effect is permanent immigration, which in recent years has reverted to high rates after falling to lower levels. The second effect is the high level of immigration because of the reduction in unemployment rates and high demand for labour. The third effect is temporary immigration, which has increased with globalisation. However, Collins's analysis of the effect of immigration on Australia seems to provide only a partial picture of what is actually happening. This is evident in the lack of emphasis he placed on the immigration of unskilled migrants, which presents social cohesion challenges. This has led to changes in immigration policies, not only in Australia, but also in other migrant-receiving countries, such as the US, the UK and Canada. These policy changes are designed to attract more well-educated professionals and skilled workers, while controlling the admission of unskilled migrants and asylum seekers. Further, to keep Australia's economy growing, economic realities dictate that immigration must continue, so that the country has the required skills to achieve economic growth and play a significant role in the global labour market (Easson 2013). This reality highlights the need to manage a diverse workforce effectively so that organisations in specific sectors and in the Australian economy in general can reap the benefits offered by having a multicultural workforce.

It should also be mentioned that the increasing number of immigrants in a national economy poses some serious challenges. Thus, it is important to discuss the flow of immigrants into Australia and the difference they have made in the development of Australia, including their effect on employment as newcomers. Immigrant groups vary and their lives do not fit neatly within national borders. Questions have arisen in relation to the influx of immigrants and whether these new arrivals pose a threat to the jobs of other citizens, welfare state, national identity, way of life, freedom and security, or whether their diversity enriches the economy, culture and society. Thus, certain measurements have been taken to assess the possible advantages and disadvantages of bringing in more immigrants, how much Australia values diversity, the level of fear concerning inter-ethnic clashes and how much flexibility Australia has to embrace the changes immigration causes (Legrain

2007). Immigration policy plays an important role in the influx of skilled immigrants to fill the labour shortages in Australia, yet still places the onus on management to provide a workable strategy to manage diversity in the workplace, as the demographics of organisations are changing under the pressure of increasing levels of diversity in Australia as a migrant-receiving country. This leads to an increased level of uncertainty in the existing Australian workforce. Workplaces in Australia are significantly different from what they were a decade ago with regard to diversity among staff, and organisations must acknowledge and adjust to this diversity.

The political discourse also confirms the development of Australia as a multicultural society. For example, former Prime Minister Bob Hawke (quoted in Foster and Stockley 1988) stated that Australia has been developing as a multicultural society for 200 years as a result of the wave of immigrants that added to the diversity of Australian culture. Another former Prime Minister Malcolm Fraser (2011) stated that diversity through multiculturalism is a quality to be embraced, as well as a source of social wealth and dynamism. Fraser (2011) further argued that multiculturalism encourages all Australians to learn and benefit from each other's heritage because multiculturalism focuses on diversity and interaction, and not division and isolation; thus, it considers respect for law and democratic institutions and processes.

However, with the election of the new Liberal Commonwealth Government in September 2013, there was a shift in multicultural policy in Australia. This shift was evidenced by the change of the name of the relevant federal government department from the 'Department of Immigration and Citizenship' to the 'Department of Immigration and Border Protection', as well as the transfer of the multicultural affairs portfolio from this ministry to the Ministry of Social Services (Abbott 2013). In addition, the previous Prime Minister Tony Abbott (2012) depicted himself as a convert multiculturalist by stating that multiculturalism allows migrants to assimilate gradually as they wish. It is evident that Abbott's concept of multiculturalism in Australia, with its emphasis on assimilation, does not align with the common understanding of multiculturalism in the literature, which is not based solely on assimilation. The effect of Abbot's new policy of multiculturalism on organisations and the diverse workforce is yet to be seen. Thus far, there is no evidence of any legislation enacted by this new government that would affect the management of diversity in the workplace. As detailed in the following paragraphs, there are advocates and opponents of multiculturalism in Australia, and their views provide insights into how multiculturalism is regarded in social and political contexts.

In relation to changes in the understanding of diversity, it is argued that Australia has moved from the age of inequality to the age of equity in the past four decades, as differences have been acknowledged and organisations have deliberately benefited from the diversity of their workforces, as illustrated in Figure 1.2.

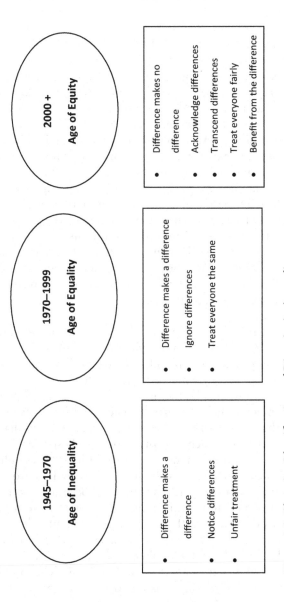

Figure 1.2 Changing Identifications of Diversity in Australia

Source: Silk et al. (2000, 8).

The changing nature of diversity in Australia raises important questions regarding the strategic management of diverse workforces. It also poses serious challenges to organisations, particularly in reshaping their organisational practice to acknowledge and transcend differences and use the benefits offered by a multicultural workforce. Cultural experiences and skills are important to Australian organisations because of the ongoing changes of demographics in the Australian workforce; however, they must be carefully managed.

Some managers cannot distinguish diversity from inclusion. Diversity implies that organisations employ people from different backgrounds and subsequently become diverse, while inclusion involves recognising the differences and values of each employee. Interestingly, inclusion has started to appear as a new paradigm in Australian social policy (Chidiac 2015). Social inclusion is an old idea that promotes building communities in which all people feel that they belong, can contribute and are valued. In principle, social inclusion would ensure a fair go for everyone, irrespective of family of origin. Workplace diversity and inclusion cover many positive aspects of life, such as removing barriers to ensure that all employees participate fully in the workplace, and recognising the value of the cultural differences that each employee brings to the work environment, and how to manage them. Therefore, diversity and inclusiveness are essential business tools in the workplace today. Clearly, the acknowledgement of cultural diversity enables managers to maximise and capitalise on the different skills of employees from different cultures.

As discussed in detail by Shore et al. (2011), the inclusion paradigm is important to organisations when dealing with diverse workforces. According to this paradigm, in a multicultural and inclusive organisation, the organisational strategy, operation and management, as well as the organisational values and success, are shaped by the diversity knowledge and perspectives brought by the members of different groups. The adoption of social inclusion was a feature of the government under John Howard in Australia between 1996 and 2007, and was widely advanced by the Australian Council of Social Service. The government under Kevin Rudd in 2008 established the Australian Social Inclusion Board as the main advisory body to the Commonwealth Government, and pursued a proactive social inclusion policy by asserting that Australians must be given the opportunity to secure employment, access services, connect with others through family, deal with personal crises and have their voices heard. In the current policy, the then Prime Minister Tony Abbott declared the abolition of the Social Inclusion Board in a press release on 23 September 2013 (Chidiac 2015). This could be seen as evidence of the removal of emphasis on social inclusion by the current Australian government, or that the current government considers this is no longer an issue requiring significant or special consideration. Either way, the practice of social inclusion should be further investigated. Social, cultural and demographic changes in Australia over the last two decades will continue to affect the workforce in terms of social inclusion, given that inequality can be exacerbated by differences in gender, culture, ethnicity and location (Hugo 2011). Despite recent changes, cultural and linguistic diversity remain core features of contemporary Australian social and business life, and provide cultural and business advantages to organisations (Chidiac 2015).

Advocacy is about influencing and changing policies, programs and barriers that affect participation in a diverse workforce. This understanding of advocacy was expanded to multicultural societies by Cattalini (1995), who conjectured that the purpose of the three policies—assimilation, integration and multiculturalism—was to embrace the concept of 'oneness', which has many elements, such as 'one people', 'one nation' and being a 'true Australian'. He further argued that Australian assimilation demanded and encouraged a 'oneness' that implied 'sameness', and was characterised by 'exclusive policies'. Multiculturalism recognised various cultures in Australia and subsequently created 'inclusiveness' as a policy for 'all Australians' (Cattalini 1995). A prominent advocate of multiculturalism in Australia, Professor George Zubrzycki—once called 'the father of multiculturalism'—played a significant role in developing multiculturalism in Australia in the 1970s, when the policy was first developed (Jupp 2009). Multiculturalism is intended to enable mixed populations to live together in major cities, while having different ethnic, cultural and religious backgrounds or other distinct features (Jupp and Clyne 2010).

Admittedly, multiculturalism means different things to different people. While some people regard it as a contested concept, others view it as a means of assimilating immigrants into a majority culture. Australian multicultural society is the result of massive waves of immigrants after World War II. The word 'multicultural' was first officially used in Australia in August 1973 in a speech delivered by Al Grassby (quoted in Soutphommasane 2012, 2–3), the then Minister for Immigration under the Gough Whitlam Labor Government. This speech was titled, 'A Multicultural Society for the Future', and contemplated the appearance of Australia in the year 2000:

> Our prime task at this point in our history must be to encourage practical forms of social interaction in our community. This implies the creation of a truly just society in which all components can enjoy freedom to make their own distinctive contribution to the family of the nation. In the interest of the Australians of the year 2000, we need to appreciate and preserve all those diverse elements which find a place in the nation today.

Multiculturalism has received strong support from political circles in Australia. For example, the former Immigration and Citizenship Minister Chris Bowen (quoted in Levey 2012, xv) asserted in a speech, titled 'The Genius of Australian Multiculturalism', that:

> [if] Australia is to be free and equal, then, it will be multicultural. If it is to be multicultural, Australia must remain free and equal. Multiculturalism is a matter of liberalism.

At the beginning of 2001, when opening an exhibition, 'Belonging: A Century Celebrated', at the State Library of New South Wales, William Deane (quoted in Headon 2007, 180), former Governor-General of Australia, presented what he termed the 'Three strands of our Australian identity', one of which was Australia's multicultural inclusiveness:

> The first is the national ethos of mutual acceptance and respect which binds us Australians together notwithstanding our diverse origins—that multicultural inclusiveness sustains our nation. The second of these strands is what I think of as 'the spirit of ANZAC' [Australian and New Zealand Army Corps] . . . courage and endurance, and duty, and love of country, and mateship, and good humour, and the survival of a sense of self-worth and decency in the face of dreadful odds. It also means mutual dependency. . . . The third strand is the generosity and the sense of fair play that are so common among Australians.

However, there is no evidence supporting the view that multiculturalism leads to a free and equal society. This book argues that the success of Australian multiculturalism is attributable to three factors. The first factor is the insistence in Australian multicultural policy for 'respect for traditional Australian values' as stated by the former Immigration and Citizenship Minister (Levey 2012). The traditional Australian values include liberal democratic values, such as freedom of the individual, gender equality, tolerance, the rule of law, parliamentary democracy and English as the national language. The second factor is the Australian 'citizenship-based model', where full rights and benefits are afforded to those who pledge commitment as citizens. The third factor is the bipartisan support for the policy, whereby both Labor and Liberal Governments have supported and guided multiculturalism policy. The extent to which these three political factors have led to a healthy environment for organisations to effectively access the benefits offered by a diverse workforce is yet to be determined. Political support for multiculturalism in Australian policy can lead to positive outcomes, whereby organisations can benefit from immigrants' skills. However, to achieve this, organisations should implement appropriate policies to harness the benefits offered by diverse workforces.

In Australia, opponents exist alongside the proponents for multiculturalism. Opposition to multiculturalism began in the early stages of its introduction, and for example, Collins (1988) argued that giving minorities rights tends to cause division in society, and that granting special rights to minorities threatens to divide the nation into many tribes. He further stated that multiculturalism is costly because it has given the 'ethnic industry' the ability to influence government spending in its favour, away from other Australians. Similarly, Clancy (2007) argued that, prior to 1970, Australia enjoyed core social values similar to other English-speaking and European nations, yet the introduction of multiculturalism caused a profound change.

In addition, Clancy stated that, prior to 1970, Australia enjoyed a social consensus—a general acceptance of rights and responsibilities—yet multiculturalism destroyed this balance, and equal treatment under accepted laws no longer exists. In contrast to Clancy, many believe that multiculturalism did not destroy the balance of rights and responsibilities—instead, it has, at least in principle, extended the rights enjoyed by Anglo-Celtic Australians to all Australians, regardless of their ethnic origins.

Opposition to multiculturalism is evident in the claim by critics from the left and right sides of politics that Anglo-Australians do not recognise themselves in the new narrative of multicultural Australia. Hodge and O'Carroll (2006) argued that opponents of multiculturalism are viewed as being on the right spectrum of politics, while the Australian left maintains a negative attitude to multiculturalism. An opponent of multiculturalism is the Aboriginal poet and activist, who was originally named Kath Walker, yet changed her name to Oodgeroo Noonuccal (quoted in Hodge and O'Carroll 2006), and claimed that Australia has consistently been a 'dumping ground' for foreign cultures. Noonuccal (quoted in Hodge and O'Carroll 2006, 111) called multiculturalism the 'blind prejudice to cultural differences' of Australia. Thus, in multicultural Australia, there has been opposition to multiculturalism from various sections of the community who hold diverse opinions about what it represents. Further, Patterson (2007) went to the extreme by claiming that Australia is simultaneously faced with the threats of multiculturalism and 'Asianisation', and that this is a threat to Australian unity, harmony and coexistence. Patterson advocated the defence of British and national heritage. Over the last 10 years, multiculturalism has been criticised by opponents who have called for a retrieval of the earlier policies of assimilation and integration. The opponents of multiculturalism essentially prefer the 'old days' of assimilation to social tension and divisiveness (Koleth 2010).

In addition to opposition to multiculturalism from different social groups, political opposition to multiculturalism is very active in Australia. Waves of opposition to multiculturalism led to the rise of the One Nation Party, formed by Pauline Hanson in the late 1990s, which demonised multiculturalism and called for its abolition on the basis that it signified a threat to Australian 'culture' (Dellal 2013). A Sri Lankan-born pastor, Daniel Nalliah, also launched a political party, the Rise Up Australia Party, based on opposition to multiculturalism, and committed to keeping 'Australia for Australians' (Medhora 2013). Further opposition was apparent in 2007 when the term 'multiculturalism' was eradicated from official discourse by removing the word from the newly renamed Department of Immigration and Citizenship (Ho 2013). Therefore, in the Australian context, multiculturalism has become a political issue, and the result of recent elections supports that view. It can also be argued that, despite the anti-discrimination laws that have been enacted in the past three decades, anti-multicultural political discourse still receives public support in Australia.

Given the major points raised by the opponents and proponents of multiculturalism, it is important to examine workplace demographics and the associated diversity management considerations. These considerations have become important issues for governments and private enterprises because of the free movement of labour as a result of globalisation, and the struggle for human rights by minority groups in the employment sector. The social and political tensions between the opponents and proponents of multiculturalism have affected organisational practices relating to the management of diversity.

Summary

This chapter explains multiculturalism and civil rights movements, and the different meanings of multiculturalism, including European approaches to multiculturalism. It discusses the immigration and multicultural policies and elimination of divisions between the majority and minorities and the acceptance of others.

The shift that occurred in global structures after the attacks on 11 September 2001 is explained by focusing on, and becoming concerned about, immigration. Further attacks occurred in Madrid, London and the Netherlands which created a conflict between radical Islam and democracy. It is further explained how the waves of newcomers into the US changed the social fabric, and the moves that lead to multicultural and multiracial American society. In addition, details of the implementation of multiculturalism in Canada are explained, as well as the recognition of other cultures into the country and the benefits of immigration, by accepting migrants and embracing their cultures.

This chapter also highlights how the UK became culturally diverse, and how immigrants entered the UK contributing to the multicultural fabric of society. Issues of great concerns are raised in relation to British citizens and their religious loyalties which created friction and conflict. Additionally, this chapter outlines the emergence of multiculturalism in Australia, the benefits brought by the influx of immigrants leading to the development of a multicultural society in the country. The role of immigration, which provided skills, is emphasised with the significant change that occurred in the workplaces.

References

Abbott, T. 2012. 'AMC Lecture—Vote of Thanks by the Hon Tony Abbott MHR, then Leader of the Opposition'. Australian Multicultural Council. Accessed 10 March 2014. www.youtube.com/watch?v=Y3cuC1r0iA0&feature=player_embedded.

———. 2013. 'The Coalition will Restore, Strong, Stable and Accountable Government'. Accessed 14 April 2015. www.liberal.org.au/latest-news/2013/09/23/coalition-will-restore-strong-stable-and-accountable-government.

Abdullah, Melissa Ng Lee Yen. 2013. 'Embracing Diversity by Bridging the School-to-Work Transition of Students with Disabilities in Malaysia'. In *Cultural and Social Diversity and the Transition from Education to Work*, edited by Guy Tchibozo, 163–83. Dordrecht: Springer Netherlands.

ABS. 2012. *Reflecting a Nation: Stories from the 2011 Census*. Canberra: ABS.

———. 2014. *Australian Historical Population Statistics, 2014*. Canberra: ABS.

———. 2016. *2016 Census*. Accessed 16 December 2017. www.abs.gov.au/websit edbs/D3310114.nsf/Home/Census?OpenDocument&ref=topBar.

Alba, Richard. 2016. 'Assimilation in the Past and Present'. In *The Oxford Handbook of American Immigration and Ethnicity*, edited by Ronald H. Bayor, 183–96. New York: Oxford University Press.

Andrew, Caroline. 2007. 'City and Cityscapes in Canada: The Politics and Culture of Canadian Urban Diversity'. In *Managing Diversity: Practices of Citizenship*, edited by Nicholas Brown and Linda Cardinal, 115–36. Ottawa: The University of Ottawa Press.

Ang, I., J. Brand, G. Noble and J. Sternberg. 2006. *Connecting Diversity*. Artarmon: Special Broadcasting Service Corporation.

Appelbaum, Steven H., Oleksandr Kryvenko, Mauricio Rodriguez Parada, Melina Rodica Soochan and Barbara T. Shapiro. 2015. 'Racial-Ethnic Diversity in Canada: Competitive Edge or Corporate Encumbrance? Part Two'. *Industrial and Commercial Training* 47 (7): 386–93.

Asari, Eva-Maria, Daphne Halikiopoulou and Steven Mock. 2008. 'British National Identity and the Dilemmas of Multiculturalism'. *Nationalism and Ethnic Politics* 14 (1): 1–28.

Banting, K. and W. Kymlicka. 2010. 'Canadian Multiculturalism: Global Anxieties and Local Debates'. *British Journal of Canadian Studies* 23 (1): 43–72.

Barrett, James R. 2016. 'The World of the Immigrant Worker'. In *The Oxford Handbook of American Immigration and Ethnicity*, edited by Ronald H. Bayor, 261–85. New York: Oxford University Press.

Bayor, Ronald H. 2016. 'The Making of America'. In *The Oxford Handbook of American Immigration and Ethnicity*, edited by Ronald H. Bayor, 1–13. New York: Oxford University Press.

Berry, John W. 2013. 'Research on Multiculturalism in Canada'. *International Journal of Intercultural Relations* 37 (6): 663–75. doi: http://dx.doi.org/10.1016/j.ijintrel.2013.09.005.

Bliss, M. 1994. *Right Honourable Men: The Descent of Canadian Politics from Macdonald to Mulroney*. Toronto: Harper Collins.

Bukowczyk, John J. 2016. 'New Approaches in Teaching Immigration and Ethnic History'. In *The Oxford Handbook of American Immigration and Ethnicity*, edited by Ronald H. Bayor, 489–507. New York: Oxford University Press.

Carter, Gregory T. 2016. 'Race and Citizenship'. In *The Oxford Handbook of American Immigration and Ethnicity*, edited by Ronald H. Bayor, 166–82. New York: Oxford University Press.

Cattalini, H. 1995. 'Australian Immigration'. Proceedings of the Global Cultural Diversity Conference, 26–28 April 1995, Sydney, Australia.

Chidiac, Emile. 2015. 'A Study of the Strategic Management of Ethnic and Cultural Diversity in Australian Settings: A Multiple Case Study' (PhD thesis, Southern Cross University).

Clancy, G. 2007. 'The Enigma of Multiculturalism'. Accessed 14 May 2007. http://jimball.com.au/Features/Enigma-MultiC,htm.

Collins, J. 1988. *Migrant Hands in a Distant Land: Australia's Post-War Immigration*. Sydney: Pluto Press.

———. 2008. 'Globalisation, Immigration and the Second Long Post-war Boom in Australia'. *Journal of Australian Political Economy* 61: 244–66.

Cooper, C. 2012. 'The Immigration Debate in Australia: From Federation to World War One'. Accessed 29 April 2014. www.aph.gov.au/About_Parlia ment/Parliamentary_Departments/Parliamentary_Library/pubs/BN/2012-2013/ ImmigrationDebate.

Crowder, George. 2013. *Theories of Multiculturalism: An Introduction*. Cambridge: Polity Press.

Dellal, H. 2013. 'Advancing a Multicultural Standpoint'. In *For Those Who've Come Across the Seas: Australian Multicultural Theory, Policy and Practice*, edited by Andrew Jakubowicz and Christina Ho, 128–36. North Melbourne: Australian Scholarly Publishing.

Diversity Council Australia. 2011. 'The New Australian Multiculturalism'. Accessed 13 March 2014. www.dca.org.au/News/All/The-new-Australian-multiculturalism/158.

Dunn, K. M., J. Forrest, I. Burnley and A. McDonald. 2004. 'Constructing Racism in Australia'. *Australian Journal of Social Issues* 39 (4): 409–27.

Easson, M. 2013. 'Skilled Migration is the Key to a Thriving and Cohesive Economy'. *The Australian*. Accessed 29 November 2013. www.theaustralian.com.au/national-affairs/opinion/skilled-migration-is-the-key-to-a-thriving-and-cohesive-economy/story-e6frgd0x-1226573810800#.

Foster, L. and D. Stockley. 1988. *Australian Multiculturalism: A Documentary History and Critique*. Avon: Multilingual Matters.

Fraser, J. M. 2011. 'From White Australia to Today'. Accessed 15 February 2012. www.asrc.org.au/media/documents/how-australia-can-solve-its-asylum-seeker-problem.pdf.

Garcea, Joseph, Anna Kirova and Lloyd Wong. 2008. 'Introduction: Multiculturalism Discourse in Canada'. *Canadian Ethnic Studies Ethniques Au Canada* 40 (1): 1–10.

Goodhart, D. 2008. 'Has Multiculturalism Had Its Day?'. *Literary Review of Canada* 16 (3): 3–4.

Grillo, Ralph. 2010. 'British and Others: From "Race" to "Faith"'. In *The Multiculturalism Backlash*, edited by Steven Vertovec and Susanne Wessendorf, 50–71. Wessendorf: Taylor and Francis.

The Guardian. 2010. 'Angela Merkel: German Multiculturalism Has "Utterly Failed"'. Accessed 7 June 2017. www.theguardian.com/world/2010/oct/17/angela-merkel-german-multiculturalism-failed.

Guiora, Amos N. 2014. *Tolerating Intolerance: The Price of Protecting Extremism*. Oxford: Oxford University Press.

Hackney, S. 1997. *One America, Indivisible: A National Conversation on American Pluralism and Identity*. Washington, DC: National Endowment for the Humanities.

Handzlik, Izabela. 2014. 'Muslim Communities in the United States: A Multicultural Puzzle'. In *Found in Multiculturalism: Acceptance or Challenge?*, edited by Izabela Handzlik and Łukasz Sorokowski, 63–90. Frankfurt: Peter Lang.

Headon, David. 2007. 'Howard's Way or Dean's Way: Culture Wars in Contemporary Australia'. In *Managing Diversity: Practices of Citizenship*, edited by Nicholas Brown and Linda Cardinal, 165–84. Ottawa: The University of Ottawa Press.

Hiranandani, V. 2012. 'Diversity Management in the Canadian Workplace: Towards an Antiracism Approach'. *Urban Studies Research*: 1–13.

Ho, C. 2013. 'From Social Justice to Social Cohesion: A History of Australian Multicultural Policy'. In *For Those Who've Come Across the Seas: Australian Multicultural Theory, Policy and Practice*, edited by Andrew Jakubowicz and Christina Ho, 31–44. North Melbourne: Australian Scholarly Publishing.

Hodge, B. and J. O'Carroll. 2006. *Borderwork in Multicultural Australia*. Crows Nest: Allen & Unwin.

Howarth, C. and E. Andreouli. 2016. ' "Nobody Wants to Be an Outsider": From Diversity Management to Diversity Engagement'. *Political Psychology* 37: 327–40.

Hsu, Madeleine Y. 2016. 'Asian Immigration'. In *The Oxford Handbook of American Immigration and Ethnicity*, edited by Ronald H. Bayor, 53–66. New York: Oxford University Press.

Hughes, R. 1993. *Culture of Complaint: The Fraying of America*. New York: Oxford University Press.

Hugo, G. 2011. 'Social, Demographic and Cultural Trends'. Accessed 5 February 2014. www.awpa.gov.au/events/documents/hugo_briefing.pdf.

Hutchins-Viroux, R. 2009. 'Multiculturalism in American History Textbooks Before and After 9/11'. In *American Multiculturalism After 9/11: Transatlantic Perspectives*, edited by D. Rubin and J. Verheul, 133–46. Amsterdam: Amsterdam University Press.

International Organization for Migration. 2010. 'World Migration Report 2010—The Future of Migration: Building Capacities for Change'. Accessed 3 December 2012. https://publications.iom.int/system/files/pdf/wmr_2010_english.pdf.

Ivison, Duncan. 2010. 'Introduction: Multiculturalism as a Public Ideal'. In *The Ashgate Research Companion to Multiculturalism*, edited by Duncan Ivison, 1–18. Farnham: Ashgate.

Jahanbegloo, R. and B. Parekh. 2011. *Talking Politics: Bhikhu Parekh in Conversation with Ramin Jahanbegloo*. India: OUP.

Jawor, Anna. 2014. 'Is a Rainbow Society Possible? Sociological Challenges in the Age of Postmodern Multiculturalism'. In *Found in Multiculturalism: Acceptance or Challenge?*, edited by Izabela Handzlik and Łukasz Sorokowski, 121–40. Frankfurt am Main: Peter Lang Edition.

Joppke, C. 1996. 'Multiculturalism and Immigration: A Comparison of the United States, Germany and Great Britain'. *Theory and Society* 25 (4): 449–500.

Jupp, J. 2009. 'An advocate for multiculturalism'. *The Age*. Accessed 7 February 2014. www.theage.com.au/comment/obituaries/an-advocate-for-multiculturalism-20090525-bktv.html

Jupp, J. and M. Clyne. 2010. *Multiculturalism and Integration: A Harmonious Relationship*. Canberra: ANU Press.

Kalisch, David W. 2016. *2016 Census: Multicultural*. Accessed 8 October 2017. www.abs.gov.au/ausstats/abs@.nsf/lookup/Media%20Release3.

Kim, Nam-Kook. 2011. 'Deliberative Multiculturalism in New Labour's Britain'. *Citizenship Studies* 15 (1): 125–44. doi: 10.1080/13621025.2010.534938.

Koleth, Elsa. 2010. *Multiculturalism: A Review of Australian Policy Statements and Recent Debates in Australia and Overseas*. Canberra: Parliament of Australia, Department of Parliamentary Services.

Lauter, Paul. 2009. 'Multiculturalism and Immigration'. In *American Multiculturalism After 9/11: Transatlantic Perspectives*, edited by D. Reuben and J. Verheul, 23–34. Amsterdam: Amsterdam University Press.

Legrain, P. 2007. *Immigrants: Your Country Needs Them*. Princeton: Princeton University Press.

Lever-Tracey, C. and M Quinlan. 1988. *A Divided Working Class: Ethnic Segmentation and Industrial Conflict in Australia*. London: Routledge & Kegan Paul.

Levey, G. B. 2012. 'Australian Multiculturalism Rides Again'. In *Political Theory & Australian Multiculturalism*, edited by Geoffrey Brahm Levy, xii—xviii. Oxford: Berghahn Books.

Markus, A. B. 2011. 'A Context for the Asylum Debate'. *Gesher* 4 (2): 44–7.

Marshall, E. Anne, Suzanne L. Stewart, Natalee E. Popadiuk and Breanna C. Lawrence. 2013. 'Walking in Multiple Worlds: Successful School-to-work Transitions for Aboriginal and Cultural Minority Youth'. In *Cultural and Social Diversity and the Transition from Education to Work*, edited by Guy Tchibozo, 185–201. Dordrecht: Springer Netherlands.

Medhora, S. 2013. 'New Party Seeks to Curb Muslim Immigration'. Accessed 16 March 2014. http://theantibogan.wordpress.com/tag/anti-multiculturalism/.

Modood, Tariq. 2007. *Multiculturalism: A Civic Idea*. Cambridge: Polity Press.

Modood, Tariq and Nasar Meer. 2012. 'Interculturalism, Multiculturalism or Both?'. *Political Insight* 3 (1): 30–3. doi: 10.1111/j.2041-9066.2012.00097.x.

Mudde, Cas. 2016. 'Putting Canada in a Comparative Context: Still the Multiculturalist Unicorn'. *Nationalism and Ethnic Politics* 22 (3): 351–7. doi: 10.1080/13537113.2016.1203710.

Mulder, Marlene and Harvey Krahn. 2005. 'Individual- and Community-Level Determinants of Support for Immigration and Cultural Diversity in Canada'. *Canadian Review of Sociology/Revue Canadienne de Sociologie* 42 (4): 421–44. doi: 10.1111/j.1755-618X.2005.tb00848.x.

Ng, Eddy S. and Irene Bloemraad. 2015. 'A SWOT Analysis of Multiculturalism in Canada, Europe, Mauritius, and South Korea'. *American Behavioral Scientist* 59 (6): 619–36.

Nkomo, S. and Jenny M. Hoobler. 2014. 'A Historical Perspective on Diversity Ideologies in the United States: Reflections on Human Resource Management Research and Practice'. *Human Resource Management Review* 24 (3): 245–57.

Office for National Statistics. 2011. *Census 2011*. Office for National Statistics. Accessed 12 November 2015. www.ons.gov.uk/census/2011census.

Palmer, Howard. 2002. 'Reluctant Hosts: Anglo-Canadian Views of Multiculturalism in the Twentieth Century'. In *Readings in Canadian History: Post-Confederation*, edited by R. Douglas Francis and Donald B. Smith, 116–30. Toronto: Nelson.

Patterson, A. 2007. 'The Fight for Australian Culture'. Accessed 7 May 2009. http://home.alphalink.com.au/eureka/cult.html.

Pew Research Center. 2015. *Modern Immigration Wave Brings 59 Million to U.S., Driving Population Growth and Change Through 2065: Views of Immigration's Impact on U.S. Society Mixed*. Washington, DC: Pew Research Center.

Price, H. B. 1992. 'Multiculturalism: Myths or Realities'. *The Phi Delta Kappan* 74 (3): 208–13.

Ryan, P. 2010. 'Does Canadian Multiculturalism Survive Through State Repression?'. *Nationalism and Ethnic Politics* 22 (3): 342–50.

Shore, Lynn M., Amy E. Randel, Beth G. Chung, Michelle A. Dean, Karen Holcombe Ehrhart and Gangaram Singh. 2011. 'Inclusion and Diversity in Work Groups: A Review and Model for Future Research'. *Journal of Management* 37 (4): 1262–89.

Silk, C., R. Boyle, A. Bright, M. Bassett and N. Roach. 2000. *The Case for Cultural Diversity in Defence*. Canberra: Australian Defence Organisation.

Soutphommasane, Tim. 2012. *Don't Go back to Where You Came from: Why Multiculturalism Works*. Sydney: New South Publishing.

Statistics Canada. 2006. 'Census of Population'. Accessed 4 September 2017. http://www12.statcan.gc.ca/census-recensement/2006/index-eng.cfm

———. 2011. 'National Household Survey: Immigration and Ethnocultural Diversity in Canada'. Accessed 6 September 2017 http://www12.statcan.gc.ca/nhs-enm/2011/as-sa/99-010-x/99-010-x2011001-eng.cfm.

———. 2016a. 'Census Profile, 2016 Census'. Accessed 6 September 2017. http://www12.statcan.gc.ca/census-recensement/2016/dp-pd/prof/index.cfm?Lang=E.

———. 2016b. 'Visible Minority, 2016 Census'. Accessed 6 September 2017. http://www12.statcan.gc.ca/datasets/index-eng.cfm?Temporal=2016

St-Onge, Sylvie. 2015. 'Accommodations in Religious Matters: Quebec and Canadian Perspectives'. In *Managing Religious Diversity in the Workplace*, edited by Stefan Groschl and Regine Bendl, 9–30. Surrey: Gower Applied Business Research.

Taylor-Gooby, Peter and Edmund Waite. 2014. 'Toward a More Pragmatic Multiculturalism? How the U.K. Policy Community Sees the Future of Ethnic Diversity Policies'. *Governance* 27 (2): 267–89. doi: 10.1111/gove.12030.

Thompson, Debra. 2012. 'Making (Mixed-) Race: Census Politics and the Emergence of Multiracial Multiculturalism in the United States, Great Britain and Canada'. *Ethnic and Racial Studies* 35 (8): 1409–26. doi: 10.1080/01419870.2011.556194.

Trudeau, Justin. 2015. 'Diversity is Canada's Strength'. Accessed 7 September 2017. http://pm.gc.ca/eng/news/2015/11/26/diversity-canadas-strength.

UNESCO. 2006. *UNESCO Guidelines on International Education*. Paris: UNESCO Section of Education for Peace and Human Rights.

Wegner, P. E. 2009. ' "The Dead are Our Redeemers": Culture, Belief, and United 93'. In *American Multiculturalism After 9/11: Transatlantic Perspectives*, edited by D. Rubin and J. Verheul, 81–92. Amsterdam: Amsterdam University Press.

Wood, P. K. and L. Gilbert. 2005. 'Multiculturalism in Canada: Accidental Discourse, Alternative Vision, Urban Practice'. *International Journal of Urban and Regional Research* 29 (3): 679–91.

Xu, Liton Weili. 2013. 'Cultural Diversity in a School-to-work Transition Programme for Undergraduate Students'. In *Cultural and Social Diversity and the Transition from Education to Work*, edited by Guy Tchibozo, 203–22. Dordrecht: Springer Netherlands.

Zepeda, J. 2002. *Rich Cultures—One Workplace*. Woolloongabba: Multicultural Development Association.

2 Diversity in the Workforce

Facts and Figures

Diversity in the US Workforce

The formation of the working class in the US was complicated by the influx of immigrants from the nineteenth century to the present, which was led by ethnic differences and 'ethnically hybrid' cultures distinguished by class. The consecutive waves of migration over 200 years brought their own cultures, languages and organisations. By the middle of the nineteenth century, some industrial workers demanded better wages and shorter hours to make the US more egalitarian. Between the 1880s and mid-1920s, more than 25 million 'new immigrants' arrived and joined the earlier generations in the US. Further, internal migrants brought millions of African American and Mexican workers with their families to join the industrial communities, thereby forming the contemporary American working-class population. While some communities lived in 'ethnic ghettos', others seemed to be physically integrated, yet culturally segregated, having their own ethnic cultures and institutions, and mixing with other ethnic groups (Barrett 2016). The historical data shown in Table 2.1 indicates that the level of ethnic diversity in the US has been steadily increasing since the 1960s. While the share of white population was 84% in 1960, it had decreased to 62% in 2015. In the same period, all other ethnicities have increased their shares in the US population. The two ethnicities that have shown very high levels of increase in the US population have been Hispanics and Asians, whose share increased from 3% to 19% and from 0.6% to 6%, respectively, from 1960 to 2015.

Organisations in the US are dominated by middle-aged white heterosexual men, and it is essential to create a more diverse workplace, as organisations would benefit from a wider range of personnel. AA, which started over 40 years ago, has been one of the driving forces in increasing diversity, with the purpose of improving employment and educational opportunities for specific groups, including women, ethnic minorities and people with disabilities. AA has achieved many changes in the public sector and military; however, it has been unsuccessful in education, with a number of disadvantaged students still unable to access adequate resources. Private-sector organisations tend to follow their own policies, yet can still be sued through anti-discrimination laws for failing to give individuals' fair opportunities (ATMA Global 2014).

Table 2.1 Occupation Distribution of Recently Arrived Immigrants in the US

Occupation	% among recently arrived immigrants					
	1970	*1980*	*1990*	*2000*	*2007*	*2013*
Managerial and professional	20	18	17	19	19	28
Technical, sales and administrative support	22	22	23	22	19	23
Service	17	19	23	21	24	24
Farming, forestry and fishing	3	5	6	6	7	5
Precision production, craft and repairs	10	10	10	11	13	7
Operatives and labourers	28	27	21	21	19	13

Source: Pew Research Center (2015).

Globalisation, migration and social justice have affected the representation of diverse groups in organisations, especially in the US, where the demographic diversity of the workforce has greatly increased. Implemented policies—included AA and EEO—seem to have helped underrepresented groups gain access to some jobs from which they were previously excluded (Tsui and Gutek 1999). The election of the first African American president in the US in 2008 proved that American's painful history of racial subjugation can be overcome, with President Barack Obama becoming the most diverse president in American history. However, diversity exists in the people's imagination, yet many men and women of colour have attained great business success and made significant contributions to their various positions held in organisations.

In the mid-1990s, research showed that white people were more favoured in the workplace than black people. Regarding the promotion of 1,268 managerial and professional employees, black and Asian people were rated lower than white people (Reed 2011). In addition, female employees were rated lower than male employees by managers. The fact that one-third of the Fortune 100 firms have struggled with this issue since 1995 indicates that race is still a main factor in promotions. In 2009, the female executive officers at Target represented 30%—the highest proportion of women in the white group of companies (Reed 2011). In 2009, about 8% of the white executive officers in the Fortune 100 companies were born in Canada, Europe or the Middle East, and brought with them the attraction of international markets (Reed 2011). These findings reveal that some organisations are not interpreting diversity as a melting pot, but as a smorgasbord to choose what they need and ignore the rest. As an employment concept, diversity has failed to solve white job segregation at the top level of organisations. As a result of globalisation and expansion into foreign countries, organisations recruit the right people who can speak the necessary languages and know how to respond to foreign markets. Organisations view diverse people as enormous assets to gain market superiority through local knowledge, experience and language ability, and these qualities have helped these people climb to the highest leadership ranks in organisations (Reed 2011).

The fact that the US workforce is becoming more diverse is an indication of the importance of diversity to the economy and society. As of June 2012, people of colour comprised 36% of the US labour force. To break the working population into race and ethnicity, about 99,945,000 (64%) in the labour force are non-Hispanic white, 24,679,000 (16%) are Hispanic, 18,775,000 (12%) are African American and 8,202,000 (5%) are Asian. About 4,801,000 people (3%) in the labour force are not identified in any racial or ethnic categories. It is anticipated that the proportion of people of colour will increase as the country becomes more racially and ethnically diverse. Census data reveal that, by 2050, there will be no racial or ethnic majority in the US. Additionally, between 2000 and 2050, new immigrants and their children will form 83% of growth in the working-age population. Of Hispanics in the labour force, the rate stands at 58% for men and 42% for women. For African Americans in the labour force, the rate is 53% for women and 47% for men (Burns, Barton and Kerby 2012). While attempts to attain racial equality in the US have caused ethnic mixture in several organisations, there is still more work to be done in this area. As late as the 1980s, black workers were only employed in low-paying manual jobs. However, greater racial diversity does not denote equal opportunities or equal pay. Inequality arises from education levels, yet this trend is slowly changing (ATMA Global 2014).

These data indicate that the diversity of the US population is naturally reflected in the diversity of the US workforce, which is one of the world's most diverse national workforces in terms of individual differences, such as culture, sex, ethnicity and sexual orientation. The 2012 data show that the American workforce consists of 64% non-Hispanic white, 16% Hispanic, 12% African American and 5% Asian employees (Burns, Barton and Kerby 2012). In the US context, both civil rights legislation and AA have changed the demographic composition of the American workforce, resulting in high diversity in organisations. Considerable efforts have been made to ensure people from diverse backgrounds have equal access to public jobs in the workplace. Since the *Civil Rights Act of 1964*, the US federal government has endeavoured to include both women and minorities in the employment of federal agencies, and to correct the problem of underrepresentation therein. The term 'American Labor'—which has been synonymous with the white male working class for a long time—has undergone a sound change since the 1960s, which also led to the formation of a different labour movement. In the late 1980s, white males comprised more than half of the unionised workforce, yet now represent only one-third of this workforce, while the proportion of black workers ranges from 13% to 15%. Thus, the new labour movement has emerged as increasingly immigrant and female (Barrett 2016). Table 2.2 provides recent data for employment status in the US workforce by race.

In their book, *Workforce 2020*, published in 1997, Judy and D'Amico (1997) predicted that organisations in the US would face four major

Table 2.2 Employment Status of the US Civilian Non-institutional Population by Age and Race, 2016

	Percentage of population	Employed	Unemployed
		Percentage of population	Percentage of labour force
Total			
16 years and over	62.8	59.7	4.9
16 to 19 years	35.2	29.7	15.7
20 to 24 years	70.5	64.6	8.4
25 to 54 years	81.3	77.9	4.2
55 to 64 years	64.1	61.8	3.6
65 years and over	19.3	18.6	3.8
White			
16 years and over	62.9	60.2	4.3
16 to 19 years	37.4	32.1	14.1
16 to 17 years	25.5	21.4	16.1
20 to 24 years	72.4	67.2	7.2
25 to 54 years	82.1	79.1	3.6
55 to 64 years	65.4	63.2	3.3
65 years and over	19.5	18.8	3.7
Black or African American			
16 years and over	61.6	56.4	8.4
16 to 19 years	29.0	21.3	26.7
20 to 24 years	67.7	57.8	14.5
25 to 54 years	78.9	73.3	7.1
55 to 64 years	55.1	52.2	5.4
65 years and over	16.6	15.6	5.8
Asian			
16 years and over	63.2	60.9	3.6
16 to 19 years	21.2	18.8	10.9
20 to 24 years	53.0	49.4	6.9
25 to 54 years	78.7	76.2	3.2
55 to 64 years	67.4	65.1	3.4
65 years and over	20.0	19.3	3.2

Source: Bureau of Labor Statistics (2016).

macro-environmental opportunities. First, rapid technological change would create more jobs for knowledge employees, and reduce the opportunities for women and older American people. Second, the expanding economies in Asia and Latin America would lead to increased competition for low-skilled jobs and increase the instability of the American economy. Third, baby boomers would work beyond their retirement age, and thus constitute a major consumer segment in the economy. Fourth, the US labour force would be more diversified, with minorities forming more than half of new net entrants and a minimum of one-third of all entrants to the workforce. In the American context, it is claimed that, with the fast growth in demographic diversity in the workplace, organisations would have to 'embrace and value' diversity and acknowledge that human resources are an advantage if and when workplace diversity programs are effectively managed (Oyler and Pryor 2009).

Diversity in the Canadian Workforce

Canada became the first country in the world to adopt a multicultural policy through the *Multiculturalism Act* in 1988, aiming to encourage immigrants to retain their cultural heritage, rather than assimilate. The *Multiculturalism Act* is a policy of inclusion that recognises the potential of all Canadians, and encourages participation in Canada's social, cultural, economic and political life. This recognition makes Canadians more open to and accepting of diverse cultures. Thus, the Canadian government is accountable and ensures that they 'carry on their activities in a manner that is sensitive and responsive to the multicultural reality of Canada' (*Canadian Multiculturalism Act 1985*, 4). Consequently, Canadian organisations are urged to consider multiculturalism when hiring and promoting employees from different backgrounds in order to serve a diverse public. Eighty-four per cent of Canadians are in favour of multiculturalism and immigration (Ng and Metz 2015).

When a multiculturalism policy was first introduced in Canada in 1971, the census data revealed that 96% of the Canadian population were of ethnic European origin, yet, by 2011, only 63% of Canadians reported the same. Originally, immigrants to Canada came from Europe; however, in the last 30 years, Asia and the Pacific region have been the principal source of immigrants. As diversity grows in Canada, federal institutions continue to support equal treatment and full participation in society, and enhance policies and programs that enable individuals and communities of all backgrounds to contribute to Canada's evolution. Despite the challenges met by some small institutions in endeavouring to meet their obligations pursuant to the Canadian *Multiculturalism Act* because of limited resources, they remain committed to finding solutions and pooling their resources. The Department of Canadian Heritage remains supportive of efforts to enable all people to help build an inclusive society. However, Canada's success as a diverse and inclusive nation was not built without effort, as diversity and inclusion have made Canada strong and free in practice (Trudeau 2015). Table 2.3 shows labour market data for the racialised population in Canada.

As a major migrant-receiving country with an officially adopted multiculturalism policy, Canada has an ethnically and culturally diverse population. Before 1967, more than 80% of immigrants to Canada came from Europe; however, this has since declined to one in five (Mulder and Krahn

Table 2.3 Participation, Employment and Unemployment Rates by Racialised Groups in Canada, 2006

	Participation rate (%)	Employment rate (%)	Unemployment rate (%)
Total racialised population	67.3	61.5	8.6
Chinese	62.0	57.3	7.5
South Asian	68.5	62.6	8.6
Black	70.7	63.2	10.7
Filipino	76.6	72.8	5.0
Latin American	71.9	65.4	9.0
Southeast Asian	68.9	63.1	8.5
Arab/West Asian	64.1	56.3	12.1
Korean	54.8	50.1	8.5
Japanese	61.6	58.5	5.1
Visible minority, nie	71.1	65.6	7.8
Multiple visible minority	72.7	66.5	8.5
Non-racialised	66.7	62.6	6.2

Source: Statistics Canada (2006).

2005). Since 1979, more than half of all immigrants to Canada (54%) came from Asia. Around 79% of all newcomers settle in Canada's three largest centres—Montreal, Toronto and Vancouver—and subsequently enhance the cultural diversity of these three 'capitals of immigration' and other communities. In 2001, visible minorities comprised more than one-third of Toronto's population, yet only 17% of Calgary's population (Mulder and Krahn 2005). In 2006, it was anticipated that by 2017, 20.25% of all Canadians would be members of minority groups by 2017, and increase to as much as over 50% of the population in some major cities, such as Toronto and Vancouver (Dib 2006). Immigrants will be the source of all population growth in Canada by 2025. It seems that both Aboriginal peoples and visible minorities have more youthful populations and higher fertility rates than do the general Canadian population, who have an average of less than 1.5 children per woman (Dib 2006).

The Canadian census data show that immigrants comprised two-thirds of Canada's population growth of 2 million people between 2006 and 2011, which has contributed to Canada's economic growth (Ng and Metz 2015). Today, Asia and the Middle East lead the list, with seven in 10 immigrants coming from these regions. It is anticipated that one in three workers will be foreign born by 2031. In the meantime, Canada endeavours to promote the multicultural heritage of Canadians. As a result, the majority of immigrants (80%) in Canada speak languages other than English and French, with Chinese, Punjabi, Spanish, Arabic and Tagalog representing most of the languages spoken by immigrants at home (Ng and Metz 2015). Canada's people, including a great number of visible minorities, contribute to the prosperity of the country. The ethno-cultural diversity of Canada's population is expected to increase by 2031, and, in the *Canada Year Book 2011*, Statistics Canada (quoted in Conference Board of Canada 2013) reported that:

> By 2031, 2.9% to 32% per cent of Canada's population—between 11.4 and 14.4 million people—could belong to a visible minority group, which is nearly double the proportion (16%) and more than the number (5.3 million) reported in 2006.

At a time when Canada is facing labour shortages and projected shrinking labour because of the retirement of significant numbers of baby boomers, Canada needs to depend on immigrants to fill the gap in its labour force. A 2004 study by the Conference Board of Canada (2013) revealed that, between 1992 and 2001, visible minorities formed over 0.3% per year of growth in potential output, as well as real gross domestic product. It is expected that the contribution of visible minorities and the total elimination of this existing 14.5% wage gap will benefit visible minorities and the overall economy in Canada (Conference Board of Canada 2013). A skills shortage will be noticeable in certain professions as retirements begin to occur. Moreover, it seems that the fertility rate has declined below the rate needed to maintain the population, thereby resulting in fewer Canadians to replace the retirees. This change has placed pressure on immigration to establish a labour force, and it is reported that Canada will need about 225,000 newcomers each year to keep pace with economic growth and to enjoy the same standard of living to which it has been accustomed over the last 30 years (Rotundo 2012). Therefore, immigration will be useful to address skills shortage in specific professions and trades (Rotundo 2012).

A 2006 survey on diversity-related practices and priorities in Canadian private- and public-sector organisations conducted by the Conference Board of Canada (2013) revealed that diversity has become an integral part of strategic planning and operation of Canadian organisations. According to the study, there appeared to be strong commitment to diversity by the participating organisations, yet a gap between policy and performance because of many organisations' failure to adhere to their commitment to diversity and provide inclusive work environments (Conference Board of Canada 2013). More recent research confirms the findings of the 2006 survey by revealing that two-thirds of Canadian organisations either adopt a collaborative (40%) or inclusive (11%) approach to diversity management, or embrace diversity (20%), while struggling to optimise its outcomes. Only a minority of Canadian organisations have a compliance culture, and hence view diversity as a problem (24%), or have a singular culture (4%) (Garr,

Shellenback and Scales 2014, 14). This is contrary to the findings in the US, which revealed that 11% of US organisations have a compliance culture. Similarly, the regulatory laws in Canada serve as a driver for organisations to deal with diversity and inclusion. The percentage of 11% confirms that Canadian organisations are still at the compliance level. However, 49% of the Canadian survey respondents stated that their organisation had begun concentrating on non-compliance diversity and inclusion in the last five years (Garr, Shellenback and Scales 2014). The research further indicated that almost half of Canadian organisations started to implement inclusion efforts beyond compliance during the last five years (Garr, Shellenback and Scales 2014). Table 2.4 indicates the diversity and inclusion of staff size in the Canadian workplace.

According to recent statistics, members of *EEA*-designated groups, who encompass women, people with disabilities, Aboriginal people and visible minorities, represent increasing numbers of the Canadian labour market. From 2006 to 2011, two-thirds of labour market growth in Canada was spurred by the majority of newly arrived immigrants. In 2015, women formed 46.7% of the total employed labour force in Canada (Cukier et al. 2017). Meanwhile, research has revealed that, although members of the designated groups exist at the senior management and middle management levels, they are still considered underrepresented at both levels in comparison to their availability in the labour force (Cukier et al. 2017). When the *EEA* was implemented in Canada, the idea of diversity management emerged in the US as an outstanding characteristic of change in the workplace demographics of the workforce. The Royal Bank of Canada (quoted in Cukier et al. 2017, 1034) announced that, economically, 'how well Canada continues to meet the challenges of diversity will determine our future success in attracting talented immigrants as global competition for talent intensifies'.

Table 2.4 Diversity and Inclusion Staff Size by Employer Size

	Number of dedicated staff members				
	None	Less than one	One to three	Four to six	More than six
Large companies (more than 25,000 employees)	24	24	29	12	12
Medium companies (5,000 to 25,000 employees)	42	8	42	–	8
Small companies (less than 5,000 employees)	60	13	27	–	–

Source: Garr, Shellenback and Scales (2014).

Diversity in the UK Workforce

The UK labour market has become diverse with the participation of ethnic and religious minorities in the workforce; however, equality among different groups is yet to be achieved. Previous studies indicate that ethnic and religious minorities still experience occupational segregation and pay gaps. Muslims comprise the religious minority with the lowest employment rate (47% for men and 24% for women), while black graduates experience a 24% earnings penalty (Klarsfeld, Ng and Tatli 2012). In relation to employment equity legislation in the public and private sectors in the UK, the *Equality Act 2010* covers age, disability, gender reassignment, pregnancy and maternity, race and ethnicity, religion or beliefs and sexual orientation. However, research indicates that public sector organisations in the UK enforce the equality legislation more strongly and subsequently minimise evasion, while the interpretation and implementation of the *Equity Act* is more voluntary in private-sector organisations (Klarsfeld, Ng and Tatli 2012).

Black, Asian and minority ethnic (BAME) groups in the UK seem to be underrepresented at all management levels in the workplace. About one in eight of the working-age population come from a BAME background, yet only one in 10 are working, and only one in 16 top management positions are held by an ethnic minority person (Kerr 2015). While British people with a BAME background seem to enjoy their work, they are not rated as the best performers when compared with their white colleagues. When asked about the term BAME 'black and minority ethnic' that these groups prefer, there are differences in opinion among ethnic minority groups, and no consensus on the preferred terminology (Kerr 2015).

Race affects individuals in the workplace in many ways, such as their rates of employment. For example, in the UK, 13% of ethnic minorities are unemployed, compared with only 8% of the general population. Further, research indicates that ethnic minority workers in the UK experience a pay gap in their earnings when compared with white workers.

The 'Race at Work' report (Kerr 2015) gives a better understanding of the underrepresentation of ethnic minorities in the workplace and at senior level. This report examined the experiences of 24,457 ethnic minority and white employees aged 16 and over and currently employed in the UK. Via a YouGov survey (6,076 respondents) and public open survey (18,381), the participants indicated that:

- BAME people are more likely to enjoy their work and have far greater ambition than their white colleagues: 64% of BAME and 41% of white employees emphasised the importance of their career progress. Similarly, the open survey showed that 84% of BAME employees and 63% of white employees stated that it is important to progress (Kerr 2015).
- Racial harassment and bullying in the workplace is prevalent: '30% of those employees who have witnessed or experienced racial harassment

or bullying from managers, colleagues, customers or suppliers report it has occurred in the past year alone' (Kerr 2015, 3).

- **Many UK employees do not feel valued or inspired:** Many employees without career role models or inspiration feel they are unappreciated by their managers. The absence:

  of role models in the workplace is stark for Black Caribbean (11%), other black group employees (7%), Chinese and mixed-race employees lacking role models both inside and outside of the workplace (Kerr 2015, 3).

- **Employees feel uncomfortable discussing race at work:** UK employees might feel comfortable discussing age and gender, but not race. Employers need more confidence dealing with race in the workplace and understanding its effect on individuals and their ability to reach their full potential—especially because race also affects organisational success and survival (Kerr 2015).

People in the UK are three times more likely to take the racial bias test than any other country in relation to age, gender or sexuality because of what they have read in the media. This led to a race equality campaign to determine what is occurring in regard to race in workplaces in the UK. The target was to hear from 10,000 employed people in the UK, aged 16 or above (Kerr 2015). More than 2,000 comments on discrimination and 3,000 on leadership were submitted, with 6,076 respondents representing UK employees and 18,381 respondents to the open survey—a total of 24,457 respondents. The changing demographic of the UK workforce includes its age, education background and ethnicity, which indicates that employers have to provide workplaces that truly reflect equality for all today and tomorrow, and that now is the time to act (Kerr 2015). Organisations in the UK are seeking to prioritise diversity, yet the solutions seem complex and more must be done in relation to recruitment, professional and mentoring issues. It is also important to consider customers, suppliers, employers, shareholders and the public, who have a stake in creating a fairer, more equal environment in the UK (DiversityUK 2016). Clearly, it will take some time to achieve fair representation of ethnic minorities in public and private sectors (DiversityUK 2016).

Diversity in the Australian Workforce

Successful adaptation to diversity depends on the small and everyday actions taken by the individuals in organisations at all levels (Kreitz 2007); however, diversity poses challenges to organisations in many fields today. Demographic changes in the workforce are affected by global markets and international competition, and increase the level of diversity in organisations. This increased diversity needs to be managed internally at an organisational level, where increased diversity is caused by demographic changes in the compositions of the workforce, and externally at a customer level, where increased diversity is caused by demographic changes in customer populations, combined with the globalisation of markets. Riccucci (2002) regarded diversity as the next step needed to create a more integrated workforce. Whether and the extent to which this is occurring in Australia constitutes one of the main issues explored in this book.

Developing a clear understanding of workplace demographics is essential to examine how the dynamics of change affect national economies, and how organisations adapt and manage such changes in the face of constantly increasing levels of diversity in the workplace. The Community Relations Commission for Multicultural New South Wales (2011) stated that Australia has become a productive culturally diverse nation with an annual migrant intake that targets the skills and demands of the labour market, as well as the integration and success of second-generation migrants. According to the commission, this has been achieved because of successive governments' recognition of the need to implement policies for the national economic interest, and because of the settlement programs that have been conducted with fairness and integrity in Australia's migration program (Community Relations Commission for Multicultural New South Wales 2011). It is apparent that the fairness and integrity of the settlement program does not necessarily lead to effective management of diversity in the workplace; thus, the ways that organisations are managing their increasing levels of diverse workforce requires further investigation.

Australian workplace statistics have also revealed the multicultural features of the national demographics, which are naturally reflected in the Australian workforce. This was evident in the release of 2016 Census of Population and Housing data, published by the ABS. The 2016 census (ABS 2016) revealed that almost one-third (33.3%) of Australians were born overseas and the majority of immigrants belong to working-age groups. Thus, the question of whether diversity in the workplace is managed effectively becomes a real issue.

Diversity management has become a necessity, and can be seen as a natural outcome of globalisation. There is acknowledgement that diversity is an effect of globalisation, which is the 'defining political economic paradigm of our time' (Bratton and Gold 2007, 120), and, with this increasing internationalisation, diversity is becoming a strategic success factor for leading companies. The importance of a diverse workforce is also indicated by the claim that managing workforce diversity is important for success and penetration of the global market (Henry and Evans 2007). Globalisation has had a significant effect on the migration of people from various cultural backgrounds who have joined the Australian workforce and now form a substantial proportion of diversity in the workplace. However, while governments are facilitating the circulation of goods and services around the globe, they are endeavouring to impose higher national barriers to restrict the free movement of people. This affects immigrants from various backgrounds who form the workforce, yet it remains unclear how this is experienced in the workplace.

As discussed, the demographics of the Australian workforce have changed dramatically over the years, as has the global marketplace. The success of the strategic management of diversity in the workplace depends on the recognition of employees' differences and skills, and using them to their full potential. The more we investigate diversity, the more we find that diversity is a concept that is linked to population distribution, socio-political features and the workforce. Thus, the attributes of workplace diversity relate to employees who come from different backgrounds and possess these attributes in varying degrees.

Summary

This chapter deals with waves of immigrants into the US over a long period of time who brought with them their cultures and languages, and how, over a period of time, it created a diverse workplace. The various policies in the private and public sectors are discussed, together with the factors that impacted on diversity in organisations. The importance of diversity in the US is explained and how equal opportunities are afforded to individuals.

This chapter then discusses how Canada adopted its multicultural policy, and why Canada depended on its immigrants in the labour force to overcome skills shortages and fertility rates. Further discussions covered the stages of compliance levels of Canadian organisations, and acceptance of diversity by the population. Additionally, the inequality experienced in the UK labour force is revealed and how organisations should provide equality in the workplace, regardless of individuals' ethnic or religious backgrounds. Race seems to be an issue with the diverse workforce which prompts organisations in the UK to deal with race to ensure the organisations' survival and success. Furthermore, the issues that Australian organisations had to consider in relation to global markets and competition are dealt with, as well as the steps required for an integrated workforce. The importance of managing a diverse workforce and the impact of globalisation on immigration are outlined. The recognition of immigrants from different cultural backgrounds and their skills are investigated in order to highlight the benefits of a diverse workforce.

References

———. 2016. *2016 Census.* Accessed 16 December 2017. www.abs.gov.au/websit edbs/D3310114.nsf/Home/Census?OpenDocument&ref=topBar.

April, Kurt and J. Syed. 2015. 'Race and Ethnicity in the Workplace'. In *Managing Diversity and Inclusion: An International Perspective*, edited by J. Syed and M. F. Ozbilgin, 134–80. London: SAGE Publications.

ATMA Global. 2014. 'USA Diversity in the Workplace'. New York: ATMA Global. Accessed 16 September 2017. http://search.alexanderstreet.com/view/work/ bibliographic_entity%7Cbibliographic_details%7C2383729.

Barrett, James R. 2016. 'The World of the Immigrant Worker'. In *The Oxford Handbook of American Immigration and Ethnicity*, edited by Ronald H. Bayor, 261–85. New York: Oxford University Press.

Bratton, J. and J. Gold. 2007. *Human Resource Management: Theory and Practice.* 4th ed. Basingstoke: Palgrave Macmillan.

Bureau of Labor Statistics. 2016. 'Employment Status of the Civilian Noninstitutional Population by Age, Sex, and Race'. Accessed 12 December 2017. www.bls. gov/cps/cpsaat03.htm.

Burns, Crosby, Kimberly Barton and Sophia Kerby. 2012. *The State of Diversity in Today's Workforce: As Our Nation Becomes More Diverse So Too Does Our Workforce.* Washington, DC: Center for American Progress.

Canadian Multiculturalism Act 1985. R.S.C., 1985, c. 24 (4th Supp.).

Community Relations Commission for Multicultural New South Wales. 2011. *The Economic Advantages of Cultural Diversity in Australia.* Sydney: Community Relations Commission for Multicultural New South Wales.

Conference Board of Canada. 2013. 'How Canada Performs: Acceptance of Diversity'. Accessed 17 October 2017. www.conferenceboard.ca/hcp/details/society/acceptance-of-diversity.aspx.

Cukier, Wendy, Suzanne Gagnon, Erin Roach, Mohamed Elmi, Margaret Yap and Sara Rodrigues. 2017. 'Trade-Offs and Disappearing Acts: Shifting Societal Discourses of Diversity in Canada Over Three Decades'. *The International Journal of Human Resource Management* 28 (7): 1031–64.

Dib, K. 2006. 'Canada's 150th Anniversary Multiculturalism and Diversity: Vehicles for Sustainable Socio-Economic Progress'. *Canadian Ethnic Studies Ethniques Au Canada* 38 (3): 143–59.

DiversityUK. 2016. 'Diversity in the UK'. Accessed 11 November 2017. https://diversityuk.org/diversity-in-the-uk/.

Garr, S. S., K. Shellenback and J. Scales. 2014. 'Diversity and Inclusion in Canada: The Current State'. Deloitte Development LLC. Accessed 18 September 2017. https://www2.deloitte.com/content/dam/Deloitte/ca/Documents/human-capital/ca-en-human-capital-diversity-and-Inclusion-in-canada.pdf

Henry, O. and A. J. Evans. 2007. 'Critical Review of Literature on Workforce Diversity'. *African Journal of Business Management* 1 (4): 72–6.

Judy, Richard W. and C. D'Amico. 1997. *Workforce 2020: Work and Workers in the 21st Century.* Washington, DC.: ERIC Clearinghouse.

Kerr, Sandra. 2015. *Race at Work 2015.* London: Business in the Community.

Klarsfeld, A., E. Ng and A. Tatli. 2012. 'Social Regulation and Diversity Management: A Comparative Study of France, Canada and the UK'. *European Journal of Industrial Relations* 18 (4): 309–27.

Kreitz, P. A. 2007. 'Best Practices for Managing Organizational Diversity' (PhD thesis, Simmons College, Stanford University).

Mulder, Marlene and Harvey Krahn. 2005. 'Individual- and Community-Level Determinants of Support for Immigration and Cultural Diversity in Canada'. *Canadian Review of Sociology/Revue Canadienne de Sociologie* 42 (4): 421–44. doi: 10.1111/j.1755-618X.2005.tb00848.x.

Ng, E. and I. Metz. 2015. 'Multiculturalism as a Strategy for National Competitiveness: The Case for Canada and Australia'. *Journal of Business Ethics* 128: 253–66.

Oyler, Jennifer D. and Mildred Golden Pryor. 2009. 'Workplace Diversity in the United States: The Perspective of Peter Drucker'. *Journal of Management History* 15 (4): 420–51.

Pew Research Center. 2015. *Modern Immigration Wave Brings 59 Million to U.S., Driving Population Growth and Change Through 2065: Views of Immigration's Impact on U.S. Society Mixed.* Washington, DC: Pew Research Center.

Reed, Susan E. 2011. *The Diversity Index: The Alarming Truth about Diversity in Corporate America . . . and What Can Be Done about It.* Saranac Lake: Amacom Books.

Riccucci, N. M. 2002. *Managing Diversity in Public Sector Workforces.* Boulder: Westview Press.

Rotundo, Maria. 2012. 'Building a Culture of Inclusion at the Royal Bank of Canada: Strategies for Aboriginal Peoples and Newcomers to Canada'. In *Global Human Resource Management Casebook*, edited by James C. Hayton, Michal Biron, Castro Christiansen and Bard Kuvaas, 331–42. New York: Routledge.

Statistics Canada. 2006. *2006 Census.* Catalogue Number 97–562-XCB2006013. Ottawa: Statistics Canada.

Trudeau, Justin. 2015. 'Diversity is Canada's Strength'. Accessed 14 July 2017. http://pm.gc.ca/eng/news/2015/11/26/diversity-canadas-strength.

Tsui, A. S. and B. A. Gutek. 1999. *Demographic Differences in Organizations: Current Research and Future Directions.* Lanham, MD: Lexington.

3 Strategic Management of Diversity

Benefits and Challenges

Strategic Management of Diversity

One of the features of democracy is the rule of law, under which everyone must be dealt with in accordance with the law—although, in some cases, different groups enjoy different rights and duties. For example, rights and duties given to young people may differ in some respects from those afforded to adults. The main issue is that everyone is to be treated as stipulated by the law. There are three ways in which democracies vary. The first variation involves the method of voting for elected political representatives. In some countries, voting is a right (such as in the US) and the government has to provide conditions for individuals to practise this right. In contrast, in other countries (such as Australia), voting is considered a duty, and it is the individual's responsibility to perform this duty. The second variation of democracy involves economic inequalities. However, the amount of money held by citizens is irrelevant, as long as they enjoy equal rights in the courts and political sphere. The third important variation is the management of cultural diversity, which is the focus of this book. Democracies have embraced different policies for managing cultural diversity, and these policies can be conceptualised as either complete assimilation—where all cultural differences are melded to create cultural and linguistic homogeneity—or full multiculturalism—where cultural differences and linguistic diversity are followed and supported (Moghaddam 2008).

This chapter considers the strategic management of diversity in the workplace as a means to determine organisational goals, roles, objectives and responsibilities, as well as the integration of a diverse labour force into the organisation. As detailed in the previous chapters, workplace diversity emerged onto the equality scene in the US in the 1990s, and spread its influence to encompass public and private organisations. In the 1990s, three types of organisations were described: monolithic, pluralistic and multicultural. Monolithic organisations employ and are managed by white males, with women and racial/ethnic minorities performing duties in stereotypical jobs, such as factory work and domestic employment. Pluralistic organisations encompass general diversity, yet lack structural and role integration (Motel

2016). However, in the 2000s, criticisms arose against the dominance of US diversity that did not align with other countries and their legislations, such as Denmark (Risberg and Soderberg 2008), Australia (Strachan, Burgess and Sullivan 2004) and New Zealand (Jones, Pringle and Shepherd 2000). This resulted in the current 'country contexts' perspective on workplace diversity (Klarsfeld 2010; Klarsfeld et al. 2014). As managing diversity was gaining momentum, criticism of the displacement of social justice began to emerge, led by two scholars—Liff (1997) and Dickens (1999), the 'depoliti-cised and ahistoric conception of difference' (Tatli 2011, 246) upon which diversity management was established.

Diversity approaches provide a pattern for success in the workplace in relation to thinking, feeling and interactions with employees from different backgrounds. The idea of a one-size-fits-all approach to discuss diversity is doubtful. The level of representation-based concerns experienced by individuals will determine whether diversity approaches that focus on differences (versus equality) will enhance performance and persistence. The diversity approach that minimises the prominence of social group membership, and instead concentrates on the importance of equality, is known as a value in equality approach, which improves representation-based concerns, and thus increases performance and persistence. It is expected that a diversity approach focusing on the importance of social group differences—which is referred to as a value in difference approach—will also increase performance and persistence (Apfelbaum, Stephens and Reagans 2016).

Diversity management is sometimes seen as a voluntary measure for organisations, and, without the support of legislation, tends to be ineffective (Ozbilgin and Syed 2015). Additionally, since domestic formulations of diversity cannot be transferred to other national contexts, attempts have been made to formulate global approaches for diversity to deal with management differences. Historically, labour markets have been riddled with inequality, which could be described today as discrimination. This inequality has been experienced in different countries and has changed over time (Jain, Sloane and Horwitz 2003; Kennedy-Dubourdieu 2006). In the nineteenth century, women and minority groups struggled for equality and social justice (Cassell 1996), until the *Declaration of Human Rights 1948*, which led to just conditions for work without discrimination. In addition, conventions by the UN and International Labour Organization made recommendations regarding the elimination of all discriminations. Such recommendations included the UN *International Convention on the Elimination of All Forms of Racial Discrimination 1965* and the UN *Convention of Discrimination on the Elimination of All Forms of Discrimination against Women 1979*. In some countries, legislation was introduced to cover specific ethnic groups and women in the labour market (Klarsfeld et al. 2014).

The rise of diversity management has developed significantly in the history of the workplace, and the shift from equal opportunity to diversity management 'meant a shift from the ethical and legal case to business case arguments' (Tatli 2011, 242). The spread of diversity management was rapid and 'by the late 1980s, equal employment opportunity/affirmative action (EEO/AA) specialists were recasting EEO/AA measures as part of DM [diversity management] and touting the competitive advantages offered by these practices' (Kelly and Dobbin 1998, 972). The shift from equal opportunity to diversity management and beyond led to new terms being coined, with some researchers adding the concept of inclusion to denote a shift from removing obstacles to organisational belonging and full participation. When employees feel included, they tend to feel part of the organisation by having access to information and sharing in decision making. While diversity management is introduced in organisations voluntarily and implemented in various ways, it must be operated with appropriate and pertinent national legislation, such as anti-discrimination and industrial relations law (Klarsfeld 2010). In addition, managing diversity is different from AA because it is a voluntary corporate approach concerned with increasing heterogeneity in the workplace, instead of being imposed by the government (Ng and Burke 2005).

Strategic management of diversity in action shows how managers use diversity to manage the workforce and reinforce class relations. Strategic diversity management is broadly defined as a planned commitment by organisations to employ, retain and promote a heterogeneous group of employees (Henry and Evans 2007). Stuber (2009) conceptualised diversity management as a principle consisting of four main components: diversity, respect, inclusion and added value. Cox and Blake (1991) defined the concept as referring to various management issues and activities pertaining to the hiring and effective use of employees from different cultural backgrounds. The concept is also defined as:

> the strategic alignment of workforce heterogeneity to include and value each employee equally on the basis of their diverse characteristics, and to leverage organisational diversity to enhance organisational justice and achieve better business outcomes.
>
> (Ozbilgin et al. 2011, 27)

Therefore, diversity management should be seen as managerially initiated programs and/or HRM policies and practices aimed at empowering the diverse workforce through effective integration to increase business productivity. Thus, diversity management is a process of managing people's similarities and differences, and recognising that employees' differences in the workplace represent a potential strength. At the same time, the existence of diversity among groups of people arises from differences in both culture and structure. These differences affect perceptions, feelings and attitudes. This adds to the needs and expectations of different management styles for different cultures, including language, custom, conventions and normative behaviour (DiTomaso 1999).

The term 'diversity management' began in North America and has now spread to other countries. The term is defined in reference to 'the voluntary organizational actions that are designed to create greater inclusion of employees from various backgrounds into the formal and informal organizational structures through deliberate policies and programs' (Mor Barak 2005, 208). Motel (2016, 332) defined workforce diversity as: 'ways in which people in a workforce are similar and different from one another', encompassing legally protected characteristics, such as race, gender and 'background, education, language skills, personality, sexual orientation, and work roles'. However, as discussed before, defining diversity in the workplace is a challenging task because there appears to be no clear or commonly agreed definition of workplace diversity in the literature, as diversity is a concept that means many things to many people, with both positive and negative connotations. Cultural diversity constitutes the representation of groups and individuals, regardless of their racial, ethnic, linguistic, national and religious backgrounds and sexual orientation, in a community that consists of culturally diverse members of different groups (Amadeo 2013).

The categorisation-elaboration model defines diversity as 'differences between individuals on any attribute that might lead to the perception that another person is different from self' (Guillaume et al. 2017, 279). The model proposes that the positive or negative outcomes of diversity depend on three factors: (i) variables that highlight demographic differences, (ii) variables that create or hinder intergroup prejudice and (iii) variables that improve or impair information-elaboration (Guillaume et al. 2017). In the 'integrating diversity' approach, diversity is a reality inside and outside organisations, where companies voluntarily adopt actions to deal with social expectations. This approach improves both employee motivation and corporate image. Nevertheless, conflicts in the workplace which affects all employees' levels of satisfaction and lead to resignation, may emerge between employees from different backgrounds, and, by dedicating opportunities to specific groups, reverse discrimination may eventuate. The 'leveraging variety' approach aims to achieve a competitive edge by learning from the various competencies and knowledge-related differences (Ravazzani 2016).

Therefore, workplace diversity is a multifaceted concept that includes people of culturally and linguistically diverse (CALD) backgrounds, and members of different religions and groups, who have their own languages and ethnicity. These are not mutually exclusive categories, as one employee might belong to more than one or even all of these categories at the same time. In addition, employees can belong to groups with political and personal affiliations, thus adding to the diversity of the workplace. In Western societies, workplace diversity can be seen as a natural reflection of diverse populations based on ethnicity, language, race, culture, religion, group affiliations and sexual orientation. Plurality is a stronger concept than diversity because it is more dynamic and less static. Plurality is the condition of human action, given that human beings are all the same (human), yet are all different from each other. In a sense, the one factor that all human beings share in common is their difference, which also applies to cultures (Gillespie 2007).

Diversity has richly added to the social fabric of migrant-receiving countries. The expression 'managing diversity' is a reminder that:

> citizenship might have become too right-centred and not sufficiently concerned with self-government and the sharing of power in both national and postnational contexts. Thus, any reference to a 'governance perspective' should not serve to abolish the need for politics. On the contrary, the more groups are involved in the management of diversity, the more they can use their experiences and redefine their political roles in broader terms.
>
> (Brown and Cardinal 2007, 4)

Strategic management requires all employees to understand the values and direction of the organisation to facilitate the passing of clear and effective strategic decisions to lower levels for implementation. The espoused values implemented by management as part of the corporate image enable employees to understand the organisation and how to perform daily duties. In this manner, the organisational culture is viewed as being the glue that holds employees together with shared values and common purpose (Chandler 2017). The relevant literature indicates that strategic management of diversity has different features that organisations must implement in the workplace. One of these features is the notion of training as a common activity adopted by organisations to enhance awareness of both diversity and management (Vickers-Willis, Connelly and Halliwell 2009). To ensure that organisations take full advantage of the positive aspects of cultural diversity, their training programs should focus on four areas: awareness, attitude, knowledge and skills (Ahmed et al. 2011). First, awareness is a skill that requires individuals to overcome stereotypes and learn about their own reactions to people who are different. Second, attitude enables people to scrutinise their values and beliefs about cultural differences, and understand their origins. Third, knowledge is an essential skill that deals with behaviour and how it relates to fairness and workforce effectiveness. Fourth, skills allow organisational leaders and employees to achieve cultural competence and create a new work environment based on understanding, communication and cooperation (Ahmed et al. 2011). These four areas form an integral part of cultural diversity and equip organisations with a competent understanding of employees' positive contributions under efficient and capable management. The first three also require a certain level of acknowledgement and cooperation by employees, which might be seen as an important obstacle to implementing this training strategy successfully.

A potential benefit of diversity is a workforce of higher quality, leading to competitive advantages. Organisations that hire minority employees may recruit top-performing minorities, while newly employed non-minorities may not be subjected to similar performance standards, thereby resulting in better performance in organisations with minorities. It is expected that organisations that manage diversity well may also manage the workforce well, and minority employees tend to be attracted to organisations with better workplace practices. Racial diversity is valued favourably by shareholders, who recognise the organisation's workforce and its potential benefits to improve returns in the marketplace. Ethnic diversity is considered at multiple levels within the organisation, such as the board level, managerial level and workforce level, with some implications affecting these three levels (Ellis and Keys 2015).

Apart from the recruitment, training and promoting of underrepresented groups, Hollwell (2007) added that the focus of strategic management of diversity should also be on taking full advantage of employees' skills and abilities in the organisation. Similarly, Chinnery and Bothwick (2005) stated that diversity management aims to recognise that people are different, and to support their differences to enable them to achieve their best.

There are several reasons for organisations to manage diversity, which differ depending on the organisation's culture, the structure of the organisation's workforce and the organisation's aims. It is assumed that cultural diversity management should improve the environment in the organisation, provide positive effects of cultural diversity and minimise possible conflicts. Diversity management is a measure taken by organisations to ensure equal treatment and equal opportunities for employees, and as a deterrent to discrimination. Shortage of skilled labour is driving organisations to be more concerned with cultural diversity and to recruit workers internationally to fill vacant positions. However, in an organisation where the owner is running the business and as such, holds multiple roles, he may not have primary focus on diversity in the workplace. This role is overloaded; thus, diversity management may not receive the attention it requires. Therefore, there should be a person in charge of diversity issues to ensure effectiveness. Additionally, managing cultural diversity effectively is a long-term approach that will include changes in the entire business (Kühlmann and Heinz 2017). In developing such a long-term plan, two primary strategies are required to incorporate diversity into the workplace, and they include 'the creation and development of employee resource group and having women and minorities in decision-making and policy-making roles' (Canas 2014, 54).

With the increased workforce diversity, contemporary organisations have increased the variety of their diversity management strategies. Different practices are adopted by organisations depending on their beliefs and expectations of diversity and its role (Kulik and Li 2015). The 'identity blind' option is the dominant approach to diversity management taken up by most organisations. Employees are encouraged to view people of different cultural backgrounds as the same, and to ensure that such differences 'do not count' (Kulik and Li 2015, 568). Under this approach, the decision-making procedure in human resources is the same for each individual. It evaluates people for their achievements and merit, rather than their social identities, and such principles of equality are greatly valued by employees. In a blind approach to diversity management, organisations do not refer to social group identity when making decisions in HRM. The identity blind approach perceives that members of specific groups can be kept away from the organisations because of prejudice; however, with equal access and fair treatment pursuant to the law, inequities can be rectified. Thus, organisations that are equal opportunity providers in recruiting and promoting employees inhibit prejudicial attitudes and eliminate discrimination in their operations. It has been reported that HRM practices reduce discrimination and bias, and provide equal opportunities for employees (Kulik and Li 2015).

In the 'identity conscious' approach to diversity management, organisations consider social group identity when human resource decisions are made. Such organisations take measures to eliminate discriminatory language from job descriptions and remove bias from their decision procedures, and replace them with other practices incorporating recruitment materials designed to appeal to members of underrepresented identity groups. Such practices are targeted to appeal to women, racial minorities, people with disabilities and other underrepresented groups in organisations, and to give them a voice in organisational decisions (Kulik and Li 2015). Organisations that adopt an identity conscious approach to diversity management are proactive and go beyond legal compliance. Organisations that adopt this approach believe that different employees bring different knowledge, which is relevant and important because it gives the organisation a competitive edge and different perspectives on how work should be undertaken. The identity conscious perspective acknowledges employees' differences as potential valuable resources that can generate learning and adaptive change. It allows employees to use their skills and experiences gained by virtue of being members of an identity group (Kulik and Li 2015).

In addition to business-related benefits, which are examined more closely later in this chapter, in a political context, diversity management aims for social justice and supports equal opportunities and long-term sustainable employment (Bleijenbergh, Peters and Poutsma 2010). In addition, managing diversity in the workplace is often linked to EEO and AA initiatives. While diversity has evolved from these two concepts, it is significantly different because EEO aims to prevent discrimination in the workplace on the basis of characteristics such as race, colour, religion, gender, national origin, ability and age (Riccucci 2002). In contrast, AA embodies proactive efforts to redress past discrimination and diversify the workplace in terms of similar factors and characteristics. Riccucci (2002) provided a rather narrow definition of diversity management as a successor to AA or equal opportunities program. In contrast, the broader definition provided by Bleijenberg, Peters and Poutsma (2010) views it as a more inclusive approach to attracting new employees and involving a wider understanding of people's differences, including sexual orientation, skills and experience. As discussed, diversity further encompasses several aspects of differences in the workforce, such as gender, ethnicity and culture, which need to be considered when examining the strategic management of diversity in the workplace. This book argues that there is a difference between managing diversity and EEO. While EEO requires the elimination of discrimination from the workplace, managing diversity goes beyond this process of management to recognise the differences between people as a source of strength and competition. In this sense, managing diversity supersedes EEO by addressing the organisational need to align organisational objectives with the objectives of diverse employees (Stone 2014).

The success of cultural diversity depends on various factors—one of which is the way diversity is managed, which can help organisations benefit by increasing productivity. The implementation of certain measures can minimise conflicts based on cultural differences due to insufficient integration of immigrant employees. Cultural diversity management involves both management *of* and management *for* a culturally diverse workforce. While management *of* cultural diversity promotes awareness and respect of cultural diversity at work and fosters intercultural competence, management *for* cultural diversity involves providing a diverse workforce and equal opportunities. In addition, cultural diversity management must ensure that immigrant employees can contribute their skills to the utmost and are afforded equal opportunities. Most measures have a positive effect on the organisational and individual levels. If the value of cultural differences is appreciated, then demographic changes will be an opportunity, rather than a challenge, for the organisation (Kühlmann and Heinz 2017). Table 3.1 provides detailed information on the differences between the principles of equal opportunity and diversity management.

Table 3.1 Differences between Principles of Equal Opportunity and Diversity Management

Equal opportunity	Diversity management
Reliance on legal regulation and bureaucratic procedures to eliminate discrimination	Systematic, cultural transformation of the organisation to promote the value of workforce diversity
Highlights discrimination and the penalties that organisations face under the law	Uses positive imagery and celebratory rhetoric
Efforts justified by reference to legal compulsion and the social justice case	Efforts justified by reference to the business case
Social group-based differences are the focus, such as gender, race/ethnicity and disability	Individual differences are emphasised, including lifestyle, appearance and work style

Source: Greene and Kirton (2009).

It appears that globalism and diversity go beyond the tolerance of cultural differences which is considered an ethical and political issue by organisations—not only in theory, but also in practice. Therefore, the way to manage the workforce depends on many factors, including the degree to which an organisation is prepared to accept culturally diverse employees' social identities. It has become apparent that managing diversity is underpinned by an acceptance that the workforce consists of a diverse population, and that diversity includes visible and non-visible differences, such as sex, age, background, race, disability, personality and work style. Such differences create a productive environment in which employees feel valued and have their talents fully used, while organisational goals are being met (Kandola and Fullerton 1998). In this context, the relationship between race and diversity becomes essential. While race is considered a function of physical or biological variations, ethnicity may not be connected with these variations. There is no evidence of the use of 'race' in science. However, the fact is that the external appearance of individuals—such as skin colour and facial features—is associated with treating people differently, based on what is assumed to be racial identity (April and Syed 2015).

Racial and ethnic discrimination relates to ongoing stereotypes in society, which are described as 'beliefs about the characteristics, behaviour and attributes of members of certain groups' (April and Syed 2015, 135). Such beliefs may affect employment, promotion and other decisions, leading to sophisticated discrimination in the workplace. Adverse generalisations can result from discrimination, such as 'Indian people have poor time management', 'Americans are domineering', 'Black Caribbean people are lazy', 'French people are obnoxious', 'Nigerians are aggressive' and 'Singaporeans are uncreative'. These generalisations may affect employers or managers to make decisions that: (i) do not adapt to the law or spirit of equal opportunity; (ii) discriminate against individuals during recruitment and career advancement; and (3) affect the selection of offices, plants and manufacturing sites (April and Syed 2015).

While diversity involves hiring minorities and foreign nationals because of the workforce demographic trend, in addition to demographic differences, cultural differences are also important in managing diversity in the workplace. With respect to cultural differences, Querling, Stuart and Butler (2008) stressed that Western society is not divided by differences, but by an inability to respect and learn from these differences. Being exposed to diversity has the power to bring people together; however, diversity can create fear if people focus on differences and ignore similarities. Fear is further increased by the inability to communicate effectively with other people who tend to disagree about certain issues—political, religious, cultural and so forth. Thus, fear of the unknown can damage the strategic management of diversity in the workplace (Saxonhouse 2001). Given the seriousness and potential effect of fear on diversity, other cultures must be understood and the barriers of difference should be overcome. Thus, it seems that one of the central issues that must be analysed in contemporary studies is the effect of fear and how it becomes a challenge to management.

Around two decades ago, Prasad and Mills (1997) stated that the management of diversity is under-researched and under-theorised in the management literature. Despite the increasing number of studies in the field, the gap in the literature still seems to exist. This book attempts to address the ways leaders are beginning to realise the organisational benefits and competitive advantages of diversity management by discussing the benefits and challenges of strategically managing diversity.

Benefits of Strategic Management of Diversity

The relevant literature provides rich insight into the benefits of diversity management. For example, DiTomaso (1999) argued that diversity creates positive results for organisations when differences among people lead to more qualified workers, creative problem solving, productive human resources and a better understanding of markets and competitors. Business leaders are beginning to realise the organisational benefits, potential competitive advantage and importance of different views leading to improved organisational performance, decision making, creativity and innovation. As an attempt to deal with the increasing levels of diversity in the workforce, diversity management has become a positive tool in organisations that can solve and prevent negative group dynamics. According to De Cieri and Kramar (2007), strategic management of diversity creates an environment that permits all employees to contribute to organisational goals and experience personal growth in the process. Another supporting element is the view that managing diversity recognises that employees' differences in the workplace are a potential strength that can enhance business results (Kelly and Dobbin 1998).

Diversity management aims to provide tangible benefits to the company. It is viewed as a business strategy that aims to use the full potential of employees in the organisation to achieve a competitive advantage. In contrast, employees of different backgrounds (such as race/ethnicity or gender) were previously considered unqualified by managers if they failed to adhere to the values of the majority. Diversity allows members of organisations to bring to the workplace their unique perspectives for the benefit of the organisation (Mor Barak 2017).

Benefits of diversity to organisations can be featured in three main points. First, the *voluntary nature* of diversity management means that it may not last during economic difficulties. It has been reported that, if organisations must choose among competing expenditures, diversity programs may be reduced or removed because it takes too long to reap their benefits. Second, the *broad definitions of diversity* mean that vulnerable people—such as racial minority groups, people with disabilities and women—may not enjoy the protection they merit because the resources have to be divided among many groups. Finally, the *practical benefits* denote that, once it is realised that diversity is no longer of any benefits to organisations, it will disappear. Thus, diversity must be established on the principle of giving tangible benefits to organisations, as well as based on moral and ethical obligations to diversity (Mor Barak 2017).

Further benefits of strategic management of diversity include improved employee relations and securing new sources of talent (Gordon 2007). Similarly, McLauren (2009) argued that an organisation with a good reputation for workplace diversity has a higher chance of attracting and retaining the best available talent in the market. Strategic management of diversity can also lead to a work environment in which conflicts are less likely to arise. McLauren (2009) further claimed that strong strategic management of diversity results in effective problem solving and efficiency for organisations because management can use the diverse workforce as a pool of multiple solutions and ideas to address problems and challenges.

The literature indicates that international organisations take advantage of the linguistic and cultural backgrounds of their employees to enhance communication and product alteration. In addition, language plays an important role in diversity management. Responsible written and verbal communication is imperative to ensure understanding and identification of key cultural differences. Thus, training employees to be aware of these differences is vital. Diversity is no longer only about fairness or imposing moral, ethical or legal rules, but also about valuing diversity and the diverse workforce, and managing these well for the organisation's advantage (Litvin 2006). These views suggest that diversity management offers mutual benefits to both employers and employees. For this reason, it is imperative to study whether organisations are aware of these mutual benefits, and whether they effectively manage their diverse workforces to maximise these benefits.

Additionally, international organisations are more affected by the globalisation of management, and will adopt diversity management for flexibility. Organisations that aim for equal opportunities and have recently included diversity management have revealed a lack of competencies and resources, compared with organisations seeking competition and foreign multinationals (Ravazzani 2016). With the globalising economy, diversity management refers now to the workforce within other nations. *International diversity management* deals with managing a diverse workforce of citizens and immigrants in a single national organisational context, such as an Australian organisation implementing policies and training programs for its employees to offer employment to minority groups and immigrants in the workforce. The second type, *cross-national diversity management*, refers to the management of a workforce of citizens and immigrants in another country, such as a Canadian organisation with branches in China and Malaysia introducing diversity policies and training that will also apply in its headquarters and subsidiaries in these countries. Each of these types requires different policies and programs, and cross-national diversity management requires employers to comply with the legislation in different countries. For example, while US organisations may provide training and promotion to young women in accordance with anti-discrimination legislation, its Korean subsidiaries may consider this a waste of time. Thus:

> the challenge of diversity is not simply to have it but to create conditions in which its potential to be a performance barrier is minimised and its potential to enhance performance is maximised.
>
> (Cox 2001, 16)

White (1999) discussed some common themes that support diversity in the workplace. The first theme is that multicultural organisations attract and retain the best human resources from diverse cultural backgrounds, and subsequently gain competitive advantage. Similarly, several other authors (Carrell, Elbert and Hatfield 2000; Hollwell 2007; Silk et al. 2000) have claimed that organisations that successfully manage diversity tend to attract the best personnel, thereby leading to organisational benefits and improvements. The second theme indicates that a multicultural organisation is able to understand and penetrate more widely into improved markets, employ diverse workforces internally and serve diverse external clients. In this context, a potential benefit of diversity is in marketing customer relationships, and diverse organisations will gain market share, especially if customers prefer dealing with diverse employees. It has also been revealed that ethnically diverse upper management have better knowledge of marketplace factors and create new product markets. Thus, racial diversity is important to organisations and can generate more customers, more sales income and increased market share (Ellis and Keys 2015).

Kandola and Fullerton (1998) also explained that managing diversity offers great benefits to organisations by enabling them to make better use of their employees. This can include developing an improved understanding of the political, social, legal, economic and cultural environments of the countries from which employees originated. Therefore, a potential benefit lies in the increased interaction between management and employees at other levels in the organisation, and diverse organisations tend to have organisational flexibility and improved problem solving. It has been suggested that positive benefits related to diversity are a result of improved workforce practices (Ellis and Keys 2015).

In Western developed countries, language (both oral and written) is used in work interactions and has become a skill required of workers. Knowing a particular language represents an added economic value of communication skills in the workplace. Communication allows workers to achieve their goals and control their destinies. Language has been placed at the forefront in the service sector, especially in the industrialised world. The interactions of migrants and minority groups in the workplace provide opportunities in the workforce. In addition, knowing more than one language or being competent in English is a valued skill that must be possessed by individuals to obtain specific types of employment. The ability to write well in two or more languages has also emerged as a criterion for recruiting employees, and serves as a protection of one's job in times of crisis (Moyer 2017).

The third theme supporting diversity in the workplace states that multicultural organisations display higher creativity and innovation, and that the talents of gender and ethnically diverse organisations are invaluable. The fourth theme argues that multicultural organisations have a better ability to problem solve (Adler 1991). The fifth theme states that multicultural organisations are more adaptable to change and more flexible than non-multicultural organisations (White 1999). These themes provide the basis of useful steps to support workplace diversity to build stronger and more competitive organisations. However, the effectiveness of the ways these features have been acknowledged and internalised in organisational management activities is an open question that this book attempts to address.

Organisations should be aware of the importance of employees and their communication skills by encouraging them to be part of the decision-making team and to use their communications skills to improve productivity. Kuga (1996) argued that diverse work groups can be a source of new ideas and opportunities, a means of growth for individuals and a new challenge for people who lead and manage diversity. In addition, enhancing communication skills and productivity can increase a team's effectiveness. Further, Kuga (1996) added that the communication process may be influenced by cultural and religious background, age, gender and first language. Therefore, creating an organisational environment where management converts diversity from a challenge to a source of productivity and communication is a critically important task, which can only be achieved through the successful strategic management of diversity.

It has been suggested that support for diversity is an economically sound business practice that results in competitive advantages, including increased innovation and creativity in the workplace. Organisations that require specific skills and experience may benefit from a diverse workforce at upper levels because managers and directors decide on innovations by virtue of their authority (Ellis and Keys 2015). Businesses that embrace their nation's changing demographics will gain the economic benefits of diversity and inclusion in the workplace. It is claimed that 'a diverse economy is a strong economy' (Burns, Barton and Kerby 2012, 1) and organisations that hire a diverse workforce are likely to find the best talent to compete in the competitive economy. Combining different backgrounds, skills and experiences breeds creative solutions. In addition, the adoption of diversity significantly increases productivity and job performance (Burns, Barton and Kerby 2012).

The supporters of a business case for diversity argue that diverse organisations can: (i) achieve cost savings, (ii) recruit the best talent and (iii) have high rates of growth (Canas and Sondak 2014). Regarding cost savings, it is suggested that embracing the value of diversity and diversity management enables organisations to reduce costs and have competitive advantage. If employees feel they are respected, they will remain longer in the organisation and maintain productivity. The Society for Human Resource Management (quoted in Canas and Sondak 2014, 18) stated that an organisation's return on investment 'is reduced when commitment and productivity are lost because employees feel disregarded, time is wasted with conflicts and misunderstandings, and money is spent on legal fees and settlements'. Reducing these expenses will lower costs and increase profits in the organisation (Canas and Sondak 2014). Cost savings is crucially important because it refers to the organisation's bottom-line. Insecurity among employees causes absenteeism, and diversity initiatives tend to have a positive effect on both absenteeism rates and labour turnover. Another element of cost-savings concerns are lawsuits regarding sexual preference, age and race discrimination, and the importance of investing organisational efforts to prevent the occurrence of such lawsuits. Organisations must comply with laws related to discrimination and ensure that proper policies are implemented to deter legal actions instigated against them (O'Donovan 2017). The attraction, retention and promotion of diverse employees are referred to as the 'talent war', which is another argument for managing diversity. Further, customers, suppliers and the marketplace are becoming increasingly diverse; thus, a diverse workforce is needed to respond to their needs and penetrate new markets. Similarly, organisations can benefit by matching their sales force with their customer base (O'Donovan 2017). The concept of winning the competition for talent, as a benefit of diversity management, relates to the assumption that organisations that enjoy a strong reputation for managing a diverse workforce will appeal more to talented workers. Based on this assumption, it is an advantage to be ranked in one of the 'top diversity lists', such as Fortune's 'Best Companies for Minorities' or DiversityInc's 'Top Companies for Diversity'. Further, when considering which organisation to join, talented recruits often ask about the company's diversity programs, and this has a significant bearing on their decision to consider that organisation for employment (Canas and Sondak 2014).

In relation to high rates of growth in the diverse workforce, the assumption is that, when employees from diverse backgrounds in an organisation feel that their viewpoints are considered, creativity and problem solving are likely to be enhanced. In addition, the skills of flexibility and adaptability acquired from a diverse workforce will improve employees' ability to communicate successfully in a complicated and global economy (Canas and Sondak 2014).

Another benefit of productive diversity is that it establishes better relationships between management and employees (Silk et al. 2000). However, to make these factors an essential element of the strategic management of diversity, organisations must value and pursue diversity effectively in the workplace. This will lead to attracting and retaining employees, and encouraging their contributions to better serve their customers and suppliers and satisfy their shareholders. Gandz (2001) indicated that there are two processes needed to achieve diversity in organisations: (i) moving from a non-diverse workforce to a diverse workforce and (ii) managing diversity by realising its benefits at a minimal cost. However, this requires acknowledgement of the costs associated with a diverse workforce and an effective strategy to address them. Gandz's study did not directly address the question of how these processes can be achieved.

Challenges of Strategic Management of Diversity

While the benefits are clear, diversity and its management are not without challenges. Just as the opponents to diversity have been vocal, the challenges must also be considered to provide a balanced perspective. The literature on managing diversity in the workplace provides extensive insights on the benefits and challenges associated with managing a diverse workforce. According to Bhadury, Mighty and Damar (2000), the effect of diversity management on organisations does not depend on diversity itself, but on the type of diversity climate that exists in organisations. Hence, organisations that have well-designed diversity management strategies can effectively manage the challenges derived from the diversity climate in which they operate. These approaches can also convert diversity into a strategic tool to increase organisational effectiveness.

The other side of diversity in the workplace encompasses negatives and risks, which may lead to misunderstandings, suspicions and conflicts, resulting in absenteeism, low work morale, loss of competitiveness and problems in employees' social integration. Immigrants may also have a language barrier that can weaken communication in the organisation or increase risks emanating from cultural differences. The European public has a negative attitude towards immigrants. Based on these problems, the task of diversity management involves eliminating the negative elements of diversity in the workplace. Increasing the diverse workforce in an organisation and acquiring special skills by executives who can manage diversity provide an environment for respect and equality for all employees. Therefore, among executives, it is essential to increase awareness of diversity and the importance of cooperation to ensure the organisation's success. The executives can then manage diversity from the top down, where a change in the culture will affect all levels. Training at all levels is also necessary for all individuals, and organisations should implement policies and programs in the field of HRM to incorporate steps against bullying, and monitoring the organisation's goals in relation to equal opportunities. The measures taken by the organisation should increase respect and understanding and eliminate discrimination throughout the organisation (Urbancová, Čermáková and Vostrovská 2016).

In relation to gender participation in the workplace, Jamieson and O'Mara (1991) observed that, in the early twentieth century, white males dominated the workforce in the US. In Australia, the workforce was similarly male dominated during this period, as shown by the 1911 labour participation rates published by the ABS (2000). These data show that the participation of women in the workforce was below 50% between the ages of 15 and 64, and below 20% at the age of 35 and onwards (ABS 2000). However, today, both women and various cultural groups are now more visible in the labour force in Western societies, including Australia, and employees of different cultural backgrounds have a variety of values, work ethics, and ethnically and culturally rooted behaviour. Thus, it is argued that, in managing the diverse workforce, the challenge for an organisation is to integrate, not assimilate, the rapidly growing number of employees from diverse cultures into the workplace. As Henry and Evans (2007) stated, diversity can be an important source of conflicts in organisations. These conflicts are mostly triggered by prejudice, derogatory comments and feelings of superiority. To tackle such challenges, organisations should manage diversity to benefit the organisation; otherwise, conflicts can prevent the realisation of the full potential of both organisation and employees (Henry and Evans 2007). In relation to challenges in the workplace, Jamieson and O'Mara (1991) also proposed several organisational strategies, such as rethinking communication techniques by considering employees' unfamiliarity with the English language, or providing rewards that are valued by different cultural groups. However, these strategies do not present clear-cut solutions to the challenges associated with a diverse workforce, as the climates of diverse organisations differ from each other. As a result, organisations need to introduce specific solutions tailored to the type of diversity in their operations.

Furthermore, exclusion is one of the substantial problems faced by today's diverse workforce, where the reality experienced by many individuals and perception of many employees is that they are not considered part of the organisation. The inclusion–exclusion continuum is defined as follows:

> The concept of *inclusion-exclusion* in the workplace refers to the individual's sense of being a part of the organizational's system in both the formal processes, such as access to information and decision-making channels, and the informal processes, such as 'water cooler' and lunch meetings where information and decisions informally take place.
>
> (Mor Barak 2005, 149)

Therefore, the concept of inclusion–exclusion considers how employees perceive their experience and position in the organisation in relation to its 'mainstream' group. Traditionally, human beings depend on one another for livelihood and basic needs, such as food, shelter, clothing and social inclusion, which have been essential survival functions for many years (Mor Barak 2005).

In addition to the inclusion and exclusion duality, Wrench (2015) elaborated that racial/ethnic discrimination occurs in the workplace surreptitiously, without the victims always being aware of it. Employers may exhibit a 'no problem here' attitude in relation to discrimination. Reluctance to acknowledge the existence of discrimination at work drives employers to make these statements to deny employment opportunities driven by hostility towards some groups. Some employers may state that although they are different, there should be no discrimination. However, ethnic discrimination can exist without racist motives. There are various 'types' of discrimination, and direct discrimination is just one of them. Surveys indicate the existence of discrimination deriving from the achievements of immigrants and their descendants, compared with the majority population (identified as 'ethnic penalty'), taking into account age, experience, educational level and other pertinent factors. The ethnic penalties are identified as only *indirect* indicators of discrimination, and have specific relevance to the dominant 'no problem here' assumption (Wrench 2015). One direct indicator of ethnic discrimination at work is the documentary evidence given by tribunals and court cases, and so any discrimination in employment is outlawed by legislation introduced by the government. Formal complaints by victims about discrimination are rarely made because of the financial costs and difficulties of obtaining evidence. The cases that reach tribunals and courts present strong indications of the *nature* and *forms* of ethnic discrimination, yet these complaints and cases do not constitute a good indicator of the *extent* of discrimination (Wrench 2015).

Cultural diversity in the workplace is now a reality, and culturally diverse work groups form an integral part of organisations around the world. Interaction between multiple cultures requires intercultural understanding to manage and avoid conflicts, and reach employees' performance potential. Conflict is detrimental to organisations and requires attention to determine the causes and find resolutions (Korovyakovskaya and Chong 2016):

> Whilst relationship conflict is an awareness of interpersonal incompatibilities that includes emotions, task conflict is an awareness of differences in opinions regarding a group task, process conflict is an awareness of differences regarding the way for a task to be accomplished.
> (Korovyakovskaya and Chong 2016, 30)

Additionally, research on cultural diversity reveals that members of culturally different groups are not attracted to each other and have more communication problems with each other than do members of a culturally homogenous group (Korovyakovskaya and Chong 2016).

The relevant literature indicates that communication-related problems seem to be an important source of challenge for organisations with diverse workforces. Good communication skills are vital if the workplace is to operate effectively and avoid misunderstandings. The failure to ensure effective communication between management and employees and among employees will lead to suspicion, lack of confidence and even hostility (Aytemiz Seymen 2006). These feelings present differing challenges to be managed by organisations. It has also been shown that the most common type of conflict in diverse workforces is conflict between employees (Kuusela 2013). The ways in which organisations deal with such conflicts are dictated by the types of diversity management they have in place. If these conflicts are seen as being merely due to character differences, while ignoring the cultural factors, the underlying cause of the conflict cannot be addressed effectively by management. The skill level of managers plays an important role, given that managers lacking the required skills may not be able to arrange conversations between employees to resolve conflicts.

Kuga (1996) suggested that communication in the workplace can be made more effective through knowledge of people's backgrounds. Based on their varying perspectives and experiences, employees might have different interpretations of words and phrases, and this can be seen as a significant workforce challenge. Diverse work groups have different communication styles, and the challenge is to acknowledge these differences and choose the right approach to avoid the escalation of conflicts. Another challenge identified by Kuga (1996) concerns feedback, which is discouraged in some cultures, especially in the case of a younger person having to communicate feedback to an older person. However, feedback is important because it is an indication of effective communication and a confirmation that the message sent was received as intended. Therefore, feedback mechanisms implemented in an organisation constitute one of the most important aspects of diversity management. Stuart (2013) recommended points for effective communication, such as listening to others to know what they are thinking, and having empathy to help oneself be open to others' opinions. Stuart further recommended being patient with others and ensuring clarity to help them get to the intended message. A further recommendation is maintaining a positive attitude at work, and being aware that self-improvement is necessary, with practice to improve communication skills (Stuart 2013). These recommended points are a challenge to any organisation with a diverse workforce because they require management to introduce implementation and monitoring policies.

Similar to Stuart (2013), Edewor and Aluko (2007) argued that, to manage an effective and harmonious diverse workforce, organisations should introduce specific strategies in the workplace. These strategies include setting a good example to address issues such as myths and stereotypes, and communicating in writing to prevent prejudice and discriminatory behaviours. Further strategies include implementing training programs, recognising individual differences and actively seeking input from minority groups (Edewor and Aluko 2007). Additional recommended strategies include revamping reward systems, making room for social events, creating a flexible work environment and conducting continuous monitoring. Each aspect of the effective management of a diverse workforce presents further challenges for organisations, based on various factors, such as the willingness to bear the associated costs and continuous commitment to implement these measures consistently.

In relation to diversity in the workplace, a major difference—commonly described as the 'hearable difference'—is one of the core issues upon which this book focuses. Language is a means of communication that enables workers to know what their managers want or what other colleagues say. In their empirical study, Zanoni and Janssens (2004) examined an international automotive organisation in Flanders, the Dutch-speaking part of Belgium, which employed Moroccan workers who could not speak Dutch. As a result of the division of tasks, workers were dependent on each other to perform tasks, and this could only be done if they understood each other or employed someone who could speak their language to work with them, thereby creating teamwork. The organisation solved this problem by employing someone who spoke Moroccan to provide the necessary communication (Zanoni and Janssens 2004). In the Australian context, this suggests the need for a language other than English in the workplace to facilitate communication with clients and between employees. The literature further indicates that international language management in transcultural organisations is an indication of successful diversity management, since language is one of the strongest indicators of group identity and is a powerful element of ethnic conflicts (Christiansen and Sezerel 2013).

Riccucci (2002) raised a key point by referring to the ability of senior management to develop programs and strategies to accommodate and manage diversity in their workplaces. This involves the ability to harness the diverse human resources available to create a more productive and motivated workforce (Riccucci 2002). Similarly, El Shearif (2013) claimed that organisations today face the challenge of accommodating reasonable adjustments, maximising and harnessing the potential of all employees, and recognising and valuing the cultural and linguistic diversity in the workplace. These are all important challenges faced by organisations that employ diverse workforces. Programs to address diversity in the workplace should be designed in a way that makes them sensitive enough to address various factors, such as culture, ethnicity, gender and age. For example, Simlin (2006) indicated the negative relationship between age and perceptions of diversity openness. To address this challenge, management must conduct training and workshops for older employees regarding the presence and necessity of diversity in organisations. Whether and to what extent organisations can reap the benefits of a diverse workforce and address the challenges associated with this workforce depend on how differing values, beliefs and work practices derived from the diverse workforce are managed by organisations. The following section focuses on the implementation of diversity programs to shed more light on the strategic management of diversity.

Implementation of Diversity Programs

The purpose of diversity management is to direct organisations towards attaining diversity in the workplace. Diversity management programs come in various forms, yet have one purpose—to appeal to and develop a multicultural workforce by focusing on women and ethnic minorities. Moreover, a common component of diversity management programs is to educate and train employees (Madera, Dawson and Neal 2016). There is no single uniform method for implementing a successful diversity program for all companies. Diversity efforts vary and must be tailored to suit each organisation's needs and goals. In implementing a diversity program, pragmatic programs and policies consisting of strategic management tools used by organisations are essential to achieve job satisfaction and the optimal performance of diverse employees. Such programs and policies aim to achieve the effective integration of employees from diverse backgrounds. They are also used as tools in both pre- and post-hiring processes by introducing opportunities, such as flexible working hours and collaborative working arrangements (Pitts et al. 2010). These policies constitute a good example of one of the three diversity management program types, *managing for diversity*, which focuses on 'pragmatic management policies for helping employees to succeed at work' (Pitts 2007, 1578). The other two types of diversity management programs are *AA* (focusing mainly on the legalistic side of diversity) and *valuing diversity* (with an emphasis on norms and values in creating an inclusive and tolerant work environment) (Pitts 2007). Both the type and nature of the program and policies adopted are open to interpretation by management, based on individual needs and targets.

Organisations that promote themselves as valuing diversity appeal to members for being egalitarian, with equal opportunities offered to all employees in an environment that maintains an unbiased, inclusive, multicultural workforce. Employees wish to feel they are looked after by the organisation, that they are safe at work and that their organisation endorses egalitarian values and evaluates workplace fairness, which will yield positive outcomes for all its employees. Thus, it is claimed that investing in diversity management will increase organisational attraction and people will want to work there (Madera, Dawson and Neal 2016).

The recruitment and development of human resources forms an integral part of diversity management. Growth of workforce diversity places pressure on managers to develop an organisational culture that helps employees from different environments to succeed. To be competitive, organisations seek talented workers, even among students, and target groups, such as women on maternity leave. Supporting mothers is a part of supporting equal opportunities and providing temporary employment positions shortens the period of unemployment and helps lead to long-term employment, which helps mothers returning from maternity leave transition back into the workforce (Urbancová, Čermáková and Vostrovská 2016).

In terms of maximising and sustaining employee effectiveness, diversity training has been used as an important element in the implementation of diversity programs. Diversity training refers to a set of programs and activities that show the differences between employees and offer strategies and ways to handle them. Robbins (1998) claimed that diversity training helps participants learn how to value their differences, increase cross-cultural understanding and overcome stereotypes. The important issue for organisations is to develop a diversity training strategy tailored to the organisation's specific needs and targets, and to implement the training activities effectively as a supporting tool of an overall diversity management strategy. However, some diversity management initiatives are more effective than others, and the key to success lies in the implementation itself.

Regarding diversity training, it has been found that training is important for managers and corporate-level executives because the latter influence personnel policies. Frontline managers constitute a vital link between diversity management and employees, since the selection, training, appraising and rewarding of frontline employees are the responsibility of frontline managers. It is also argued that managers' different views can affect the acceptance of diversity management programs, and influence members' attitudes towards the organisation. It is assumed that individuals and organisations become more effective when the values of both the individual and organisation are harmonious. In addition, diversity practices lead to a competitive advantage in three particular areas: 'attraction, increased productivity, and a reduction in turnover' (Madera, Dawson and Neal 2016, 22).

Romanenko (2012) warned that there is a gap between what organisations are doing and what they should be doing. The literature indicates that the way most organisations are presently acting regarding the management of diversity involves mere compliance with government legislation. However, as argued in the following chapters, more effective implementation of diversity policy requires a self-tailored policy that is sensitive to the benefits and challenges associated with organisations' own diverse workforces.

Summary

Strategic management of cultural diversity is investigated in this chapter showing how workers are treated and enjoy equal rights in accordance with the law. Diversity approaches emphasise the importance of equality and performance, and the need for legislation to support diversity management in organisations. The discussions further include the historical development of diversity management in the workplace, how it differed from AA and the subsequent emergence of inclusion. In the absence of a clear definition of workplace diversity, the need for various management styles for different cultures is presented in this chapter and the way to deal with similarities and differences of a diverse workforce is discussed. Issues have been covered regarding the measures that organisations can take to eliminate discrimination, attract employees and provide equal opportunities.

Furthermore, the extent of globalism and diversity, the benefits and challenges in the workplace and what constitute competitive advantages in organisations are considered with the impact of interaction with visible and non-visible minorities. This chapter considers the concept of inclusion-exclusion, the importance of communication and the implementation of diversity management in the organisations as well as the process involved for an effective policy.

References

ABS. 2000. *Population Characteristics: 20th Century—Beginning and End*. Canberra: ABS.

Adler, N. J. 1991. *International Dimensions of Organizational Behavior*. Boston: PWS-Kent Publishing.

Ahmed, S., K. B. Wilson, R. C. Henriksen Jr. and J. Windwalker Jones. 2011. 'What Does it Mean to be a Culturally-competent Counselor?'. *Journal for Social Action in Counseling and Psychology* 3 (1): 23–4.

Amadeo, K. 2013. 'Cultural Diversity, How it Boosts Profits'. Accessed 16 February 2014. http://useconomy.about.com/od/suppl1/g/Cultural-Diversity.htm.

Apfelbaum, Evan P., Nicole M. Stephens and Ray E. Reagans. 2016. 'Beyond One-size-fits-all: Tailoring Diversity Approaches to the Representation of Social Groups'. *Journal of Personality and Social Psychology* 111 (4): 547–66.

April, Kurt and J. Syed. 2015. 'Race and Ethnicity in the Workplace'. In *Managing Diversity and Inclusion: An International Perspective*, edited by J. Syed and M. F. Ozbilgin, 134–80. London: Sage Publications.

Aytemiz Seymen, Oya. 2006. 'The Cultural Diversity Phenomenon in Organisations and Different Approaches for Effective Cultural Diversity Management: A Literary Review'. *Cross Cultural Management: An International Journal of Manpower* 13 (4): 296–315.

Bhadury, J., E. J. Mighty and H. Damar. 2000. 'Maximising Workforce Diversity in Project Teams: A Network Flow Approach'. *Omega: The International Journal of Management Science* 28 (2): 143–53.

Bleijenbergh, I., P. Peters and E. Poutsma. 2010. 'Diversity Management Beyond the Business Case'. *Equality, Diversity and Inclusion: An International Journal* 29 (5): 413–21.

Brown, Nicholas and Linda Cardinal. 2007. 'Introduction'. In *Managing Diversity: Practices of Citizenship*, edited by Nicholas Brown and Linda Cardinal, 1–16. Ottawa: The University of Ottawa Press.

Burns, Crosby, Kimberly Barton and Sophia Kerby. 2012. *The State of Diversity in Today's Workforce: As Our Nation Becomes More Diverse So Too Does Our Workforce*. Washington, DC: Center for American Progress.

Canas, Kathryn. 2014. 'An Integrated Approach to Managing Diversity in Organizations'. In *Opportunities and Challenges of Workplace Diversity: Theory, Cases and Exercises*, edited by Kathryn Canas and Harris Sondak, 45–64. New Jersey: Pearson Education.

Canas, Kathryn and Harris Sondak. 2014. 'Diversity in the Workplace: A Theoretical and Pedagogical Perspective'. In *Opportunities and Challenges of Workplace Diversity: Theory, Cases and Exercises*, edited by Kathryn Canas and Harris Sondak, 3–21. New Jersey: Pearson Education.

Carrell, M., N. Elbert and R. Hatfield. 2000. *Human Resource Management: Strategies for Managing a Diverse and Global Workforce*. 6th ed. Dryden: Harcourt College Publishers.

Cassell, C. 1996. 'A Fatal Attraction? Strategic HRM and the Business Case for Women's Progression at Work'. *Personnel Review* 25: 51–66.

Chandler, Nick G. 2017. 'Cultural Complexity in Large Organisations'. In *Managing Organizational Diversity: Trends and Challenges in Management and Engineering*, edited by Carolina Machado and J. Paulo Davim, 49–65. Cham: Springer International Publishing.

Chinnery, C. and F. Bothwick. 2005. 'Sharing a Diversity Initiative at Lehman Brothers'. *Strategic Communication Management* 9 (4): 18–21.

Christiansen, B. and H. Sezerel. 2013. 'Diversity Management in Transcultural Organizations'. *Global Business Perspective* 1 (2): 132–43.

Cox, T. 2001. *Creating the Multicultural Organisation: A Strategy for Capturing the Power of Diversity*. San Francisco: Jossey-Bass.

Cox, T. and S. Blake. 1991. 'Managing Cultural Diversity: Implications for Organizational Competitiveness'. *The Executive* 5 (3): 45–56.

De Cieri, H. and R. Kramar. 2007. *Human Resource Management in Australia: Strategy, People, Performance*. 2nd ed. Sydney: McGraw-Hill.

Dickens, L. 1999. 'Beyond the Business Case: A Three-pronged Approach to Equality Action'. *Human Resource Management Journal* 9 (1): 9–19.

DiTomaso, N. 1999. 'Managing Diversity in Organisations'. Accessed 16 February 2012. http://ditomaso.rutgers.edu/syllabi/managing%20diversity.pdf.

Edewor, P. A. and Y. A. Aluko. 2007. 'Diversity Management, Challenges and Opportunities in Multicultural Organizations'. *The International Journal of Diversity in Organizations, Communities and Nations* 6 (6): 189–96.

El Shearif, F. 2013. *Diverse Backgrounds, Workplace Diversity Strategy 2011–13*. Canberra: Australian Government, Department of Immigration and Citizenship.

Ellis, Kimberly M. and Phyllis Y. Keys. 2015. 'Workforce Diversity and Shareholder Value: A Multi-level Perspective'. *Review of Quantitative Finance and Accounting* 44 (2): 191–212.

Gandz, J. 2001. *A Business Case for Diversity. Richard Ivey School of Business*. Toronto: The University of Western Ontario.

Gillespie, Paul. 2007. 'Conclusion: Managing Diversity in a Post-Nationalist World'. In *Managing Diversity: Practices of Citizenship, edited by Nicholas Brown and Linda Cardinal*, 185–208. Ottawa: The University of Ottawa Press.

Gordon, Christopher. 2007. 'Managing Diversity in the Garda Siochana'. *An Garda Siochana Management Journal*. Accessed 18 September 2017. hwww.garda.ie/Documents/User/communiquedec2007.pdf

Greene, A. M. and G. Kirton. 2009. *Diversity Management in the UK: Organisational and Stakeholder Experiences*. New York: Routledge.

Guillaume, Yves R. F., Jeremy F. Dawson, Lilian Otaye-Ebede, Stephen A. Woods and Michael A. West. 2017. 'Harnessing Demographic Differences in Organizations: What Moderates the Effects of Workplace Diversity?'. *Journal of Organizational Behavior* 38 (2): 276–303.

Henry, O. and A. J. Evans. 2007. 'Critical Review of Literature on Workforce Diversity'. *African Journal of Business Management* 1 (4): 72–6.

Hollwell, B. J. 2007. 'Examining the Relationship between Diversity and Firm Performance'. *Journal of Diversity Management* 2 (2): 51–60.

Jain, H., P. Sloane and F. Horwitz. 2003. *Employment Equity and Affirmative Action: An International Comparison*. Armonk: ME Shape.

Jamieson, D. and J. O'Mara. 1991. *Managing Workforce 2000: Gaining the Diversity Advantage*. San Francisco: Jossey-Bass Publishers.

Jones, D., J. K. Pringle and D. Shepherd. 2000. 'Managing Diversity Meets Aotearoa/New Zealand'. *Personnel Review* 29: 364–80.

Kandola, R. and J. Fullerton. 1998. *The Diversity Mosaic in Action: Managing the Mosaic*. 2nd ed. Trowbridge: The Cromwell Press.

Kelly, E. and F. Dobbin. 1998. 'How Affirmative Action Became Diversity Management: Employer Response to Anti-Discrimination Law: 1961–1996'. *American Behavioral Scientist* 41 (7): 960–84.

Kennedy-Dubourdieu, E. 2006. *Race and Inequality: World Perspectives on Affirmative Action*. Aldershot: Ashgate.

Klarsfeld, A. 2010. *International Handbook on Diversity Management at Work Country Perspectives on Diversity and Equal Treatment*. Cheltenham: Edward Elgar.

Klarsfeld, A., L. Booysen, E. Ng, I. Roper and A. Tatli. 2014. *International Handbook on Diversity Management at Work: Country Perspectives on Diversity and Equal Treatment*. Vol. 2. Cheltenham: Edward Elgar.

Korovyakovskaya, Inessa and Hyonsong Chong. 2016. 'An Investigation of the Relationships between Three Types of Conflict and Perceived Group Performance in Culturally Diverse Work Groups'. *Journal of Organizational Culture, Communications and Conflict* 20 (1): 30–46.

Kuga, L. 1996. *Communicating in a Diverse Workplace*. Irvine: Richard Chang Associates.

Kühlmann, Torsten M. and Ramona Heinz. 2017. *Managing Cultural Diversity in Small and Medium-Sized Organizations: A Guideline for Practitioners*. Wiesbaden: Springer Gabler.

Kulik, Carol T. and Yiqiong Li. 2015. 'The Fork in the Road: Diversity Management and Organizational Justice'. In *The Oxford Handbook of Justice in the Workplace*, edited by Russell S. Cropanzano and Maureen L. Ambrose, 561–76. New York: Oxford University Press.

Kuusela, K. 2013. 'Diversity Management—Challenges and Possibilities' (Bachelor of Business Administration Thesis. Helsinki: Metropolitan University of Applied Sciences).

Liff, S. 1997. 'Two Routes to Managing Diversity: Individual Differences or Social Group Characteristics'. *Employee Relations* 19 (1): 11–26.

Litvin, D. R. 2006. 'Diversity: Making Space for a Better Case'. In *Handbook of Workplace Diversity*, edited by A. M. Konrad, P. Prasad and J. K. Pringle, 75–94. London: SAGE Publications.

Madera, J. M., M. Dawson and J. A. Neal. 2016. 'Why Investing in Diversity Management Matters: Organizational Attraction and Person-Organization Fit'. *Journal of Hospitality & Tourism Research*. First Published Online 24 June 2016. doi:10.1177/109634801665497.

McLauren, David. 2009. 'Benefits of Workplace Diversity'. Accessed 17 June 2014. http://www.davidmclauren.com/Connector_April_2009.pdf.

Moghaddam, Fathali M. 2008. *Multiculturalism and Intergroup Relations: Psychological Implications for Democracy in Global Context*. Washington, DC: American Psychological Association.

Mor Barak, Michàlle E. 2005. *Managing Diversity: Toward a Globally Inclusive Workplace*. Thousand Oaks, CA: SAGE Publications.

———. 2017. *Managing Diversity: Toward a Globally Inclusive Workplace*. 4th ed. Thousand Oaks, CA: SAGE Publications.

Motel, Laura. 2016. 'Increasing Diversity through Goal-setting in Corporate Social Responsibility Reporting'. *Equality, Diversity and Inclusion: An International Journal* 35 (5/6): 328–49.

Moyer, Melissa G. 2017. 'Work'. In *The Oxford Handbook of Language and Society*, edited by Ofelia García, Nelson Flores and Massimiliano Spotti, 505–24. New York: Oxford University Press.

Ng, E. S. W. and R. J. Burke. 2005. 'Person–Organisation Fit and the War for Talent: Does Diversity Management Make a Difference?'. *The International Journal of Human Resource Management* 16 (7): 1195–220.

O'Donovan, D. 2017. 'Diversity Management 2.0'. In *Managing Organizational Diversity: Trends and Challenges in Management and Engineering*, edited by Carolina Machado and J. Paulo Davim, 1–28. Cham: Springer International Publishing.

Ozbilgin, M. F., T. A. Beauregard, A. Tatli and M. P. Bell. 2011. 'Work-life, Diversity and Intersectionality: A Critical Review and Research Agenda'. *International Journal of Management Review* 13 (2): 177–98.

Ozbilgin, M. F. and J. Syed. 2015. 'Conclusion: Future of Diversity Management'. In *Managing Diversity and Inclusion: An International Perspective*, edited by J. Syed and M. F. Ozbilgin, 336–48. London: Sage.

Pitts, David W. 2007. 'Implementation of Diversity Management Programs in Public Organizations: Lessons from Policy Implementation Research'. *International Journal of Public Administration* 30 (12–14): 1573–90.

Pitts, David W., Alisa K. Hicklin, Daniel P. Hawes and Erin Melton. 2010. 'What Drives the Implementation of Diversity Management Programs? Evidence from Public Organizations'. *The Journal of Public Administration Research and Theory* 20: 867–86.

Prasad, P. and A. Mills. 1997. 'From Showcase to Shadow: Understanding the Dilemmas of Managing Workplace Diversity'. In *Managing the Organisational Melting Pot: Dilemmas of Workplace Diversity*, edited by P. Prasad, A. Mills, M. Elmes and A. Prasad, 3–29. Thousand Oaks: SAGE Publications.

Querling, L., M. Stuart and M. Butler. 2008. 'Diversity: An Overview'. Accessed 21 October 2013. http://www.pearsonhighered.com/assets/hip/us/hip_us_pearson highered/samplechapter/0321952294.pdf.

Ravazzani, Silvia. 2016. 'Understanding Approaches to Managing Diversity in the Workplace'. *Equality, Diversity and Inclusion: An International Journal* 35 (2): 154–68.

Riccucci, N. M. 2002. *Managing Diversity in Public Sector Workforces*. Boulder: Westview Press.

Risberg, A. A. and A. M. Soderberg. 2008. 'Translating a Management Concept: Diversity Management in Denmark'. *Gender in Management: An International Journal* 23: 426–41.

Robbins, S. P. 1998. *Organization Theory: Structure, Design and Applications*. New Jersey: Prentice-Hall International.

Romanenko, A. 2012. *Cultural Diversity Management in Organisations: The Role of Psychological Variables in Diversity Initiatives*. Hamburg: Diplomica Verlag.

Saxonhouse, A. W. 2001. *Fear of Diversity: The Birth of Political Science in Ancient Greek Thought*. Chicago: The University of Chicago Press.

Silk, C., R. Boyle, A. Bright, M. Bassett and N. Roach. 2000. *The Case for Cultural Diversity in Defence*. Canberra: Australian Defence Organisation.

Simlin, J. 2006. *Organization Culture and Impact of Diversity Openness in the IT-ITES Sector*. Karnataka: Christ College Institute of Management.

Stone, J. R. 2014. *Human Resources Management*. Milton: John Wiley & Sons Australia.

Strachan, G., J. Burgess and A. Sullivan. 2004. 'Affirmative Action or Managing Diversity: What is the Future of Equal Opportunity Policies in Organizations?'. *Women in Management Review* 19: 196–204.

Stuart, F. 2013. 'Most Effective Communication Skills in the Workplace'. ACPE. Accessed 7 December 2013. http://blog.acpe.edu.au/index.php/careers/effective-communication-skills-workplace/.

Stuber, M. 2009. *Diversity—Das Potenzial-Prinzip*. Köln: Luchterhand.

Tatli, A. 2011. 'A Multi-layered Exploration of the Diversity Management Field: Diversity Discourses, Practices and Practitioners in the UK'. *British Journal of Management* 22: 238–53.

Urbancová, Hana, Helena Čermáková and Hana Vostrovská. 2016. 'Diversity Management in the Workplace'. *Acta Universitatis Agriculturae et Silviculturae Mendelianae Brunensis* 64 (3): 1083–92.

Vickers-Willis, T., A. Connelly and D. Halliwell. 2009. 'Managing Diversity'. Accessed 30 January 2014. http://www.vwcorp.com.au/html/written/Workforce Diversity.pdf.

White, R. D. 1999. 'Managing the Diverse Organization: The Imperative for a New Multicultural Paradigm'. *Public Administration and Management* 4 (4): 469–98.

Wrench, J. 2015. 'Discrimination Against Immigrants in the Labour Market'. In *Routledge Handbook of Immigration and Refugee Studies*, edited by Anna Triandafyllidou. 118–24. Abingdon: Routledge.

Zanoni, P. and M. Janssens. 2004. 'Deconstructing Difference: The Rhetoric of Human Resource Managers' Diversity Discourses'. *Organization Studies* 25 (1): 55–74.

4 Diversity Management in the US, Canada, the UK and Australia
Legal and Political Analysis

The increasing diversity in the workforce because of worker immigration is one of the most notable occurrences of the twenty-first century. Immigrants form a significant percentage of the workforce in Australia (32%), Canada (22.4%), New Zealand (21.9%), the US (13.3%) and the UK (8.7%) (Ng and Stephenson 2015). Researchers argue that workforce diversity, if managed well, can improve business performance through the use of talents. Diversity refers to differences among people, including attributes that distinguish one individual from another. These differences include, yet are not limited to, 'age, gender, race, ethnicity, disability, sexual orientation, religion, social class, education/function, national origin, and language' (Ng and Stephenson 2015, 236). This chapter examines the legal and political aspects of managing such differences in the US, Canada, the UK and Australia.

Diversity Management in the US: Political and Legal Analysis

Before 1875, the US Congress was happy to leave immigration issues to be managed by the individual states. In early 1819, the federal government was responsible for keeping records of new arrivals, while state laws regulated the influx. In 1849, when the US Supreme Court (1849) withdrew state laws announcing that immigration legislation was a federal issue, Washington legislators began to establish a uniform system at the beginning of 1875, with the legislation of the *Page Act*. Many years later, in response to growing hostility towards Chinese immigrants, Congress passed the first of several laws related to immigration, and established a bureaucracy to monitor the entry of immigrants. Legislators endeavoured to create a nation on the basis of ethnicity and nationality (Reimers 2016).

Chinese labourers were the first immigrants to be barred, yet thousands of Chinese men (and a few women) flooded into America following the discovery of gold in 1849 in California, where they met little opposition. The Chinese people called California 'the Gold Mountain'. However, when thousands of miners from other parts of the US, Australia and Europe failed to fulfil their dreams of great wealth, they turned against the Chinese.

Additionally, laws were passed in California to penalise Chinese miners and force them to leave the mines. The Chinese people were not even welcome in the west, where they experienced riots and were forced to leave. White racism in the nineteenth century extended this hostility to include all Asians, not only Chinese immigrants, claiming Asians to be inferior to white Americans and unable to assimilate. White Californians were able to gain support for these beliefs, and convinced Congress to enact the *Chinese Exclusion Act of 1882*, which prohibited the admission of Chinese labourers to the US for 10 years, after which the law was extended and made permanent in 1903. In contrast, diplomats, students, temporary visitors and merchants and their wives were entitled to enter the US (Reimers 2016).

When the *Immigration Act of 1952* was introduced, it was criticised by both Presidents Harry S. Truman and Dwight David Eisenhower for discriminating against Southern and Eastern Europeans by having low quotas for the number of immigrants allowed to enter the US. Congress passed another *Refugee Act* in 1953, and then, when liberals and Lyndon Johnson gained victory in 1964, Congress enacted the *Hart-Celler Act*, which abolished national origin quotas for the Eastern Hemisphere and replaced them with a system based on family unification. When President Lyndon Johnson signed the *Immigration Act of 1965*, he remarked:

> This is not a revolutionary bill. It does not affect the lives of millions. It will not reshape the structure of our daily lives, or add importantly to our wealth and power. . . . The days of unlimited immigration are past. But those who come will come because of what they are—not because of the land from which they sprung.
>
> (Bayor 2016, 7)

Diversity management started in the 1960s in the US with the commencement of EEO laws, followed by AA programs to protect the underrepresented minorities. A three-step evolutionary model was presented, including AA, valuing and managing diversity, the recognition of individuals' full potential, and matters related to organisational culture and values (Ravazzani 2016). The political history of diversity management in the US began with President John F. Kennedy's *Executive Order No. 10925* of 1961, by which federal contractors were required to take AA to end discrimination. AA and equal employment law in the US were intended to preclude future discrimination in employment. AA aimed to end discrimination on the basis of race, colour, creed or national origin, under Kennedy's *Executive Order No. 10925* (Hammerman 1984). Johnson's *Executive Order No. 11246* in 1965 extended the coverage to include work undertaken by contractors and subcontractors, followed by his *Executive Order No. 11375* in 1967, which added sex to the list of protected categories (Burstein 1985). Both *Executive Orders 10925* and *11246* urged employers to end discrimination, and encouraged them to devise programs to hire, train and promote people from disadvantaged groups. Further, Title VII of the *Civil Rights Act of 1964*, which outlawed discrimination in employment, also enabled employees to sue employers for discrimination during hiring or promotion, and established the EEOC to deal with claims and monitor compliance. Additionally, during the 1970s, active federal enforcement of EEO and AA law were introduced. As a result of ambiguity regarding compliance, employers were uncertain how to comply with these laws, and hired EEO and AA specialists to design EEO/AA programs and protect organisations from any litigation (Dobbin et al. 1993). Table 4.1 provides a list of the major US legislation dealing with the different aspects of workplace diversity.

Table 4.1 Major US Legislation Related to Workplace Discrimination

Year	Legislation	Summary
1864	*Immigration Act of 1864* (also known as the *Act to Encourage Immigration*)	This Act made contracts for immigrant labour formed abroad enforceable by US courts. It also created a Commissioner of Immigration, appointed by the President to serve under the Secretary of State.
1875	*Immigration Act of 1875* (also known as *Page Law* or *Asian Exclusion Act*)	This Act prohibited the immigration of criminals and made it a felony to bring to the US or contract forced Asian labourers. It was the nation's first restrictive immigration statute.
1882	*Chinese Exclusion Act of 1882*	This Act banned Chinese labourers from immigrating for the next 10 years and authorised deportation of unauthorised Chinese immigrants. Any Chinese immigrant who resided in the US as of 17 November 1880 could remain, yet was barred from naturalising. The *Geary Act of 1892* extended this law for an additional 10 years and required that Chinese nationals obtain identification papers.
1891	*Immigration Act of 1891*	This Act expanded the list of exclusions for immigration from prior laws to include polygamists and people with a contagious disease. It permitted the deportation of any unauthorised immigrants or those who could be excluded from migration based on previous legislation. It made it a federal misdemeanour to bring unauthorised immigrants into the country or aid someone who was entering the US unlawfully.

Year	Legislation	Summary
1903	Immigration Act of 1903 (also known as Anarchist Exclusion Act)	This Act banned anarchists, beggars and importers of prostitutes from immigrating. It was the first US law to restrict immigration based on immigrants' political beliefs.
1917	Immigration Act of 1917 (also known as Asiatic Barred Zone Act)	This Act banned immigration from most Asian countries, except the Philippines, which was a US colony, and Japan, whose government voluntarily eliminated the immigration of Japanese labourers as part of the Gentlemen's Agreement of 1907. Required immigrants over the age of 16 had to demonstrate basic reading ability in any language.
1921	Emergency Quota Act of 1921	This Act was the first US law to create numerical quotas for immigration based on nationality. Quotas were equal to 3% of the foreign-born population of that nationality in the 1910 census. Immigration from Asian countries continued to be barred. Nationality quotas did not apply to countries in the Western Hemisphere, government officials or temporary visitors. Under this law, the total annual immigration was capped at 350,000.
1941	Executive Order 8802 (1941)	Signed by President D Roosevelt on the eve of World War II, this order prohibited government contractors from engaging in employment discrimination based on race, colour or national origin.
1942	Bracero Agreement of 1942	This was a bilateral agreement between the US and Mexico to permit Mexican nationals to serve as temporary agricultural workers during World War II labour shortages. It required employers to pay a wage equal to that paid to US-born farmworkers and provide transportation and living expenses. It was in effect until 1964.
1943	Magnuson Act of 1943 (also known as Chinese Exclusion Repeal Act of 1943)	This Act repealed the Chinese Exclusion Act and established a quota of about 105 Chinese immigrants per year. It was in contrast to other quotas, which were based on ancestry. Chinese residents were also eligible to naturalise.

(Continued)

Table 4.1 (Continued)

Year	Legislation	Summary
1946	Title VII of the *Civil Rights Act of 1946*	Title VII is the federal law that prohibits most workplace harassment and discrimination, covering all private employers, state and local governments, and educational institutions with 15 or more employees. It prohibits discrimination against workers because of race, colour, national origin, religion and sex, or on the basis of pregnancy; sex stereotyping; and sexual harassment of employees. Currently, Title VII does not include discrimination on the basis of sexual orientation. However, in recent years, federal legislation has been proposed to add sexual orientation as a protected class against discrimination (the *Employment Non-discrimination Act*). Many states have employment discrimination and harassment laws and may include more protected classes—such as marital status and sexual orientation—than Title VII covers.
1952	*Immigration and Nationality Act of 1952* (also known as *Hart-Celler Act*)	This Act formally removed race as an exclusion for immigration and naturalisation, granted Asian countries a minimum quota of 100 visas per year (though this was still based on ancestry, not nationality; for example, a person with Chinese ancestry coming from the UK would be counted in the Chinese quota, regardless of nationality/birthplace). It updated the national origins quota to one-sixth of 1% of each nationality's population in the 1920 census. As a result, most spots were for immigrants from the UK, Ireland and Germany. Under this law, political activities, ideology and mental health, among other criteria, served as a basis for exclusion and deportation. This law also created quota preferences for skilled immigrants and family reunification.
1963	*Equal Pay Act 1963*	This Act required men and women to be given equal pay for equal work in the same establishment. Although the jobs did not need to be identical, they had to be substantially equal; it was job content, not job titles, that determined whether jobs were substantially equal.

Year	Legislation	Summary
1964	Title VII of the *Civil Rights Act of 1964*	This Act prohibited employment discrimination based on race, colour, religion, gender or national origin. It was enforced by the Commerce Clause of the US Constitution and limited to employers with 15 or more employees, state or federal employers, or companies receiving state or federal money.
1965	*Immigration and Nationality Act* (also known as *Hart-Celler Act* or 1965 amendments)	This Act replaced the national origins quota system with a seven-category preference system emphasising family reunification and skilled immigrants. No visa cap was placed on the number of immediate family members of US citizens admitted each year.
1965	*Executive Order (EO) No. 11246 of 1965*	The aim of *EO No. 11246* enacted by President Johnson was to prohibit federal government contractors and subcontractors with contracts exceeding $10,000 from discriminating against employees and applicants on the basis of race, colour, religion, sex or national origin (Buckley IV 2017).
1967	*Age Discrimination in Employment Act (ADEA) 1967*	The *ADEA* is the federal law governing age discrimination. It was enacted in 1967 to promote the employment of older workers based on ability, rather than age; prevent discrimination; and help solve the problems that arise with an ageing workforce. Many states also have laws prohibiting age discrimination and may have more restrictions than the *ADEA*. The objective of the Act is to prohibit employers with 20 or more employees from discriminating on the basis of age against employees aged 40 years or older.
1967	*EO No. 11375 of 1967*	Enacted by President Johnson as an amendment to *EO No. 11246*, *EO No. 11375* added discrimination on the basis of sex into the list of protected categories.
1969	*EO No. 11478 of 1969*	As an amendment to *EO No. 11246*, *EO No. 11478* enacted by President Richard Nixon added people with disabilities and people over the age of 40 to the list of protected categories.

(Continued)

Table 4.1 (Continued)

Year	Legislation	Summary
1978	*Pregnancy Discrimination Act of 1978*	The *Pregnancy Discrimination Act* was an amendment to Title VII of the *Civil Rights Act of 1964*—a federal discrimination law. It made it unlawful to discriminate on the basis of pregnancy, childbirth or related medical conditions. This law covered state and local private and public employers with 15 or more employees. Pregnant women or those affected by related conditions must be treated in the same manner as other applicants or employees with similar abilities or limitations. Many states also have laws regarding pregnancy discrimination and breastfeeding.
1979	*EO No. 12138 of 1979*	Enacted by President James Carter, *EO No. 12138* established the National Women's Business Enterprise and introduced provisions to require federal contractors and subcontractors to apply an affirmative approach to promote and support women's business enterprises.
1986	*Immigration Reform and Control Act of 1986* (also known as *Simpson-Mazzoli Act*)	This Act granted a pathway to permanent residency to unauthorised immigrant workers who had lived in the US since 1982 or worked in certain agricultural jobs.
1990	*Immigration Act of 1990*	This Act increased the annual immigration cap to 700,000 during the fiscal years 1992 to 1994, followed by 675,000 as of the 1995 fiscal year, and revised the preference categories.
1990	*Americans with Disabilities Act (ADA) of 1990* and *ADA Amendments Act 1990 (ADAAA)*	The *ADA of 1990* prohibited discrimination against disabled workers or job applicants, and covered all private employers with 15 or more employees and state and local governments, regardless of the number of employees. The *ADAAA*, which was signed into law in 2008, expanded the interpretation of the *ADA's* coverage and the definition of what disabilities were covered. The *ADA of 1990* applied to employers with 15 or more employees, including state and local governments, recruitment companies and labour organisations. The Act prohibited discrimination in employment against qualified disabled people and forced employers to accommodate the disabilities of job applicants and employees.

Year	Legislation	Summary
1991	*Civil Rights Act of 1991*	The *Civil Rights Act of 1991* was designed to reinstate the interpretation given by Title VII and *Civil Rights Act of 1866* against the controversial rulings by the US Supreme Court between 1989 and 1991. The changes included: (i) making punitive damages in some cases of discrimination, (ii) making jury trials if the plaintiff is seeking damages, (iii) requiring employers to show that employment practices having a negative effect on protected groups are job-related and in line with business necessity, (iv) extending the ban of race discrimination to cover discrimination that occurs before and after the hiring process and (v) extending the coverage of the Act to US citizens working for US companies abroad.
1996	*Illegal Immigration Reform and Immigrant Responsibility Act of 1996*	This Act increased enforcement at the border and in the interior, including a mandate to build fences at the highest incidence areas of the southwest border.
1998	*EO No. 13087 of 1998*	As an amendment to *EO No. 11246*, *EO No. 13087* passed by President Bill Clinton added sexual orientation to the list of protected categories.
2000	*EO No. 13152 of 2000*	As an amendment to *EO No. 11246*, *EO No. 13152* enacted by President Clinton added status as a parent into the list of protected categories.
2002	*Enhanced Border Security and Visa Entry Reform Act of 2002*	This Act required an electronic data system be used to make available information relevant to admissions and removability of immigrants, and mandated implementation of a visa entry-exit data system.
2002	*EO No. 13279 of 2002*	*EO No. 13279*, enacted by President Bush, limited the effect of *EO No. 11246* on religious and community organisations that provide social services as federal contractors or subcontractors.
2006	*Secure Fence Act of 2006*	This law mandated the construction of a double-layered fence approximately 700 miles long.

(*Continued*)

Table 4.1 (Continued)

Year	Legislation	Summary
2008	The Amendments Act of 2008	The *Amendments Act of 2008* amended the *ADA of 1990* to restore the original protections and overrule certain Supreme Court decisions. The new Act retained the definition of disability and clarified three critical terms: 'substantially limits', 'major life activities' and 'regarded as'.
2014	Deferred for Parents of American and Lawful Permanent Residents (DAPA) and Deferred Action for Childhood Arrivals (DACA) Program Expanded of 2014	This was a second executive action by President Obama that allowed unauthorised immigrant parents who have lived in the US for at least five years and have children who are US citizens or legal permanent residents to apply for deportation relief and a three-year work permit. It also expanded the eligibility for *DACA* to any unauthorised immigrant who entered the US illegally as a child. This executive action is on hold as a state challenge works through the courts.
2014	EO No. 13672 of 2014	As an amendment to *EO No. 11246* enacted by President Obama, *EO No. 13672* added sexual orientation and gender identity to the list of categories protected from discrimination.

Source: Bogardus (2007), Buckley IV (2017), HR Hero (2017), James (2014) and Pew Research Center (2015).

It should also be noted that the term 'diversity management' has many meanings, yet normally relates to the efforts made by organisations to recruit and retain employees from various backgrounds, and establish good working relationships among them. In the US, the private sector has used inclusiveness and diversity to increase profit and escape discrimination legal proceedings. Diversity management is designed to mix organisational structure with cultural diversity by introducing training and diversity initiatives (Hur and Strickland 2015).

'Diversity in the workplace' is a concept established by the federal legislature detailed in Table 4.1. Undoubtedly, federal laws forbidding discrimination and harassment in the workplace have caused a change in the country in the last 50 years. Before the introduction of such laws, there was no incentive to hire a diverse workforce. The demographics of the American workplace changed with the passage of Title VII of the *Civil Rights Act of 1964*, prohibiting 'discrimination on the basis of race, colour, religion, sex, or national origin in employment-related matters' (James 2014, 27).

In addition, Title VII prohibits discrimination in the hiring, promoting and treatment of employees. Title VII was expanded in 1967 to encompass the *ADEA*, and, today, includes eight 'protected classes', such as race, national origin, colour of skin, religion, age, disability, sex/gender and sexual orientation (James 2014).

Under Title VII, employees have certain rights and responsibilities. To succeed in a legal complaint or charge of discrimination or harassment, employees must adhere to the organisation's policies and procedures, and this is important for two reasons. First, to ascertain a discrimination or harassment complaint, it must be established that an employee has followed the organisation's complaint procedure. Second, as a productive worker, it becomes difficult for an employer to demonstrate a non-discriminatory ground for any discriminatory action. Most employees receive policy and procedure information during orientation, and by completing their jobs and following the information guide, they will have a better chance of succeeding in any charge or complaint against employers (James 2014).

When Reagan became President in 1980, he decided to curtail the enforcement of anti-discrimination laws, yet employers maintained anti-discrimination programs, with the exception of some elements related to AA law (Kelly and Dobbin 1998). EEO/AA specialists did not respond to Reagan's cutbacks, and formalised HRM through anti-discrimination measures in hiring and promotion systems and recruitment schemes, claiming that 'the capacity to manage a diverse workforce well would be the key to business success in the future' (Kelly and Dobbin 1998, 961). In the 1980s and 1990s, *EEO/AA* practices became the diversity management component of the new HRM paradigm.

Employer response to AA and EEO law was subjected to four stages, the first two of which were documented in the neo-institutional literature (Abzug and Mezias 1993; Dobbin et al. 1988; Dobbin et al. 1993). First, in the 1960s, the ambiguity and weak enforcement of these laws resulted in some changes in employment practices. The 1960s civil rights movement stimulated American managers to rush to increase employment opportunities for racial minorities. Then, in the 1980s, when more women joined the labour force, organisations started to consider diversity through a 'business case' lens, and, to obtain 'a competitive advantage', they took advantage of a diverse talented workforce (Kulik and Li 2015). The US adopted anti-discrimination regulation in 1964 in Title VII, which is the main anti-discrimination law under the *Civil Rights Act*, which made it illegal to implement workplace prejudice and discrimination based on sex, age, race, colour, religion and national origin. Additionally, to adhere to the legal requirements of Title VII, organisations in the US had to adopt EEO policies to provide fair and equal treatment to all employees, regardless of their diverse background (Gotsis and Kortezi 2015).

The second stage was between 1972 and 1980, when federal enforcement led employers to acknowledge anti-discrimination law, yet the ambiguity of compliance forced employers to hire EEO/AA specialists to formulate compliance strategies and create internal constituencies of EEO/AA measures. This was largely because the management of a diverse workforce became subject to the legally imposed perspective of AA, also known as 'positive discrimination'—a term commonly used in the UK. AA deals with the introduction of a more inclusive workplace, and its aims are more precise than EEO policies. AA increases the number of underrepresented groups in the workplace, including women and racial/ethnic minorities. Both EEO and AA are mandatory, as they are legally enforced upon organisations, which are required to adhere to legal mandates. Both EEO and AA are collectivist in nature, while diversity management is considered a more individualistic approach to workplace diversity. The collectivist approach deals with the fact that legally imposed policies cannot ignore discrimination and inequalities experienced by people such as women and racial and ethnic minorities (Gotsis and Kortezi 2015).

AA in the US requires employers to provide equal opportunity and develop types of assistance to minority ethnic groups who are deemed to have suffered legal discrimination. In addition, AA covers colour, religion, sex and national origin. In the 1970s, 'diversity' was added to prior discrimination, yet its vagueness was so great that even white racists could claim to be 'diverse'. This led to the rise of 'group rights' and demand for universal 'equal rights', which shifted the argument from the 'rights of blacks' to 'everyone's rights to have access to political institutions' (Stam and Shohat 2012, 211). Affirmative action and reparations can ideally be seen as a continuum of complementary strategies, which are designed:

(1) to combat racial inequality and discrimination; (2) to penalize acts of discrimination against people of color, gays, lesbians, and transsexuals; (3) to heal injured minority self-esteem through cultural, educational, and media affirmation; and (4) to empower women and people of color in key media and educational institutions.

(Stam and Shohat 2012, 212)

While the success of AA is recognised by some conservatives, critics argue that it is no longer required and that it implies unfairness to white males, resulting in accusations of 'reverse racism', 'race-based quotas', 'special rights for blacks', 'rigid quotas', 'preferential hiring' and so forth (Stam and Shohat 2012).

The third stage of employer responses to EEO/AA started when Reagan curtailed enforcement in the 1980s, and EEO/AA specialists began to reap the benefits of EEO/AA practices that rationalised the allocation of personnel. In the fourth stage, after 1987, the future of AA became uncertain, and neither Bush nor Clinton offered any outright support and the days of AA were numbered. As a result, EEO/AA specialists became diversity managers by promoting human resource practices with the purpose of maintaining and managing diversity in the workplace. However, a great number of procedural changes occurred, which significantly reduced the number of sanctions against violating employers (Leonard 1989), and workers' back pay fell from more than 4,000 in 1980 to 499 in 1986 in view of AA violations (Blumrosen 1993). These changes led Leonard (1989, 74) to declare that 'an administration lacking the will to enforce AA beyond rubber-stamped compliance reviews has resulted in an AA program without practical effects since 1980'.

By the late 1980s, EEO/AA specialists presented EEO/AA measures as part of diversity managers, promoted their competitive advantages and argued that diversity programs produced a strategic advantage that enabled members of diverse groups to perform to their potential (Winterle 1992). Ethnicity-related demographic changes in the US population emerged as a great concern for administrative practices in the late 1980s and early 1990s under the heading of 'managing workplace diversity' or 'valuing cultural diversity'. The demographic changes occurring during that period also became a focus of academic discussion. For example, in relation to the notion of diversity, Hawkins (1992, 33) stated that 'our human diversity is greater in the 1990s than it has been at any time in our history'. In contrast, Foster et al. (quoted in Yanow 2003) placed race-ethnic diversity in a historical context by arguing that employee diversity has been a constant theme in American workforce for many years, and the only difference from the past is changes in the groups towards which companies direct diversity activities. While from around 1870 to 1924, the so-called 'outsiders' were Italian, Polish, Irish and Russian men (who were white ethnic groups, yet considered inferior immigrants, before being gradually embraced into the white Protestant workforce by Americans), the focus of diversity in the 1980s started to change to cultural and racial minorities and women of all races (Yanow 2003).

In American academic and administrative circles, discussions around growing diversity refer to both public and private sectors. While studies of the private sector view diversity in the workplace as a competitive advantage (Cox and Blake 1991), public sector studies tend to promote diverse workforce as social justice (Kellough 1990; Schmidt 1988), although some administration journals have published articles highlighting the performance effectiveness and competitive profits (Coleman 1990). EEO and AA are criticised for creating a gender-, culture- and colour-blind workplace, and focusing more on assimilating differences than on enabling every individual to perform according to their potential. Thus, EEO and AA practices often result in the integration of culturally diverse employees to the dominant cultural paradigm in a given organisation, creating what is characterised as the American 'melting pot' (Gotsis and Kortezi 2015). Thus, in the early 1990s, there was a shift to understand what diversity and difference mean, irrespective of the continuous focus on race-ethnicity and gender. Understanding diversity has changed corporate culture in the US, and the traditional management view implied that the employee must adapt to the workplace, which is an assimilationist, Anglo-dominant, melting-pot view. This view is based on the desire for homogeneity, where all individuals' cultures melt into the single 'American' pot. Thus, 'different' meant (and means) something negative or inferior, and equality meant (and means) identical, the same, the perceived 'normal' or an unmarked state (Hanamura 1989). Culture was an identity kept outside the workplace, and bringing it into the organisation was viewed as complicating the real mission of work. This view indicated a total adherence to a single identity—a single organisational culture (Yanow 2003).

The shift from viewing the US as a 'melting pot' to the metaphors of 'mosaic' or 'tossed salad' may be responsible for how cultural diversity is viewed in organisational contexts. In this notion, managing 'diversity' seems to be the opposite of managing 'uniformity'. While the AA/EEO policies of the past focused on increasing the numbers of underrepresented groups and newcomers in the organisation, in the emerging approach of 'managing cultural diversity', the organisation is seen as a changing workforce in mutual adjustment and adaptation (Goldstein and Leopold 1990). Additionally, this view reflects two influencing factors: the bidirectional interchange between the workforce (employees) and the workplace (the organisation), and between the workplace and the family/community. In this manner, the workplace is no longer isolated from the society in which it resides (Yanow 2003).

In addition, the issue of wage inequality still exists in the American workplace, despite the existence of two laws to ensure equal pay for equal work. The first is the *Equal Pay Act of 1963*, which forbids unequal pay for equal work performed by men and women. The second is Title VII of the *Civil Rights Act of 1964*, which prohibits wage discrimination based on race, colour, sex, religion or national origin. Yet women still earn about 75% of men's earnings for the same job. This is an increase from 60% in 1980, at a time when women represented 42% of the workforce in the US. In 1990, women formed 45% of the workforce, and, in 2009, women formed almost 50% of the workforce (ATMA Global 2014).

The *Workforce 2000* report (Johnston and Packer 1987) published by Hudson Institute in 1987 revealed the importance of managing diversity to fulfil a competitive advantage. This cross-cultural and linguistic diversity has occupied the interest of scholars ever since. The 2010 Economist Intelligence Unit (2010, 5) report, based on 479 survey responses and 16 interviews with senior executives, revealed the importance of understanding and managing diversity in the workplace in a global context, now and in the future:

> Workers will come from a greater range of backgrounds; those with local knowledge of an emerging market, a global outlook and an intuitive sense of the corporate culture will be particularly valued. . . . To

build on this, many companies will send employees overseas more frequently, often for short periods, on project-based assignments or to take part in training.

Today, managers tend to value the powerful benefits of diversity in the workplace, and declare that a more diverse workforce will increase organisational effectiveness, lift morale and enhance productivity. It seems that the benefits of a diverse workforce far exceed the financial measures, creativity, organisational and individual growth (Thomas and Ely 1996). Further, diversity specialists state that demographic changes affect both labour and consumer markets and provide 'a sense of crisis, urgency and purpose' (Lynch 1997, 9) for diversity programs. Diversity specialists argue that labour markets are changing, and, to include other types of workers, organisations must accept people from different cultures and diverse backgrounds by becoming 'employers of choice' (Winterle 1992). When workers from different cultures feel appreciated and comfortable in the workplace, they will increase productivity and contribute more to the organisation. Organisations must develop new products to reach new immigrants and newly wealthy minority groups by recruiting employees from those groups (Kelly and Dobbin 1998). Eventually, business organisations have accepted diversity management as a secondary area of HRM. The Conference Board and the Society for Human Resource Management developed diversity management programs that began in 1993 (Lynch 1997). In addition, diversity specialists introduced a workplace 'culture audit', in which surveys and interviews were used to identify features of culture in diversity (Thomas and Ely 1996).

It is claimed that 'America has always handled its diversity so well', yet some ask 'Why we're the Great Melting Pot' (Carr-Ruffino 2005, 90). Diversity has succeeded for all immigrants from European countries, and, in the workplace, has succeeded for male immigrants from those countries. European immigrants were expected to assimilate and be absorbed into the American way of life, thereby creating a seamless American culture and workplace. While European men found the American culture similar to their own, and looked much alike, other people—such as Jewish, Irish, Italian and Eastern European immigrants—experienced some prejudice and discrimination, until they eventually blended into the mainstream culture within a generation or two. In contrast, people of colour and women did not look like Euro-American men, who were the dominant culture in the workplace, and subsequently failed to assimilate and melt into the mainstream (Carr-Ruffino 2005).

Newcomers in the past accepted the concept of the melting-pot belief system in the US, which led to new beliefs, such as wanting to become like the dominant group, feeling that their country is inferior and America is better, wanting to fit in at any cost and being willing to raise their children as Americans. The ideal was to ignore differences and treat everyone equally, according to the biblical 'Golden Rule': 'Do unto others as you would have them do unto you'. However, while this rule usually works in a homogeneous culture, it is different in a multicultural workplace. A more appropriate Golden Rule would be: 'Do unto others as they would have you do unto them'. To be fair, different people must be treated differently because they have different habits and values (Carr-Ruffino 2005). Some social groups, such as women and minorities, still experience social and structural problems that can affect performance in the workplace and lead to friction, despite their labour force participation in the US over the last 50 years. To overcome these challenges, organisations endeavour to implement AA plans and provide flexible work arrangements, training and sponsorship programs. These arrangements can enhance the stigmatised groups' experiences in the workplace (Apfelbaum, Stephens and Reagans 2016).

Diversity Management in Canada: Political and Legal Analysis

Canada was the first country to welcome diversity by introducing the first multiculturalism Act in 1970 in Parliament, enacted in 1988, and an immigration system based on points to examine potential immigrants who might successfully integrate into Canadian society. Canada has become well acknowledged around the world for its generous immigration influx and anti-discrimination policies. Diversity is so important in Canada that the Preamble of the *Canadian Multiculturalism Act 1988* states the following:

> The government of Canada recognizes the diversity of Canadians as regards race, national or ethnic origin, colour and religion as a fundamental characteristic of Canadian society and is committed to a policy of multiculturalism designed to preserve and enhance the multicultural heritage of Canadians while working to achieve the equality of all Canadians in the economic, social, cultural and political life of Canada.
>
> (Haq 2015, 32)

Freedoms to all Canadians are guaranteed by the *Canadian Charter of Rights and Freedoms* (*CCRF*) of the *Constitution Act 1982* (Haq 2015):

> The *Canadian Human Rights Act* prohibits discrimination on 11 grounds: race, national or ethnic origin, colour, religion, age, sex, sexual orientation, marital status, family status, disability or conviction for which a pardon has been granted.
>
> (Haq 2015, 33)

Canadian society and workplaces are also changing. The ban on Sunday shopping was lifted in Canada in 1985, challenged under the *CCRF* of the *Constitution Act 1982*, following discussions and debates about the negative influence of the religious practices of Christian workers who wished to attend church on Sundays (Haq 2015).

In the Canadian context, the concept of diversity states that 'as Canada's population grows and its demographics change becoming more diverse with cultures, religions, racial groups, languages and sexual orientations, fair treatment is a necessity' (Xu 2013, 211). The diversity management model in Canada is regarded a mixed approach that can be categorised into four approaches. The first approach is the legalistic approach, whereby the government enacts two types of appropriate legislations: positive and negative. Positive legislation deals with the pieces of legislation that protect people's natural rights. Negative legislation is intended to punish undesirable social arrangements and behaviours that threaten the rights of other people. This deterrence is explicitly expressed in the *Bill of Rights, Human Rights Act* and *CCRF*. The second approach is the reactive approach, which deals with laws and regulations to deter and punish undesirable social arrangements and behaviours through the human rights tribunal, police and court systems. The third is a proactive approach, whereby social institutions enhance and create mutual understanding and communication among different groups. The fourth is the celebratory approach, which is the most popular approach, and deals with celebrating cultural differences during various ethnic festivals, such as Chinese Lunar New Year, South Asian's Diwali and the gay pride celebrations in Vancouver and Toronto (Yan 2010). In this context, it can be argued that the Canadian human rights model of managing diversity seems to offer valuable experience for the global community. The challenges and critiques of this model by members of Canadian society have not undermined its achievements, but rather generated healthy debates that will improve this model because of Canada's open society (Yan 2010).

In terms of a legal basis of diversity management in Canada, the federal *EEA*, which is akin to AA in the US, and was passed in 1986, is the major piece of legislation aimed at improving labour force diversity. The *EEA* covers both the public and private sectors, and requires:

> employers in covered sectors (e.g., communications, transportation, and banking) to reduce disparities in employment and workforce representation between designated groups (such as women, visible minorities, aboriginal peoples, and people with disabilities) and the general workforce.
>
> (Hiranandani 2012, 2)

Table 4.2 lists the key Canadian legislation on workplace diversity.

In Canada, certain legislative requirements—such as the *Canadian Human Rights Act 1985*—ensure the protection of individuals from discrimination by employers and other members of society. While this legislation of protection exists in every Canadian jurisdiction, legislation dealing

Table 4.2 Major Canadian Legislation Related to Workplace Discrimination

Legislation	Summary
Canadian Human Rights Act 1985	For all purposes of this Act, the prohibited grounds of discrimination are race, national or ethnic origin, colour, religion, age, sex, sexual orientation, marital status, family status, disability and conviction for an offence for which a pardon has been granted or in respect of which a record suspension has been ordered (Government of Canada 1985).
Canadian Multiculturalism Act 1988	This Act established a legislative framework for the Canadian policy of multiculturalism by aiming to protect the cultural heritage of Canadians, reducing discrimination and encouraging multicultural programs and activities undertaken by public and private organisations (Elliott and Fleras 1990).
EEA 1995	'The purpose of this Act is to achieve equality in the workplace so that no person shall be denied employment opportunities or benefits for reasons unrelated to ability, and in the fulfilment of that goal, to correct the conditions of disadvantage in employment experienced by women, aboriginal peoples, persons with disabilities and members of visible minorities by giving effect to the principle that employment equity means more than treating persons in the same way but also requires special measures and the accommodation of differences' (Government of Canada 2001, 1).
Human Resources Management Standards Standard 4.3 2008	This standard ensures that employers provide a work environment free from harassment and set out confidentiality rules in complaint processes (HR Council Canada 2009).
Human Resources Management Standards Standard 4.4 2008	This standard ensures that employers commit to providing and promoting an inclusive workplace in business practices, including recruitment and selection (HR Council Canada 2009).

with promotion of equity in the workplace is limited to federally regulated employers (Cukier et al. 2017). The *Equity Act* was enacted in Canada in 1986 and amended in 1995 to achieve the following aim:

> To achieve equality in the workplace so that no person shall be denied employment opportunities or benefits for reasons unrelated to ability..., to correct the conditions of disadvantage in employment experienced by women, aboriginal peoples, persons with disabilities and members of visible minorities by giving effect to the principle that employment equity means more than treating persons in the same way but also requires special measures and the accommodation of differences.
>
> (Government of Canada 2001)

Employers covered by the *Equity Act 1995* are forced to form an employment equity plan for selected groups in the workforce, to find and eliminate barriers to equity in the workplace, and to table annual reports to the federal government (Government of Canada 2001). Adherence to this Act is controlled by audits performed by the Canadian Human Rights Commission, and heavy penalties are imposed for non-compliance. Employment equity disputes emerging among employers, employees and compliance officers are referred to a tribunal to be resolved (Government of Canada 2001).

Following the enactment of the federal *EEA* in 1986, the concept of diversity management in Canada emerged in association with the theory of 'the business case for diversity'. Diversity management introduced the concept of a diversity inclusion system that could increase productivity, expand the customer base, increase market share and maximise profits. It was further claimed that diversity management is 'more inclusive than pay equity or AA or employment equity management (which cover only specific designated group)' (Foster and Jacobs 2012, 66). Therefore, diversity management in Canada is now spread across the political spectrum and all Canadian business operations. As a result of global and national demographic changes, a diverse and inclusive workforce that can improve morale in the workplace has become imperative for the benefit of organisations. It is reported that embracing differences makes good business sense, both ethically and legally, for the advantages and varied opportunities these differences offer (Foster and Jacobs 2012).

In this context, diversity management in Canada revolves around the 'business imperative' and the necessity to deal with the shortage of a skilled labour force. The 'business imperative' refers to compelling reasons to increase diversity in Canadian organisations, including fostering creativity and innovation, where creative ideas, knowledge and innovation are considered stable sources of capital (Oliver 2005), and providing maximum access to talented people (Ferner, Almond and Colling 2005; Thomas and Ely 1996). In Canada, diversity management has also been used as a means of entering ethnic markets, with the assumption that an organisation with a workforce similar to its customer base is more competitive in ethnic markets. For example, the Bank of Montreal focused on Chinese Canadians by hiring Chinese-speaking employees who knew the community's culture. By doing so, the bank's market segment increased by 400% over a five-year period (Oliver 2005).

In Canada, political projects or solutions developed in their names are used to undermine genuine expressions of diversity. Canada has to deal with 'national' diversity, which is a challenge that other countries (such as Australia, Germany and the Republic of Ireland) do not have to manage to the same degree. As for citizenship, Canada has to address issues related to the integration of immigrants, cultural pluralism and ethno-cultural diversity, while having regard to its federal constitution (Gagnon and Iacovino 2007). It should also be noted that diversity immigration and workplace diversity are two closely related issues in Canada, where immigration is regarded as investment in human capital in the age of a knowledge-based economy. The federal *Immigration and Refugee Protection Act* states that 'the selection criteria for the Skilled Worker Class emphasise human capital attributes and flexible skills, rather than the specific intended occupations of applicants' (Government of Canada 2001). Human capital emphasises that economic growth and societal success stem from investment in people. However, with an ageing population and expected mass retirement, the number of Canadian graduates is not meeting the rising demand for specific skills and the available knowledge workers are either in shortage or nearing retirement. Alongside education and skills development, the logical solution to replace the declining population in Canada has been to increase the intake of skilled immigrants who make positive contributions (Reitz 2005). Canadian public opinion is still positive about immigration (Citizenship and Immigration Canada 2012); however, there has a change in the influx of immigrants, with fewer people arriving from Europe and more arriving from Asia, Africa and Latin America. This change has created discrimination against visible and religious minorities, and newcomers are experiencing problems with racism, recognition of academic qualifications, language and cultural adaptation (Biles and Winnemore 2007).

The Conference Board of Canada's 2004 report titled 'The Voices of Visible Minorities' found that, despite 20 years of employment equity legislation, a 'sticky floor' limits the advancement of visible minorities, and a 'glass ceiling' prevents them from achieving top positions in organisations (Trichur 2004). Shortage of skilled labour has led to the admission of more immigrants to Canada, and the report estimated that about 70% of recent immigrants to urban Canada are visible minorities, while people of colour represent nearly 50% of the populations of Vancouver and Toronto (Hiranandani 2012). However, the Conference Board's report revealed that the barriers faced by visible minorities are widening the gap between policy and practice, which will affect the Canadian economy in the future. Oliver

(2005) reported that among the 69 medium and large organisations that responded to the survey, only 3% had a visible-minority CEO and only 3% of about 900 senior executives were visible minorities. The research further revealed that nine in 10 organisations had no plans to recruit visible minorities to the board of directors, despite the fact that a majority supports the representation of visible minorities in decision-making positions in the organisation. It is also estimated that 100% of Canada's net labour force growth will depend on immigration by 2011, and visible minorities will constitute about 20% of the country's population by 2016 (Hiranandani 2012).

In 2005, the Canadian government introduced the Racism-Free Workplace Strategy as a key component of 'A Canada for All: Canada's Action Plan against Racism'. The goal of this strategy was to eliminate the systemic discriminatory barriers experienced by visible minorities and Aboriginal peoples. However, there is no perfect recipe for dealing with racism (Hiranandani 2012, 5) and the risk of an anti-racism approach between visible minorities and the dominant culture tends to validate the division of 'us' versus 'them'. Anti-racism policies in organisations need to be paralleled by government policies on a national scale (Hiranandani 2012). There are differences between the Canadian-born visible minorities and their non-visible minority counterparts who have similar education and language skills, and discrimination exists in the workplace, in addition to other factors, such as racial harassment or discrimination that tends to affect their career promotion (Pendakur and Pendakur 2002). Discrimination in Canada is plentiful and evident, and Canada's survey on ethnic diversity indicated that more than 1.4 million Canadians experienced racial discrimination or were victims of racism at some point, constituting 17% of all Canadians (Hiranandani 2012). The Canadian Human Rights Commission (quoted in Hiranandani 2012) reported that 36% of all complaints were related to racism mostly experienced in the workplace. While many organisations maintain employment equity and diversity initiatives, they can fail to provide fairness in the recruitment, retention and treatment of visible minorities. As suggested by Hiranandani (2012), anti-racism policy in the workplace needs to be part of a national anti-racism drive through government policy in Canada, with strong emphasis on education, to move away from discrimination based on skin colour, ethnicity or religious background.

The *Annual Report on the Operation of the Canadian Multiculturalism Act 2015–2016—Diversity and Inclusion in Action* aimed to advance the objectives of the *Canadian Multiculturalism Act*. When this report was presented by Canadian Prime Minister Justin Trudeau (2016), he stated:

> As the first country in the world to adopt a policy of multiculturalism 45 years ago, Canada has shown time and time again that a country can be stronger not in spite of its differences, but because of them.

The strength and success of diversity in Canada arises from its commitment to a vision. Under the *Canadian Multiculturalism Act 1988*, the:

> Government of Canada recognizes the diversity of Canadians as regards race, national or ethnic origin, color and religion as a fundamental characteristic of Canadian society and is committed to a policy of multiculturalism designed to preserve and enhance the multicultural heritage of Canadians while working to achieve the quality of all Canadians in the economic, social, cultural and political life of Canada.
>
> (Government of Canada 1988)

In summary, it can be argued that the social model in Canada is a cross between Europe and the US—it is neither a 'social state' (like the Nordic countries) nor a 'minimalist state' (like the US). Canada is unique in two principal respects. The first is that Canada is a largely immigrant country with universal social programs, yet is facing the challenge of delivering prosperity and economic growth while maintaining social justice, equal opportunity and universal social services. The second unique feature of Canada is the absence of slums, like those in Paris (Basavarajappa and Samuel 2006). Therefore, the Canadian model is recognised worldwide as a successful tool for the use of unique skilled human resources, and has been copied by other advanced industrialised countries. Several countries have sought Canada's expertise as a diverse society rich in human capital, since 'the Canadian model of multiculturalism, human rights, and employment equity would help address the challenges of citizenship and identity, human capital, and demographics' (Basavarajappa and Samuel 2006, 11–2). In a republican country, it is worth remembering the motto of the French Revolution: '*liberté, égalité, fraternité*' (liberty, equality, fraternity). The multicultural approach of Canadian liberal democracy requires that a request for accommodation should be reasonable in its nature. Reasonably accommodating neighbours has always been people's tendency in Canada. In terms of increasing diversity, the challenge remains: 'to distinguish what is reasonable from what is unreasonable' (St-Onge 2015, 26). Shortcomings have been observed in Canadian multiculturalism and the policy of Aboriginal autonomy protects groups, while the charters of rights and freedoms protect individuals (St-Onge 2015).

Diversity Management in the UK: Political and Legal Analysis

The evidence from the UK illustrates that equality and diversity policies are becoming universal, and form 99% of the policies in the public sector and 74% in the private sector (Kirton and Greene 2017). Additionally, the Workplace Employment Relations Survey (WERS; 2011) upon which the evidence of van Wanrooy et al. was based, does not differentiate between the 'equality' and 'diversity' policies developed in the UK. Therefore, in the UK, current equality legislation causes no challenge to the principle of diversity management, irrespective of the need to safeguard against discrimination (Kirton and Greene 2017).

In the UK, diversity practitioners seem to be more concerned with corporate reputation, rather than equality, social justice and employee rights. However, there is strong belief in shared management and employee interests, and that business case diversity can provide an inclusive workplace culture. Trade unions in the UK have played an important role in developing this workplace culture. They have a long history of fighting for social justice and fair treatment of workers. As such, the public sector now tends to have greater equality, more diversity policies and better working conditions (Kirton and Greene 2017). Unions remain suspicious of organisations when dealing with diversity management, in case the organisation causes harm when dealing with discrimination and inequalities, as the emphasis may be on organisational resources, rather than employee rights. Some unions argue that discrimination and harassment are detrimental to business and corporate reputation, and deter the most talented workers (Kirton and Greene 2017). There is also a significant difference between the private and public sectors in terms of the presence of trade unions which forms 19% of membership in the UK private sector, while terms and condition of work only cover 26% of private sector workers (Kirton and Greene 2017). In discussing diversity management, these data imply that unions support equality legislation in the workplace, yet employees in the private sector are opposed to unions' influence.

In the UK public sector, diversity management is viewed in the context of a business case, where diversity can bring benefits in terms of maximising employee potential, recruitment, retention and promotion (Asari, Halikiopoulou and Mock 2008). Other areas can also be addressed, such as key public services, including nursing, teaching and policing, where significant problems of recruitment and retention exist. In making a business case for diversity, there is a demand for resource constraint and budget rationalisation in the public sector under the Conservative and Labour Governments. In addition, questions arise about what happens to the status and practice of diversity policies and equality during times of economic hardship, as these policies tend to become easy targets to lose funding (Asari, Halikiopoulou and Mock 2008).

Despite the UK's framework of anti-discrimination legislation, previous research indicates that inequality exists in the UK workforce, yet is considered favourable compared with other EU member states. Attention is more focused on equality and diversity in large private sector organisations in the UK. The findings of the 2004 WERS indicated that over two-thirds of UK private sector workplaces have equal opportunities policies, with large workplaces (1,000 employees or more) significantly more likely to have a policy than small workplaces (100 employees or fewer) (94% versus 46%)

(Asari, Halikiopoulou and Mock 2008). However, the WERS data revealed a mismatch between organisational equal opportunities policies and organisational action to transfer the policy into practice (Asari, Halikiopoulou and Mock 2008). It seems that the majority of workplaces in the UK do not monitor the implementation of policy, yet the WERS survey showed that only 14% of UK private sector workplaces monitored the implementation of their policy (Asari, Halikiopoulou and Mock 2008). Moreover, the number of private sector workplaces that focus on demographic monitoring represents less than half of the number in the public sector (Asari, Halikiopoulou and Mock 2008).

Table 4.3 lists the key pieces of legislation dealing with different aspects of workplace diversity in the UK. The legalisation of non-discrimination in the UK consists of the enactment of three major areas:

> expression—meaning verbal or written forms of discrimination; access—meaning any hindrance due to one's race, culture, or religion in seeking employment, education, or house rent; and physical—meaning violence or hate crime because of a victim's race, culture, or religion.
>
> (Kim 2011, 166)

In relation to dealing with ethnic and national minority matters, it is worth noting that British deliberative multiculturalism focuses on minorities' social rights to engage in public negotiations. This leads to a decision-making process that ensures both majorities' and minorities' agreement (Kim 2011).

A close examination of the historical development of diversity management in the UK reveals that, apart from being a 'model' employer, the public sector seems to be the pioneer in the development of equality policy (Asari, Halikiopoulou and Mock 2008). In addition, the public sector enjoys a better record on equality because of its proximity to equality legislation by virtue of its dual role as employer and legislator (Greene and Kirton 2009). The public sector is, of course, more closely linked to legislation; thus, it is subject to scrutiny for compliance (Greene and Kirton 2009).

In the UK, employers are known to object to the introduction of extensive employment law, as the UK's labour market was the least regulated in the world. Thus, a tendency to resist the introduction of new legislation still exists, and employers are calling for a reduction in the existing 'regulatory burden', arguing that it prevents organisations from employing new staff and makes the UK economy less globally competitive. However, 'employment law is here to stay and that it makes good business sense to comply with its requirements'; thus, many employers in the UK have to face employment tribunal claims, and human resources professionals are left to cope with the consequences (Armstrong and Taylor 2017, 578). There has been no strategy to build modern employment law; rather, it has been constructed gradually over 50 years, with new laws implemented as a result of political pressure. European institutions were sometimes responsible for the

Table 4.3 Major UK Legislation Related to Workplace Discrimination

Legislation	Summary
Equal Pay Act 1970	In 1970, the *Equal Pay Act* was passed, prohibiting unequal pay and working conditions between men and women. The Act did not come into force until 1975. Its foundations were laid by women's industrial action at Ford car manufacturing plants in 1968, and the resulting legislation was introduced in 1970 by MP Barbara Castle. The 1970s and 1980s saw further industrial action by women and men as workers fought for their rights, regardless of gender, ethnicity and class. This Act is now superseded by the *Equality Act 2010*.
Sex Discrimination Act 1975	The *Sex Discrimination Act 1975* prohibited sex discrimination against individuals in the areas of employment; education; the provision of goods, facilities and services; and the disposal or management of premises. It also prohibited discrimination in employment against married people. It is not unlawful to discriminate against someone because they are not married. Victimisation because someone has tried to exercise their rights under the *Sex Discrimination Act* or *Equal Pay Act* was prohibited. This Act is now superseded by the *Equality Act 2010*.
Race Relations Act 1976	The **Race Relations Act 1976** was established by the UK Parliament to prevent discrimination on the grounds of race. Items covered included discrimination on the grounds of race, colour, nationality, and ethnic and national origin in the fields of employment, the provision of goods and services, education and public functions. It is now superseded by the *Equality Act 2010*.
Disability Discrimination Act 1995	The *Disability Discrimination Act 1995* ensured people were not discriminated against because of disability. The Act protected the rights of people with disabilities in different areas, including employment; education; access to goods, facilities and services, such as banks and supermarkets; and renting property. It is now superseded by the *Equality Act 2010*.
Gender Reassignment Regulations 1999	These regulations were made under Section 2(2) of the *European Communities Act 1972* and extended the *Sex Discrimination (Northern Ireland) Order 1976* to cover discrimination on the grounds of gender reassignment in employment and vocational training, following the judgement of the European Court of Justice in *Case No. C-13/94 P v S and Cornwall County Council*. They came into operation on 1 August 1999. They are now superseded by the *Equality Act 2010*.

(Continued)

Table 4.3 (Continued)

Legislation	Summary
Employment Equality (Religion or Belief) Regulations 2003	The *Employment Equality (Religion or Belief) Regulations 2003* was a piece of UK labour law designed to combat discrimination in relation to people's religion or belief or absence of religion or belief. They were introduced to comply with the EU Directive 2000/78/EC and complement similar measures on sexuality, age, disability, race and gender discrimination. The EU Directive was similar to legislation passed in the US. It is now superseded by the *Equality Act 2010*.
Employment Equality (Sexual Orientation) Regulations 2003	The *Employment Equality (Sexual Orientation) Regulations 2003* were secondary legislation in the UK that prohibited employers unreasonably discriminating against employees on the grounds of sexual orientation, perceived sexual orientation, religion or belief, and age. They are now superseded by the *Equality Act 2010*.
Employment Equality (Age) Regulations 2006 superseded by Equality Act 2010	The *Employment Equality (Age) Regulations 2006* (SI 2006/2408) was a piece of secondary legislation in the UK that prohibited employers unreasonably discriminating against employees on the grounds of age. It came into force on 1 October 2006. It is now superseded by the *Equality Act 2010*.

transfer of regulations dealing, with the protection of employees' terms and conditions, following the acquisition or merging of organisations. Additionally, governments have used employment law to increase their popularity and guarantee re-election. For example, maternity and paternity rights were introduced by the government in April 2015 before the general election. New employment law can be introduced as a result of major strikes or campaigns by trade unions and other groups (Armstrong and Taylor 2017). In 2013, the UK government issued a progress report on its programs of employment regulation, which had three distinct objectives, as follows:

- Flexible—encouraging job creation and making it easy for people to stay in work and find work;
- Effective—enabling employers to manage staff productivity;
- Fair—employers competing on a level playing field and workers benefiting from core employment protections (Armstrong and Taylor 2017, 578).

However, there is evidence of discrimination against ethnic and racial minorities in the UK labour markets (Noon 1993), in addition to the implementation gap that exists between legislation and practice (Creegan et al. 2003). It seems that equality laws cannot deal with disadvantages, including intersectionality (Healy, Bradley and Forson 2011), when employees have more than one difference to the mainstream group, such as being an ethnic minority woman employee (Ozbilgin et al. 2011). The tensions between ethnic and racial minorities and the majority are increasing in the UK, where previous liberal views in favour of immigrants from both EU countries and from non-EU developing countries are now vilified (Ozturk, Tatli and Ozbilgin 2015).

Diversity Management in Australia: Political and Legal Analysis

The multicultural nature of the Australian workforce requires sound diversity management. In the Australian context, it is important to examine how organisations transform their commitment to diversity management into action to determine whether a gap exists between what is espoused as diversity management and how it is achieved in practice. In practice, there are various methods that Australian workplaces are using to manage their diverse workforce. The first method is adapted by 'colour-blind' managers—who believe that diversity involves individuals who differ in knowledge, skills and interests—and leads to managing the workforce by being responsive to people's differing work styles and interests. A colour-blind approach to diversity management involves management treating employees equally and fairly, regardless of their background, and aims to prevent any discriminatory practices (Podsiadlowski et al. 2013). The second method is implemented by 'melting pot' managers, who believe that diversity means that people different to the 'norm' should be managed through assimilating them into the organisation's culture. However, this method is unlikely to increase employee retention (O'Leary and Sandberg 2012). The third method encompasses 'multicultural' managers, who are inclusive of people from all groups. These managers believe that employees not only come from 'different' groups, but should be managed by acknowledging that their needs are affected by their group membership. Multicultural managers have the skills and attitudes that enable them to relate to and motivate people across race, ethnicity, social attitudes and lifestyles. This method is likely to be successful in attracting and retaining employees (DuBrin, Dalglish and Miller 2006). The fourth method is adopted by 'level playing field' or 'equal footing' managers, who believe that diversity signifies a need to create 'substantive equality' for individuals from all groups. They manage their workforce by balancing 'power' among these groups. In other words, for 'equal footing' managers, managing diversity leads to substantive equality among employees. 'Equal footing' is claimed to be the most effective way to manage diversity. These management styles are critical for understanding and evaluating the types of diversity management implemented in organisations. It is believed that 'equal footing' managers are the most effective in managing diversity in the Australian context (Chidiac 2015).

Kramar (2012) argued that diversity management in Australia must be understood in terms of national contextual factors, such as legislation, government policy, the local and global economy, and multiple identities (including gender, race, social class and family status). In addition, the international contextual factors and their effect on the national practice are important. These include the relevant conventions that have been developed by the International Labor Organisation and ratified by Australia. These conventions include the 1951 Convention 100 on *Equal Remuneration*, the 1958 Convention 111 on *Discrimination (Employment and Occupation)* and the 1981 Convention 156 on *Equal Treatment for Men and Women Workers: Workers with Family Responsibilities*. The ratification of these conventions led the Australian government to undertake various actions by enacting legislation, reviewing employment policies for employees in the public sector, and establishing units in government departments to encourage and support employees to implement the spirit of the conventions. More specifically, the ratified conventions resulted in passing anti-discrimination legislation in all jurisdictions and AA or EEO legislation in the federal jurisdiction in the 1970s and 1980s (Chidiac 2015).

In the context of the strategic management of ethnic and cultural diversity, immigration has naturally become an important issue in Australia, and Australia will continue to depend on immigration to meet skills shortages and provide a revenue basis to support its ageing population. This means that diversity in the workplace will remain a core characteristic of the Australian labour market. However, not all migrants who arrive in Australia will be skilled, and some may lack English language skills and subsequently encounter problems in securing employment. As a result, Australian organisations are facing an influx of skilled and unskilled immigrants of different cultural backgrounds. Since migrants form part of the diverse workforce in Australia, it is important to investigate the effect of immigration on Australian workplaces and how organisations manage their diverse workforces.

As part of the globalisation process of the Australian economy, multinational corporations have had a great influence on Australia and made significant contributions in terms of employment, investment and trade. In addition, diversity management is regarded as an important practice in these corporations, yet there is a lack of data on the use of diversity management policies, especially in Australia. Kramar (2012) suggested that the human resources policies of the parent organisation affect its Australian subsidiaries, and that it is likely that diversity management policies will be transferred from the parent organisation to the Australian subsidiary. Diversity management is also formally integrated into corporate social responsibility (CSR) in Australia, especially in the financial sector. The major Australian banks—such as Westpac, the Australian and New Zealand Banking Group (ANZ), Commonwealth Bank and National Australia Bank (NAB)—use diversity management as an open system approach as part of their business strategy and CSR agenda. However, Kramar (2012) further claimed that diversity management in the Australian context has been viewed in terms of organisational outcomes, rather than equity considerations. In their study on employee perceptions of diversity management in the manufacturing sector, D'Netto et al. (2014) concluded that Australian organisations do not implement effective diversity management policies because there is a general tendency to consider diversity as a legal obligation to be complied with, rather than by valuing diversity as a source of benefits to the organisation.

In relation to the adoption of diversity policies, Krautil (2014) explained how some industries are affected by recent economic downturns, and argued that the adoption of these policies in Australian organisations is expected to be slow and only eventuate when small and medium-sized enterprises begin to grow. Leaders of these Australian enterprises need to educate themselves and realise that many large organisations have already adopted values that include diversity at all levels. Good diversity management goes far beyond implementing appropriate policies and requires proactive, visible, well-informed and thoughtful leaders.

Australian organisations must comply with a number of legislative requirements relating to management standards, transparency and accepted best practices. The Australian policy and legislative framework concentrates on establishing cultural diversity in the workplace, and far exceeds employment equity policies and legislation. Table 4.4 lists the historical development of Australian legislation on diversity-related issues. The changes in legislative and policy frameworks on diversity management clearly correspond with the changing identifications of diversity in Australia since the 1940s, as analysed in Chapter 1.

In Australia, diversity has transformed over many years. Since Federation, the government shifted from its White Australia policy to an assimilation policy in the 1950s and 1960s, and an integration policy in the 1960s and 1970s. In the 1980s, the main issue was dealing with discrimination in the workplace based on the then-emerging emphasis on multiculturalism, while, in the 1990s, the focus was on promoting EEO for women employees. In the new millennium, the emphasis changed to corporate responsibility and organisations addressing equity objectives. As seen in Table 4.4, the initial legislative step in Australia was related to racial discrimination, which was followed by legislation on human rights in 1986. The *Affirmative Action Act (AAA) 1986* was an important step forward in addressing women's rights in the workplace. However, its limitations were eventually magnified by John Howard's government's regulatory reform in the late 1990s, in line with the Coalition agenda of deregulation and enhancing competition among organisations and employees (North-Samardzic 2009).

Moreover, the Australian policy and legislative framework calls for recognition of individuals' contributions to the organisations in terms of skills and previous experience, not just as being members of a legislatively designated group (Silk et al. 2000). The emphasis on cultural diversity in the current Australian policy and legislative framework rejected the earlier

Table 4.4 Major Australian Legislation Related to Workplace Discrimination

Legislation	Summary
Racial Discrimination Act 1975	This Act made it unlawful for anyone to behave in any way that would involve a distinction, exclusion, restriction or preference based on race, colour or national or ethnic origin, or to offend, insult, humiliate or intimidate another person or group of people on the basis of race, colour or national or ethnic origin.
Sex Discrimination Act 1984	This Act was designed to eliminate all forms of discrimination against women; to eliminate discrimination against people on the grounds of sex, marital status, pregnancy or potential pregnancy; to eliminate discrimination involving dismissal of employees on the ground of family responsibilities; to eliminate discrimination involving sexual harassment in the workplace; and to promote recognition and acceptance in the community of the principle of the equality of men and women.
Affirmative Action Act 1986	This Act was designed to ensure appropriate action was taken to eliminate discrimination by employers against women in relation to employment matters, and that measures were taken by employers to promote equal opportunity for women in relation to employment matters. It is now replaced by the *Workplace Gender Equality Act 2012*.
Human Rights and Equal Opportunity Commission Act 1986	This Act requires commission that are committed to working across levels of government and the community to assist in removing systematic and covert discrimination, where it exists, from being established in each state and territory.
Equal Employment Opportunity (Commonwealth Authorities) Act 1987	This Act requires certain incorporated and unincorporated Commonwealth Government bodies to develop and implement an EEO program that is designed to ensure that appropriate action is taken to eliminate discrimination and to promote equal opportunity for women and people in designated groups in relation to employment matters.
Human Rights and Equal Opportunity Act 1991	This Act was extended from the 1986 Act to specifically include religion.

Legislation	Summary
Disability Discrimination Act 1992	This Act was developed to eliminate, as far as possible, discrimination against people on the ground of disability in a number of areas, including work; to ensure that people with disabilities have the same rights to equality before the law as the rest of the community; and to promote recognition and acceptance in the community of the principle that people with disabilities have the same fundamental rights as the rest of the community.
Age Discrimination Act 2004	This Act was developed to eliminate discrimination against people on the ground of age in various areas, including work; to ensure that everyone, regardless of age, has the same rights to equality before the law as the rest of the community; to allow appropriate benefits and other assistance to be given to people of a certain age, particularly younger and older people, in recognition of their particular circumstances; to promote recognition and acceptance in the community of the principle that people of all ages have the same fundamental rights; and to respond to demographic change by removing barriers to older people participating in society, particularly in the workplace, and to change negative stereotypes about older people.
Workplace Gender Equality Act 2012	This Act requires employers to promote equal opportunity for women in employment and established the Workplace Gender Equality Agency (formerly the Equal Opportunity for Women in the Workplace Agency).

legislative and regulatory framework, which is reviewed in detail later in this section. The earlier system of diversity management in Australia was based on AA and EEO policies and legislation with the concepts of quotas and mandated targets. However, the rather limited scope of the earlier legislative and regulatory system does not reduce its importance due to its historical contributions in the new paradigm named the age of equity. Even though the contemporary emphasis has shifted from AA and EEO towards the notion of equity, elements of the earlier legislative and regulatory framework are still incorporated in the contemporary system of diversity management in Australia.

Moreover, while the legislation focuses on women in the Australian private sector—especially until the enactment of the *Workplace Gender Equality Act 2012*—in the public sector, other groups are also included, such as Indigenous Australians, people with a disability and people from non-English-speaking backgrounds (Burgess, French and Strachan 2010). At present, the Australian legislation on workplace diversity and equal opportunity includes the *Australian Human Rights Commission Act 1986, Age Discrimination Act 2004, Sex Discrimination Act 2004, Racial Discrimination Act 1975, Racial Hatred Act 1995, Disability Discrimination Act 1992, Workplace Gender Equality Act 2012* and *Fair Work Act 2009*. These pieces of legislation determine the national employment standards and the state-based anti-discrimination and occupational health and safety laws. During the last 30 years or so, a wide range of legislations have been enacted in Australia to address the disadvantage suffered by some groups in the workplace. However, the emphasis in legislative and policy frameworks has shifted more towards corporate responsibility over the last decade (Strachan, French and Burgess 2010). Thus, it is important to consider specifically the Australian workforce, which was subject to increasing percentages of workers of CALD backgrounds between 1974 and 1997.

In addressing the changes in the demographics of the Australian workforce, one of the first legislative instruments introduced by the federal government was the *Racial Discrimination Act 1975*. This Act, which is still in force, ruled in Article 9 (1) that:

> It is unlawful for a person to do any act involving a distinction, exclusion, restriction or preference based on race, colour, descent or national or ethnic origin which has the purpose or effect of nullifying or impairing the recognition, enjoyment or exercise, on an equal footing, of any human right or fundamental freedom in the political, economic, social, cultural or any other field of public life.

In addition, the Australian government passed the *Australian Human Rights Commission Act 1986*, which established the Australian Human Rights Commission to make provision in relation to both human rights and equal opportunity in employment. In Article 31, this Act gives the commission the power:

(a) to examine enactments, and (when requested to do so by the Minister) proposed enactments, for the purpose of ascertaining whether the enactments or proposed enactments . . . have, or would have, the effect of nullifying or impairing equality of opportunity or treatment in employment or occupation.

(b) to inquire into any act or practice, including any systemic practice, that may constitute discrimination and.

(c) to promote an understanding and acceptance, and the public discussion, of equality of opportunity and treatment in employment and occupation in Australia.

In addition to passing such Acts dealing with the different aspects of diversity management, the federal government introduced amendments to the Australian Constitution in 1996 that guaranteed fairness and justice in society and the workplace. The *Public Service Act 1999* established the Australian Public Service (APS) employment principles and recognised 'the diversity of the Australian community and fosters diversity in the workplace'. In Article 18, the Act further rules that each federal agency must establish a workplace diversity program to ensure that the APS employment principles are effectively implemented. These workplace diversity programs go beyond the elimination of employment disadvantages and legal compliance by enforcing agencies to value the different skills of all employees (Kramar et al. 2011). The purpose of the Act is to sustain human resource policies, such as planning, recruitment, selection, performance and workplace relations which indicate that the public sector has thus far taken the lead in the development and implementation of diversity management in Australian organisations (Burgess, Strachan and French 2010). However, Soldan and Nankervis (2014, 546) argued that diversity management in the APS still suffers from a commitment-implementation gap, which results from the behaviours and actions of line managers responsible for the management and implementation of diversity policies and programs. Their findings indicated that, in the Australian context, great levels of cynicism and mistrust exist in diversity and equality policies because of the superficial commitment to such policies, with some doubts regarding the interpretation of the espoused values.

The key difference between diversity management and EEO is that the former (which is a result of executive decisions in an organisation) is voluntary, while the latter is compulsory legislation for organisations with 100 or more employees, imposed externally by law. This is not unique to Australia, with the voluntary approach to diversity management applied in the UK and US as well (Greene and Kirton 2009). Kramar and Holland (2015) further illustrated that a diversity management agenda does not deal with issues of discrimination or equity, whilst the US, the UK, Australia and other countries have passed legislation to promote an equitable labour market and organisational results for particular specified groups. In the Australian context, the extent to which private sector organisations have implemented diversity management in the workplace is not evident, given the lack of legislation to enforce such policies in the private sector. It is evident that, in the absence of compulsory policies, organisations tend to make their own judgements regarding equity for employees and profits for business. Organisations are more certain regarding how to act when policies are clearly stated in legislation. If not, their approach to diversity seems to be based on the individual organisation's ethics and values (Chidiac 2015).

As discussed in Chapter 1, the changes of workplace demographics because of globalisation and the increasing levels of migration in migrant-receiving countries (such as Australia and the US) have led to the need for legislation dealing with equity and equality in diverse workforces. In the US in the 1980s, AA was built on the premise that no person's competence and character would ever be overlooked or undervalued because of race, sex, ethnicity or physical disability (Thomas 2002). Nonetheless, Thomas (2002) argued that AA in the US tended to focus unnaturally on one group, was perceived to be the subject of abuse and was an unworkable solution to manage difference, primarily because of the quota system that it introduced, despite the great improvements that it brought about. In the Australian context, AA was practised differently. While the US legislation contained employment quotas for minority groups and women, the Australian system, legislated by the *AAA 1986*, never included such measures, as all employment decisions were merit based. Again in contrast to the US, the *AAA 1986* in Australia was a special piece of federal legislation, independent of anti-discrimination laws, that led to changes in gender equality in the workforce, albeit slowly (Braithwaite and Bush 1998, 116).

The *AAA* was first replaced by the *Equal Opportunity for Women in the Workplace Act (EOWWA) 1999*, which required employers to develop equal opportunity for women in workplace programs and established the Equal Opportunity for Women in the Workplace Agency. The *EOWWA* promoted the concept that employment for women should be based on merit, and called for workplace consultation between employers and employees on any issues related to equal opportunity for women in employment. This Act was narrow because it applied only to employers with 100 or more employees, and its coverage included managerial and non-managerial employees who happened to be women. Thus, the *EOWWA* failed to achieve equal employment opportunities for women, and was less effective than the AAA, which eventually led to devolution of Australia's EEO regulatory framework.

A few years after passing the 1999 legislation, in 2003, there was an attempt to remove the phrase 'Equal Opportunity' from the title of the Human Rights and Equal Opportunity Commission. The bill lapsed and the name was changed to the Australian Human Rights Commission in 2008. The term 'Equal Opportunity' began to disappear from workplaces in the 1990s, while the concept of diversity or 'managing diversity' began to replace 'equality' and EEO. One of the core reasons for the shift from equal opportunities to diversity is that the former was ineffective because it is divisive and old-fashioned (Gatrell and Swan 2008). While this shift was occurring in the Australian context, the political discourse of the time emphasised the view that gender discrimination no longer existed because equality had been achieved, which prompted the then Prime Minister John Howard to claim that we now live in a 'post-feminist' age (Thornton 2015).

The proactive 1999 legislation seeking equal opportunity for women in the workplace was short-lived, and was repealed and replaced by the

Workplace Gender Equality Act (WGEA) 2012, which encompasses productivity and competitiveness as objects of the Act. The *WGEA* has benefits for employees, employers and the workforce. While the Act enables employees to view data on their employers' performance, rather than policy statements or effective reporting, employers have the benefit of a private assessment regarding their position in the industry, and can assess whether their efforts for gender equality are effective in the workplace (Gaze 2014). This Act dispensed with the word 'women' in favour of gender neutrality, which is an issue that attracted criticism from feminist perspectives (Summers 2003). Many feminist scholars support men accessing flexible working hours, sharing domestic work and sharing caring responsibilities, and that such a move would support the women's rights movement (Remedios 2011; Smith and Riley 2004). Such gender-neutral policy developments are useful or even necessary for organisational culture to move away from the masculine model of work that dominates most workplaces in Australia. The emergence of gender-neutral policy developments is an emerging research area that goes beyond the scope of this book, yet needs to be examined in future studies. Another linguistic shift in the *WGEA 2012* placed work and family at the centre, with 'choice', 'flexibility' and 'work/life balance' replacing the emphasis on equal access, benefits and treatments in the EEO. This linguistic shift pleased both the neoconservative morality and neoliberalists, and the more conservative side of politics (Thornton 2015).

According to critics, the biggest downfall of the system established by the *WGEA 2012* is that organisations are not required to meet the new standards to comply with the Act, but rather improve their own performance (Charlesworth and Macdonald 2015). Failing to show improvement is construed as non-compliance with the Act, unless organisations have a legitimate reason. Organisations were given a period of two years to improve, which meant that no organisation could be considered non-compliant on this basis until 2017. The critics further claim that the *WGEA 2012* suffers from one of the most notable deficiencies of the *AAA* and *EOWWA,* which is the weakness to deal with non-compliance (Cardillo 2013; Charlesworth and Macdonald 2015). It can be argued that the *WGEA* does not offer much improvement in this regard, as it seems to retain the same 'naming and shaming' approach of the past Acts. With regard to the legislative changes in Australia since 1986, Thornton (2015) concluded that gender-related legislation from the *AAA* to *WGEA* has all been attacked, notwithstanding the fact that the *AAA* was the one that lacked substance and deferential towards employers. Additionally, the current Australian legal and policy frameworks and strategies in the workplace are ineffective because they fail to recognise the gender disadvantages experienced by different groups of women, including low-paid migrant and Indigenous women (Charlesworth and Macdonald 2015).

These concerns indicate that legislation is necessary to incorporate specific employment measures and to ensure equity and fairness to all employees, regardless of gender and background. However, apart from the federal and state legislation covering workplace diversity and equal opportunity in Australia, there is no legislation that actually *promotes* diversity. As Syed and Kramar (2010, 100) stated:

> the focus of. . . [EEO] legislation in Australia has been on one designated group only, i.e. women [because there] is no specific EEO legislation for culturally diverse workers or migrant workers.

As for equal opportunity, following the development of equal opportunity legislation in Australia, diversity management has become the 'second generation' of EEO initiatives after the anti-discrimination and AA legislation passed during the 1970s and 1980s. The 1995 Commonwealth Report by the Industry Task Force on Leadership and Management Skills reported that Australian managers indicated awareness of diversity issues in that period, yet did not prioritise the management of a diverse workforce (Commonwealth of Australia 1995). This finding was confirmed by a more recent study, which concluded that the many organisations surveyed did not seem to be gaining the commercial benefits from diversity management found in previous research (Skalsky and McCarthy 2009).

More recently, the Diversity Council Australia (2012) stated that effective management of diversity in the workplace is linked to improved performance, effectiveness and profitability in organisations. The council further outlined diversity-related issues in Australia by stating that studies in Australia and overseas have revealed that organisations in which more women are appointed as members of the board produce better financial performance. The study also referred to a survey conducted by Australian employers that indicated that the implementation of best practice in organisations resulted in major benefits from work–life initiatives. In its 2010 report, the Australian Defence Organisation drew similar conclusions which include better leadership and management, stronger decision making and problem solving, greater innovation and capacity, and reduced disputation and litigation (Silk et al. 2000).

These findings indicate a positive link between sound diversity management and organisational performance, effectiveness and profitability in the Australian context. While leaders in the management of diversity indicate that effective diversity management produces major business profits, failure to introduce effective diversity management leads to expensive discrimination complaints and lawsuits. Australian statistics demonstrate that many organisations continue to struggle to manage diversity effectively because of some issues in the workplace. These issues include the participation of people with a disability and Indigenous Australians in the workplace, the existence of discrimination and harassment, and the difficulties in achieving a satisfactory work–life balance. Therefore, it is essential for organisations to include in the workforce Indigenous Australians and people with a disability, to overcome discrimination and to enable employees to establish a manageable work–life balance.

It is also evident that different corporations have responded differently during various stages of the diversity phenomenon. In corporate Australia, diversity has been driven largely by legislation and corporate policy. For example, the decision to develop a cultural diversity strategy at IBM in Australia was driven by corporate values, respect for the individual and legal requirements (De Cieri 2008). These three essential factors may prove to be elements worth considering by other organisations when implementing diversity policies. Managers need to consider aspects of social capital when their organisation is implementing equity and diversity initiatives in order to assist migrant employees and minimise tensions arising between diverse groups in the workplace. In doing so, organisations can either take a proactive approach and save considerable time and money in the short and long term, or take a reactive approach after losing time and money (Schultz 2011). However, many organisations in Australia either do not realise the difference between reactive and proactive strategies or are not implementing either method. If an organisation has to be proactive or reactive, a proactive approach is beneficial, even though there are some workplace problems that require management to react, make decisions and subsequently become reactive. In addition, some organisations seem to adopt a reactive approach by acknowledging and responding to past events, and this adaptive method can cause problems, especially when dealing with issues as they occur, rather than avoiding conflicts that are likely to occur in the future. This book argues that a proactive approach is more effective to implement; however, it remains an open question whether organisations take one or the other approach when designing their diversity management activities.

Summary

This chapter explains the history of immigration and the development of labour in the US together with the legislation dealing with diversity. Employers' compliance with the laws following the introduction of EEO and AA in the US including the necessary steps taken to protect organisations from possible litigation are indicated. Additionally, this chapter shows what the private sector used to boost profit and avoid discrimination legal action. Other important factors include the employees' rights and responsibilities, and how they succeeded in their discrimination and/or harassment complaints. Given the role played by organisations in providing equal opportunities to minority ethnic groups, the chapter discusses the factors leading to the shift from the 'rights of blacks' to 'everyone's rights'.

This chapter explores the view of procedural changes that occurred in the US in order to minimise the number of sanctions against AA violations by employers. An assessment is made of the various diversity programs of strategic management introduced by organisations to enable employees of diverse ethnic and cultural backgrounds to perform fully in the workplace. More importantly, viewing cultural diversity in the US was a major shift adopted by organisations and the benefits of diversity seen by managers as a powerful factor in advancing organisational efficiency and productivity.

The first introduction of diversity in Canada is outlined taking into consideration the importance of diversity and the commitment of the Canadian government to a policy of multiculturalism. The concept of diversity and its development as well as the mixed approach to management model in Canada are explored. This chapter explains how diversity management emerged in Canada after the introduction of legislative requirements to protect individuals from discrimination and promote equity in the workplace. What occurred to create innovation and provide talented workers, reduce shortages of skills and enter competitive foreign markets are raised, and the importance of immigration highlighted in view of ageing population and mass retirement. In addition, the measures taken by Canada to overcome racism and discrimination against visible minorities, and the unique aspects and features of the social model in Canada are emphasised in this chapter and what made the model of multiculturalism a success worldwide.

This chapter further illustrates the development of equality and diversity in the UK and the efforts made by trade unions to enhance workplace culture. Diversity management in the public sector and the benefits obtained by organisations from talented individuals are covered. Moreover, the findings that the majority of private sector workplaces enjoyed equal opportunities are covered together with the legislation dealing with various aspects of diversity, non-discrimination and the focus on minorities' social rights in the UK. Employers' objection to employment legislation is noted with a focus on the implementation of laws through political pressure in the UK.

In this chapter, the transform and achievement of diversity management in Australia is also examined showing the different methods used in the workplace to manage a diverse workforce in Australian settings. It shows how diversity management is viewed in terms of various factors dealing with legislation and government policy. The significance and dependence of Australia on immigration to overcome skills shortages is emphasised with a focus on the impact of such immigration on Australian workplaces and their management. Furthermore, the adoption of diversity policies and the compliance of organisations with a range of legislative requirements served to explain the status quo in the workplace. Legislation focusing on gender in the Australian private sector was examined, including other groups in the public sector such as people who are culturally and linguistically diverse. In addition, the interest of the Australian government in diversity management is such that an amendment was introduced in the Australian Constitution in 1996 to secure fairness and justice in both society and the workplace. However, the absence of legislation to enforce diversity management policies in the workplace is still evident in the private sector.

The development of diversity in Australia and its shift away from White Australia policy, assimilation, integration and eventually to multiculturalism are discussed. This chapter considers the introduction of various legislative measures regarding racial discrimination and human rights, and the recognition of employees' contributions to organisations in terms of skills brought to the Australian workplace.

References

Abzug, R. and S. Mezias. 1993. 'The Fragmented State and Due Process Protections in Organisations: The Case of Comparable Worth'. *Organisation Science* 4: 433–53.

Apfelbaum, Evan P., Nicole M. Stephens and Ray E. Reagans. 2016. 'Beyond One-Size-Fits-All: Tailoring Diversity Approaches to the Representation of Social Groups'. *Journal of Personal and Social Psychology* 111 (4): 547–66.

Armstrong, Michael and Stephen Taylor. 2017. *Armstrong's Handbook of Human Resource Management Practice*. 14th ed. London: Kogan Page.

Asari, Eva-Maria, Daphne Halikiopoulou and Steven Mock. 2008. 'British National Identity and the Dilemmas of Multiculturalism'. *Nationalism and Ethnic Politics* 14 (1): 1–28.

ATMA Global. 2014. 'USA Diversity in the Workplace'. New York: ATMA Global. Accessed 3 December 2017. http://search.alexanderstreet.com/view/work/bibliographic_entity%7Cbibliographic_details%7C2383729.

Basavarajappa, K. G. and T. J. Samuel. 2006. 'The Visible Minority Population in Canada: A Review of Numbers, Growth and Labour Force Issues'. *Canadian Studies in Population* 33 (2): 241–69.

Bayor, Ronald H. 2016. 'Introduction: The Making of America'. In *The Oxford Handbook of American Immigration and Ethnicity*, edited by Ronald H. Bayor, 1–13. New York: Oxford University Press.

Biles, John and Lara Winnemore. 2007. 'Canada's Two Way Street Integration Model: Not without its Stains, Strains and Growing Pains'. *Canadian Diversity/Diversité Canadienne* 5 (1): 23–30.

Blumrosen, A. W. 1993. *Modern Law: The Law Transmission System and Equal Employment Opportunity*. Madison: University of Wisconsin Press.

Bogardus, Anne M. 2007. *PHR/SPHR Professional in Human Resources Certification Study Guide*. 2nd ed. Indianapolis: Wiley Publishing.

Braithwaite, V. and J. Bush. 1998. 'Affirmative Action in Australia: A Consensus-Based Dialogic Approach'. *NWSA Journal* 10 (3): 115–34.

Buckley IV, John F. 2017. *Equal Employment Opportunity: 2017 Compliance Guide*. New York: Wolters Kluver.

Burgess, J., E. French and G. Strachan. 2010. 'The Diversity Management Approach to Equal Employment Opportunity in Australian Organisations'. *The Economic and Labour Relations Review* 20 (1): 77–92.

Burgess, J., G. Strachan and E. French. 2010. 'The Future of Managing Diversity in Australia'. In *Managing Diversity in Australia: Theory and Practice*, edited by G. Strachan, E. French and J. Burgess, 269–74. Sydney: McGraw-Hill Australia.

Burstein, P. 1985. *Discrimination, Jobs, and Politics: The Struggle for Equal Employment Opportunity in the United States since the New Deal*. Chicago: University of Chicago Press.

Cardillo, T. 2013. 'New Obligations on Employers Imposed by the Workplace Gender Equality Act'. *Keeping Good Companies* 65 (4): 236–9.

Carr-Ruffino, Norma. 2005. *Making Diversity Work*. Upper Saddle River, NJ: Pearson/Prentice Hall.

Charlesworth, S. and F. Macdonald. 2015. 'Women, Work and Industrial Relations in Australia in 2014'. *Journal of Industrial Relations* 57 (3): 366–82.

Chidiac, Emile. 2015. 'A Study of the Strategic Management of Ethnic and Cultural Diversity in Australian Settings: A Multiple Case Study' (PhD thesis, Southern Cross University).

Citizenship and Immigration Canada. 2012. 'Canadian Multiculturalism: An Inclusive Citizenship'. Accessed 12 November 2017. www.cic.gc.ca/english/multiculturalism/citizenship.asp.

Coleman, Troy L. 1990. 'Managing Diversity at Work'. *Public Management* 72 (10): 2–5.

Commonwealth of Australia. 1995. *Renewing Australia's Managers to Meet the Challenges of the Asia-Pacific Century*. Canberra: The Industry Task Force on Leadership and Management Skills.

Cox, T. and S. Blake. 1991. 'Managing Cultural Diversity: Implications for Organizational Competitiveness'. *The Executive* 5 (3): 45–56.

Creegan, C., F. Colgan, R. Charlesworth and G. Robinson. 2003. 'Race Equality Policies at Work: Employee Perceptions of the "Implementation Gap" in a UK Local Authority'. *Work, Employment Society* 17 (4): 617–40.

Cukier, Wendy, Suzanne Gagnon, Erin Roach, Mohamed Elmi, Margaret Yap and Sara Rodrigues. 2017. 'Trade-Offs and Disappearing Acts: Shifting Societal Discourses of Diversity in Canada over Three Decades'. *The International Journal of Human Resource Management* 28 (7): 1031–64.

De Cieri, H. 2008. *Human Resource Management in Australia: Strategy, People, Performance*. Sydney: McGraw-Hill.

Diversity Council Australia. 2012. 'Business Case for Diversity'. Accessed 22 July 2013. www.dca.org.au/why-diversity/business-case-for-diversity.html.

D'Netto, Brian, Jie Shen, John Chelliah and Manjit Monga. 2014. 'Human Resource Diversity Management Practices in the Australian Manufacturing Sector'. *The International Journal of Human Resource Management* 25 (9): 1243–66.

Dobbin, F., L. Edelman, J. W. Meyer, W. R. Scott and A. Swidler. 1988. 'The Expansion of Due Process in Organisations'. In *Institutional Patterns and Organisations: Culture and Environment*, edited by Lynne G Zucker, 71–100. Cambridge: Ballinger.

Dobbin, F., J. Sutton, J. Meyer and W. R. Scott. 1993. 'Equal Opportunity and the Construction of Internal Labor Markets'. *American Journal of Sociology* 9: 396–427.

DuBrin, A. J., C. Dalglish and P. Miller. 2006. *Leadership*. 2nd Asia-Pacific ed. Milton: John Wiley & Sons.

Economist Intelligence Unit. 2010. 'Global Firms in 2020: The Next Decade of Change for Organisations and Workers'. Accessed 8 May 2017. http://perspectives.eiu.com/strategy-leadership/global-firms-2020.

Elliott, Jean Leonard and Augie Fleras. 1990. 'Immigration and the Ethnic Mosaic'. In *Race and Ethnic Relations in Canada*, edited by Peter S. Li, 65. Toronto: Oxford University Press.

Ferner, A., P. Almond and T. Colling. 2005. 'Institutional Theory and the Cross-National Transfer of Employment Policy: The Case of "Workforce Diversity" in US Multinationals'. *Journal of International Business Studies* 36 (3): 304–21.

Foster, L. and L. Jacobs. 2012. 'Workplace Practice and Diversity in Canada: Employment Policy in Global Modernity'. *Think India Quarterly* 15 (3): 57–72.

Gagnon, Alain-G. and Raffaele Iacovino. 2007. 'Federalism and the Politics of Diversity: The Canadian Experience'. In *Managing Diversity: Practices of Citizenship*, edited by Nicholas Brown and Linda Cardinal, 95–114. Ottawa: The University of Ottawa Press.

Gatrell, C. and E. Swan. 2008. *Gender and Diversity in Management: A Concise Introduction*. London: SAGE Publications.

Gaze, B. 2014. 'Gender Equality Reporting and the Future of Equal Opportunity at Work'. *Governance Directions* 66 (10): 621–4.

Goldstein, Jeffrey and Marjorie Leopold. 1990. 'Corporate Culture vs. Ethnic Culture'. *Personnel Journal* 69 (11): 83–92.

Gotsis, George and Zoe Kortezi. 2015. 'Critical Studies in Diversity Management Literature: A Review and Synthesis'. The Netherlands: Springer. Accessed 25 August 2017. www.springer.com/gp/book/9789401794749.

Government of Canada. 1985. 'Canadian Human Rights Act'. Accessed 11 November 2017. http://laws-lois.justice.gc.ca/eng/acts/h-6/.

———. 1988. 'Canadian Multiculturalism Act'. Accessed 11 November 2017. http://laws-lois.justice.gc.ca/eng/acts/C-18.7/.

———. 2001. 'Immigration and Refugee Protection Act'. Accessed 11 November 2017. http://laws.justice.gc.ca/eng/acts/i-2.5/.

Greene, A. M. and G. Kirton. 2009. *Diversity Management in the UK: Organisational and Stakeholder Experiences*. New York: Routledge.

Hammerman, H. 1984. *A Decade of New Opportunity: Affirmative Action in the 1970s*. Washington, DC: Potomac Institute.

Hanamura, Steve. 1989. 'Working With People Who Are Different'. *Training & Development Journal* 43 (6): 110–4.

Haq, Rana. 2015. 'Accommodating Religious Diversity in the Canadian Workplace: The Hijab Predicament in Quebec and Ontario'. In *Managing Religious Diversity in the Workplace*, edited by Stefan Groschl and Regine Bendl, 31–52. Surrey: Gower Applied Business Research.

Hawkins, Robert. 1992. 'Diversity and Municipal Openness'. *Public Management* 74: 33–5.

Healy, G., H. Bradley and C Forson. 2011. 'Intersectional Sensibilities in Analysing Inequality Regimes in Public Sector Organizations'. *Gender, Work and Organizations* 18 (5): 467–87.

Hiranandani, V. 2012. 'Diversity Management in the Canadian Workplace: Towards an Antiracism Approach'. *Urban Studies Research* 2012: 1–13.

HR Council Canada. 2009. *HR Management Standards*. Ottawa: HR Council Canada.

HR Hero. 2017. 'HR Hot Topics'. Accessed 11 September 2017. http://topics.hrhero.com/.

Hur, Yongbeom and Ruth Ann Strickland. 2015. 'Diversity Management Practices, Do They Make a Difference? Examining Consequences of Their Adoption in Local Governments'. *Public Administration Quarterly* 39 (2): 325–57.

James, P. C. 2014. 'Diversity in the Workplace: A Legal Perspective'. In *Opportunities and Challenges of Workplace Diversity: Theory, Cases and Exercises*, edited by Kathryn Canas and Harris Sondak, 26–44. Boston: Pearson Education.

Johnston, W. B. and A. E. Packer. 1987. *Workforce 2000: Work and Workers for the 21st Century*. Indianapolis: Hudson Institute.

Kellough, J. 1990. 'Integration in the Public Workplace: Determinants of Minority and Female Employment in Federal Agencies'. *Public Administration Review* 50 (5): 557–66.

Kelly, E. and F. Dobbin. 1998. 'How Affirmative Action Became Diversity Management: Employer Response to Anti-Discrimination Law: 1961–1996'. *American Behavioral Scientist* 41 (7): 960–84.

Kim, Nam-Kook. 2011. 'Deliberative Multiculturalism in New Labour's Britain'. *Citizenship Studies* 15 (1): 125–44. doi: 10.1080/13621025.2010.534938.

Kirton, G. and A. M. Greene. 2017. 'Understanding Diversity Management in the UK'. In *Corporate Social Responsibility and Diversity Management: Theoretical Approaches and Best Practices*, edited by Katrin Hansen and Cathrine Seierstad, 59–74. Cham: Springer.

Kramar, R. 2012. 'Diversity Management in Australia: A Mosaic of Concepts, Practice and Rhetoric'. *Asia Pacific Journal of Human Resources* 50 (2): 245–61.

Kramar, R., T. Bartram, H. De Cieri, R. A. Noe, J. R. Hollenbeck, B. Gerhart and P. M. Wright. 2011. *Human Resource Management: Strategy, People, Performance.* Sydney: McGraw-Hill Australia.

Kramar, R. and P. Holland. 2015. *Capstone HRM: Dynamics and Ambiguity in the Workplace.* Prahran: Tiled Publishing and Distribution.

Krautil, Fiona. 2014. *Inclusion and Diversity: Are these Qualities Alive in the Australian Workplace?* Melbourne: Australian Human Resources Institute.

Kulik, Carol T. and Yiqiong Li. 2015. 'The Fork in the Road: Diversity Management and Organizational Justice'. In *The Oxford Handbook of Justice in the Workplace*, edited by Russell S. Cropanzano and Maureen L. Ambrose, 561–76. New York: Oxford University Press.

Leonard, J. 1989. 'Women and Affirmative Action'. *Journal of Economic Perspectives* 3 (1): 61–75.

Lynch, F. R. 1997. *The Diversity Machine: The Drive to Change the 'White Male Workplace'.* New York: Free Press.

Ng, E. and Jacqueline Stephenson. 2015. 'Individuals, Teams, and Organizational Benefits of Managing Diversity: An Evidence-based Perspective'. In *The Oxford Handbook of Diversity in Organizations*, edited by Regine Bendl, Inge Bleijenbergh, Elina Henttonen and Albert J. Mills, 235–54. Oxford: Oxford University Press.

Noon, M. 1993. 'Racial Discrimination in Speculative Application: Evidence from the UK's Top 100 Firms'. *Human Resource Management Journal* 3 (4): 35–47.

North-Samardzic, A. 2009. 'Looking Back to Move Forward: The (D)Evolution of Australia's EEO Regulatory Framework'. *The Economic and Labour Relations Review* 20 (1): 59–76.

O'Leary, J. and J. Sandberg. 2012. 'Best Method to Manage Diversity'. Australian Institute of Management. Accessed 30 January 2014. www.aim-nsw-act.com.au/news/best-method-manage-diversity.

Oliver, D. 2005. 'Achieving Results Through Diversity: A Strategy for Success'. *Ivey Business Journal Online* 69 (4): 1–6.

Ozbilgin, M. F., T. A. Beauregard, A. Tatli and M. P. Bell. 2011. 'Work-Life, Diversity and Intersectionality: A Critical Review and Research Agenda'. *International Journal of Management Review* 13 (2): 177–98.

Ozturk, M., A. Tatli and M. F. Ozbilgin. 2015. 'Global Diversity Management: Breaking the Local Impasse'. In *The Oxford Handbook of Diversity in Organizations*, edited by Regine Bendl, Inge Bleijenbergh, Elina Henttonen and Albert J. Mills, Chp 18. Oxford: Oxford University Press.

Pendakur, K. and R. Pendakur. 2002. 'Colour My World: Have Earnings Gaps for Canadian-Born Ethnic Minorities Changed Over Time?'. *Canadian Public Policy* 28 (4): 489–511.

Pew Research Center. 2015. *Modern Immigration Wave Brings 59 Million to U.S., Driving Population Growth and Change Through 2065: Views of Immigration's Impact on U.S. Society Mixed*. Washington, DC: Pew Research Center.

Podsiadlowski, Astrid, Daniela Gröschke, Marina Kogler, Cornelia Springer and Karen van der Zee. 2013. 'Managing a Culturally Diverse Workforce: Diversity Perspectives in Organizations'. *International Journal of Intercultural Relations* 37 (2): 159–75. doi: https://doi.org/10.1016/j.ijintrel.2012.09.001.

Ravazzani, Silvia. 2016. 'Understanding Approaches to Managing Diversity in the Workplace'. *Equality, Diversity and Inclusion: An International Journal* 35 (2): 154–68.

Reimers, D. M. 2016. 'The Impact of Immigration Legislation: 1875 to the Present'. In *The Oxford Handbook of American Immigration and Ethnicity*, edited by Ronald H. Bayor, 14–33. New York: Oxford University Press.

Reitz, Jeffrey G. 2005. 'Tapping Immigrants' Skills: New Directions for Canadian Immigration Policy in the Knowledge Economy'. *Choices* 11 (1).

Remedios, M. 2011. 'Not Just a Women's Issue: Gender Diversity in the Workplace'. *Law Society Journal* 49 (5): 70–2.

Schmidt, R. J. 1988. 'Cultural Pluralism and Public Administration: The Role of Community-Based Organisations'. *American Review of Public Administration* 18: 189–202.

Schultz, C. 2011. 'Proactive vs. Reactive Approaches to Your Business and Talent'. ERE.net Today. Accessed 11 September 2013. www.ere.net/2011/06/01/proactive-vs-reactive-approaches-to-your-business-and-talent/.

Silk, C., R. Boyle, A. Bright, M. Bassett and N. Roach. 2000. *The Case for Cultural Diversity in Defence*. Canberra: Australian Defence Organisation.

Skalsky, P. and G. McCarthy. 2009. Diversity Management in Australia and its Impact on Employee Engagement. *World at Work*. Accessed 22 July 2013. http://ro.uow.edu.au/gsbpapers/22/

Smith, B. and J. Riley. 2004. 'Family-Friendly Work Practices and the Law'. *Sydney Law Review* 26 (3): 395–426.

Soldan, Z. and A. Nankervis. 2014. 'Employee Perceptions of the Effectiveness of Diversity Management in the Australian Public Service: Rhetoric and Reality'. *Public Personnel Management* 43 (4): 543–64.

Stam, Robert and Ella Shohat. 2012. *Race in Translation: Culture Wars Around the Postcolonial Atlantic*. New York: New York University Press.

St-Onge, Sylvie. 2015. 'Accommodations in Religious Matters: Quebec and Canadian Perspectives'. In *Managing Religious Diversity in the Workplace*, edited by Stefan Groschl and Regine Bendl, 9–30. Surrey: Gower Applied Business Research.

Strachan, G., E. French and J. Burgess. 2010. 'Equity and Diversity within Organisations: Putting Policy into Practice'. In *Managing Diversity in Australia: Theory and Practice*, edited by G. Strachan, E. French and J. Burgess, 57–74. Sydney: McGraw-Hill Australia.

Summers, A. 2003. *The End of Equality: Work, Babies and Women's Choices in 21st Century Australia*. Melbourne: Random House.

Syed, J. and R. Kramar. 2010. 'What is the Australian Model for Managing Cultural Diversity'. *Personnel Review* 39 (1): 96–115.

Thomas, D. A. and R. J. Ely. 1996. 'Making Difference Matter: A New Paradigm for Managing Diversity'. *Harvard Business Review* 74 (5): 79–90.

Thomas, R. R. Jr. 2002. 'From Affirmative Action to Affirming Diversity'. *Harvard Business Review* 68 (2): 107–17.

Thornton, Margaret. 2015. 'The Political Contingency of Sex Discrimination Legislation: The Case of Australia'. *Laws* 4 (3): 314–34.

Trichur, R. 2004. *Employment Equity Still Failing Minorities*. Toronto: Conference Board of Canada

Trudeau, Justin. 2016. 'Statement by the Prime Minister of Canada on Multiculturalism Day'. Accessed 27 June 2017. https://pm.gc.ca/eng/news/2016/06/27/statement-prime-minister-canada-multiculturalism-day.

The US Supreme Court. 1849. *Passenger Cases* 48 U.S. 283 (1849). Accessed 19 November 2017. https://supreme.justia.com/cases/federal/us/48/283/case.html

Winterle, M. 1992. 'Workforce Diversity: Corporate Challenges, Corporate Responses'. In *Conference Board Reports*. New York: Conference Board.

Xu, Liton Weili. 2013. 'Cultural Diversity in a School-to-work Transition Programme for Undergraduate Students'. In *Cultural and Social Diversity and the Transition from Education to Work*, edited by Guy Tchibozo, 203–22. New York: Springer.

Yan, Miu Chung. 2010. 'Managing Diversity in Canada: A Human Rights Approach'. Proceedings of the Conference on Managing Diversity within a Human Rights Framework: Social Inclusion Policy and Practice in China and Canada, Shandong, China, 11–12 December 2010.

Yanow, Dvora. 2003. *Constructing 'Race' and 'Ethnicity' in America: Category-making in Public Policy and Administration*. New York: M. E. Sharpe.

5 Diversity Management in Practice

The Practice of Strategic Management of Diversity in the US: A Review of Case Studies

As detailed in Chapter 2, diversity management emerged in the US in the early 1980s, and now many organisations encourage diversity management because of its recognition as a tool for proactive intervention to attain equal treatment of employees, irrespective of race, gender and ethnicity. In the US, diversity management has been adopted to follow organisational fairness and equality and to promote an inclusive workforce. The US economy needs skilled workers, irrespective of their cultural backgrounds, and immigrants are attracted to the US by the political freedom and economic opportunities. On that basis, millions will continue to flood American shores (Carr-Ruffino 2005). In addition, economic data indicate that the workforce will become more diverse, with racial and ethnic minorities, women, disabled people, and gay and transgender people playing a major role in the growth of the economy. Therefore, businesses should embrace diversity, given that both the American economy and society depend on it (Burns, Barton and Kerby 2012).

In regard to diversity management in the US public sector, data from the 2013 Federal Employee Viewpoint Survey showed that diversity management relates to organisational fairness in the federal workplace (Kim and Park 2017). However, female and minority employees view diversity management differently in the context of fairness. Organisations must have management strategies and policies to attract and retain skilled employees to succeed in competitive environments (Kim and Park 2017). In the US public sector, diversity management is positively implemented in practice by EEO or AA policies, whereas diversity management is implemented in the private sector. Private organisations protect employees from illegal discrimination, and provide equal opportunity in the workplace pursuant to existing statutes. However, it is difficult to achieve the initiatives and goals of diversity management without employees' support and appreciation of diversity practices in the organisation. Additionally, diversity management positively affects organisational fairness, leading employees to believe that the organisation is treating them fairly if they know that the organisation's practices and policies promote diversity in the workplace. Perceptions of diversity management among employees from different ethnic groups differ from women's perceptions of diversity management, even though both are underrepresented groups (Kim and Park 2017).

Female employees in federal agencies believe that, if diversity management is controlled, they will be treated more fairly than males in the organisation, even if they are under the impression that the organisation is unfair. Employees in senior positions believe that diversity management has no positive effect on organisational fairness, which means that highly paid groups have a negative view of diversity management in the context of organisational fairness. However, these groups maintain that they get fair treatment if diversity management is controlled (Kim and Park 2017).

In regard to diversity management in the US public sector, the Minneapolis Fire Department was one of the earliest agencies subject to legal actions aimed at providing racial diversity in its ranks. In 1970, the Court of Appeal in the Eighth Circuit made a decision to hire minorities, which was appreciated and well received by civil rights activists. The main issue was that 'when fire department leadership fails to recognize the value of diversity, they lose the ability to gain from a wide variety of views' (Carter 2017, 1). That emergency departments move beyond the boundary of their public-sector organisation and reach the community by providing quality emergency services and employing a diverse workforce. To be successful, comprehensive and inclusive programs should be introduced, highly supported and aimed at embracing cultural diversity. Contemporary fire officers need to have awareness of diversity to be effective managers and leaders, and minimise problems in their department (Carter 2017).

Diversity improves organisational productivity and increases profits, and employing a diverse workforce helps capture more markets. A good example of how success can be achieved by promoting diversity in the workplace is PepsiCo, which discovered early that tapping into multicultural markets would enable the organisation to flourish and grow, by depicting African Americans in its annual report in 1960 (Reed 2011). By 1995, PepsiCo had not promoted minorities and had no white female or male minority executive officers, although they employed one Asian woman, who was a senior vice-president in charge of strategic planning (Reed 2011). Senior management changed when Steve Reinemund became CEO and chairperson of PepsiCo in 2001, and a reshuffle led to employment of three white women, one Asian woman and two African men on Reinemund's 11-person team by 2005, thereby increasing the diversity of his executive officers to nearly 55%. Further, Reinemund (quoted in Reed 2011, 216–7) sought to create an environment in which employees could rise and meet their abilities, and expressed a desire to create an 'environment where true greatness can be achieved by valuing people for their differences, strengths, talents and callings that they bring'. Reinemund seems to have recognised the need to include women and minorities in the organisation's operations, as well as the business opportunity that would be obtained by their inclusion. Further, Reinemund (quoted in Reed 2011, 217) declared:

> That's what makes us strong. In 15 out of 17 cities in the US, the minority is the majority. . . . For most part, they are not white males. There are very diverse people in those stores.

It seems that employees at PepsiCo have a built-in incentive—they have real ownership of the business, as confirmed by a statement by PepsiCo's diversity manager: 'we expect people to act like owners, which breeds an entrepreneurial spirit and brings with it a strong sense of teamwork' (Reed 2011, 219). Additionally, PepsiCo compensates and promotes its managers based on their support and promotion of diversity and inclusion (Reed 2011).

Further, it has been reported that, for organisations to survive, there is intrinsic value in diversity. IBM's then CEO, Sam Palmisano (quoted in Maltbia and Powe 2009, 28), who was regarded as a leader of diversity, stated in 2009 that:

> diversity policies lie as close to IBM's core as they have throughout our heritage. Today, we're building a workforce in keeping with the global, diverse marketplace, to better serve our customers and capture a greater share of the on demand opportunity.

Further highlighting the global importance of diversity management, Tiane Mitchel Gordon (quoted in Mor Barak 2017), senior vice-president for diversity and inclusion at America On Line, referred to the strategic role of diversity management as the way that management can become more culturally aware of the influence and effect of the business as a global company that receives great revenue from undertaking business in overseas countries. The adoption of such diversity management is evident in many organisations that operate at a global level. For example, Jay C. Rising (quoted in Mor Barak 2017, 220), President of Automatic Data Processing, stated that 'Our goal is to have a workplace that is fully inclusive, one that enables us to leverage the talents of a multi-cultural organisation'. In addition, the mission statement of Hanes and Boone, a large law firm in the US, declares:

> Our greatest asset is our people. They make Haynes and Boone a special firm by embracing core values that foster a healthy work environment, a commitment to being the best and an attitude of service to others. While our people make a positive difference for our clients, they do the same for their local communities by dedicating substantial personal time and funds to pro bono work and community service. We are equally proud of the ethnic, gender and cultural diversity of our people and our success in hiring, retaining and promoting women and ethnic minorities.
> (Mor Barak 2017, 220)

In their case study research on diversity management in the US, Asari, Halikiopoulou and Mock (2008) examined the diversity management practices of four organisations: AFC Enterprises, Choice Hotels, Denny's and Domino's Pizza. Their findings indicated that diversity strategies in these organisations were developed based on changes in the workplace and marketplace. The case studies showed how the organisations altered their strategies to benefit from demographic change. It seems that diversity awareness is one of the essential changes experienced by businesses and how it affects the organisations. Evidently, organisations that understand the differences in their customer base and modify their strategies to meet these differences can expand and benefit (Asari, Halikiopoulou and Mock 2008). Diversity management strategies would fail without the support of senior management. Thus, these strategies should ideally be initiated by the CEO and senior management and then be extended to all employees and policies in the organisation (Asari, Halikiopoulou and Mock 2008). If a company suffers from a lack of diversity at the top level, it is an indication to senior executives to move to another company if they want a senior position. This is because the effect permeates down to all levels and limits innovation by senior executives to solve this issue (DiversityInc Staff 2010).

Dough McMillon (quoted in Walmart 2015, 4), president and CEO of Walmart Stores Inc., emphasised the importance of diversity in the workplace as follows:

> I'm proud of the intentional work we've done over the past decade to broaden our talent pool and diversify our leadership ranks. Now more than ever, Walmart reflects our diverse customer base, and that makes us a better company. We've also demonstrated that we're willing to speak out on behalf of diversity and inclusion, particularly when we need to support our company's core value of respect for the individual.

With respect to diversity, Sharon Orlopp (quoted in Walmart 2015, 5), Global Chief Diversity Officer and Senior Vice-President Corporate People at Walmart, stated:

> to me, diversity is like the ingredients to a recipe. To make a good dish, you need to have different ingredients that work together. At Walmart, we want people who come from different places, think in different ways, and look and act differently from one another. Inclusion is how we mix those ingredients together—it's the environment that we create, the real culture of the company. Inclusion is grounded in respect for the individual and requires us to value and recognise the contribution of every associate. In addition to providing a diverse and inclusive work environment, we provide unparalleled opportunities and access to jobs.

In addition to his various contributions in the communications industry, Ivan Seidenberg, former CEO of Verizon, laid the foundation for a culture of diversity and inclusive program at Verizon, which has been widely acknowledged. Verizon offers a variety of mandatory diversity training programs and is committed to offering participation opportunities to minority business enterprise suppliers. Expenditures are reported to Seidenberg quarterly, which has led to Verizon being cited by Fortune Magazine on its list of 'The 50 Best Companies for Minorities' (Canas 2014). The importance of diversity is reflected in Seidenberg's (quoted in Canas 2014, 67) statement that:

> being able to draw on the diverse life experience of our people helps us offer creative solutions to business challenges. That's why diversity is a strategic imperative for us and key to Verizon's growth.

He further stated that 'a multi-faceted approach drives Verizon's success and ability to compete' (Canas 2014, 67).

Further, Antonio Pérez, CEO of Kodak and chair of the CEO Leadership Initiative of Diversity Best Practices, has received positive recognition for using diversity in redesigning the Kodak company. Pérez (quoted in Canas 2014, 67) has diverse heritage, international experience and a passion for creating an inclusive culture, and stated: 'Diversity is incredibly valuable. It's a must, a condition without which you will not succeed, but that richness comes with complexity that needs to be accepted and managed'.

Poster slogans such as 'Diversity makes business sense', 'People are our most precious commodity', 'We are gender and color blind' and 'We do not discriminate, we incorporate' (Farnsworth Riche and Mor Barak 2005, 148) greeted Michàlle E. Mor Barak as he walked into the lobby of an international organisation in Southern California to evaluate the organisation's diversity policies, at the invitation of its CEO. He interviewed employees from various backgrounds and men and women from different levels, and discovered that the challenge was to provide a culture that is truly inclusive. The belief that the organisation was 'blind to ethnic and gender differences' was revealed to be true by the interviewees. Interestingly, members of racial/ethnic minority groups revealed lost job opportunities, missed promotions and exclusion. They also felt barred from decision-making processes. In addition, a woman discussed her experiences and how difficult it was for her to rise to her current position. She was told that she lacked communication for a managerial position because of her different culture. She claimed that she felt like a woman in a man's job (Farnsworth Riche and Mor Barak 2005).

In the case of AFC Enterprises, vice-president Ellen Hartman claimed that organisations need to know how to benefit from diversity by seeking, providing and continuously supporting opportunities through discussion and professional development. Hartman added that this must start at the top of the organisation. At AFC Enterprises, the onus is on everyone to implement diversity initiatives in operation. Hartman recommended gaining approval from top management, recruiting an experienced diversity consultant to conduct a cultural assessment of the organisation, and then writing a report on how the organisation could benefit from diversity. This should all be followed by training specifically designed for the organisation's needs, while management eliminates any impediments that may interfere with an inclusive approach. Hartman claimed that AFC Enterprises owes its success to diversity, which seems to comprise more than just 'doing the right thing'. He further added that organisations must learn how to use diversity to their benefit (Asari, Halikiopoulou and Mock 2008).

In another case study of Choice Hotels, diversity management is again undertaken at the leadership and senior management levels. The company also has a diversity committee consisting of members of the board of directors. Their overall approach to diversity focuses on the communities where business is conducted, and the company has two basic diversity programs: the first is intended for all employees, including a 'common ground understanding' of diversity, and the second is for management-level staff (Asari, Halikiopoulou and Mock 2008).

In the case of Denny's, the motivation for diversity management is quite different. Denny's Chief Diversity Officer Rachelle Hood-Phillips declared that the organisation was losing about US$100 million a year in potential sales by not considering African American consumers. This presented a great warning to senior management. With respect to leadership, when reforming the organisation, diversity must be in the top rank of the organisation, and then diversity filtered down to involve the rest of the organisation. At Denny's, they have a management committee consisting of 14 people, 33% of which are minorities. The organisation has 'WE CAN' diversity training processes to ensure its commitment to diversity and to guarantee its maintenance and communication. Additionally, the organisation maintains in-house 'trainer of trainers' to perform diversity training (Asari, Halikiopoulou and Mock 2008).

At Domino's Pizza, the company's Senior Director of Diversity, Jim Betts, stated that the motivation for diversity management has been to create an organisation that reflects the needs of the community by being inclusive. He further stated that the challenge was educating their workforce about diversity and its effect on business and employees (Asari, Halikiopoulou and Mock 2008).

Dell, one of the largest providers of enterprise computing products, is also committed to diversity and inclusion, and supports measures that ensure employees receive equal and fair treatment in the workplace. Its success is attributed to an environment that values individual differences, which helps the organisation promote the innovative workplace that has shaped its business and subsequently manifested in a diverse global marketplace (Bawaba 2014). Dell received an excellent score on the 2014 Corporate Equality Index, which is compiled by the Human Right Campaign—the largest civil rights organisation endeavouring to attain equality for lesbian, gay, bisexual and transgender (LGBT) Americans. This was the tenth consecutive year in which Dell achieved a perfect score. Dell supports LGBT issues through an employee resource group called Pride, and the organisation's diversity goes beyond sexual orientation and gender identity to include many organisations in the communities they serve (Bawaba 2014).

DiversityInc (2017), a leading organisation in the field of diversity management in the US, has announced the top 50 companies for diversity since 2001. Table 5.1 presents its latest list of the top 50 companies in the US.

The US workforce has become increasingly diverse and although many public and private organisations have developed diversity management policies and programs, there are still challenges to be addressed in the US context. The dreams of most people who migrated to the US were to transfer from a difficult past and assimilate into a better future. However, Price (1992) argued that the 'melting pot' idea only works at the peripherals and limited areas of life, and rarely works socially. The availability of jobs in the US attracted foreign workers, with the labour market demanding both skilled and unskilled workers. Immigrants had a great influence on the US economy by reducing production costs in factories and working long hours for very low wages, without any recourse to union protection (Henderson 1994). The admittance of many foreign workers into the US, mainly from developing countries, has created mixed feelings. While some people view foreign workers as a solution to a problem, others view them as a threat to the jobs of US workers (Henderson 1994). Americans who feel threatened by foreign workers create positive or negative attributes of citizens of other

Table 5.1 2017 Top 50 Companies for Diversity

1. EY	11. KPMG	21. Cummins	31. Aetna	41. Genentech
2. Kaiser Permanente	12. Deloitte	22. Target	32. Nielsen	42. General Motors
3. AT&T	13. Proctor & Gamble	23. New York Life	33. Allstate Insurance Company	43. KeyBank
4. PwC	14. Accenture	24. Wyndham Worldwide	34. Toyota Motor North America	44. Southern Company
5. Johnson & Johnson	15. Prudential Financial	25. BASF	35. Colgate-Palmolive	45. McCormick & Co.
6. Sodexo	16. Eli Lilly & Co.	26. Dell	36. The Walt Disney Co.	46. Medtronic
7. MasterCard	17. ADP	27. TIAA	37. Time Warner	47. Exelon
8. Marriott International	18. Cox Communications	28. Kellogg Company	38. TD Bank	48. BBVA Compass
9. Wells Fargo	19. Comcast Universal	29. Northrop Grumman	39. Monsanto	49. Aramark
10. Abbott	20. Anthem	30. Hilton Inc.	40. AbbVie	50. CVS Health

Source: DiversityInc (2017).

countries, depending on the group to which they belong. For example, they tend to look down on people of developing countries as being uncivilised and of lower intelligence, while people from Western industrialised countries are viewed by some Americans as civilised and intelligent. The belief that one culture is superior to another (ethnocentrism) can make it difficult for employees to interact and communicate with colleagues from other cultures, who may be considered inferior. Thus, there is an urgent need for cultural diversity and education in business (Henderson 1994). Lack of diversity initiatives is characterised as being 'political skill deficiency' (Douglas et al. 2003, 81). Allowing diverse group members to move beyond a social identity and towards group values—as has been successfully undertaken in the US Armed Forces—may improve diversity management in civilian organisations (Douglas et al. 2003). The effective management of diversity in the workplace is so important that organisations must find a way to effectively manage and use all their human resources or they will be unable to compete (Douglas et al. 2003).

The globalisation of markets has caused significant changes in the external environment of organisations, which have subsequently changed the workplace. Managers face challenges in the management of diversity and equality in the workplace. The systematic discrimination in the workplace, which leads to racial bias, is of vital importance in the management of equality and diversity in the workplace. There are four themes that could lead to the effective management of equality and diversity (Sharma 2016). The first theme is the performance appraisal approach, which is implemented to promote managerial and organisational performances with employee motivation. Black people felt a lack of acceptance in the organisations and received lower ratings from their supervisors, which affected their promotion and created lower job satisfaction (Sharma 2016). The second theme is the sociocultural approach, where HRM consists of distinctive functions and processes with the purpose of directing and maintaining organisations' human resources, and is influenced by social and cultural factors. Further, organisations experience challenges in managing diversity at both individual and group levels, particularly when employees come from diverse religions. The 11 September 2001 attack in the US produced more religious persecutions, and, according to the Council on American—Islamic Relations, led to a 15% increase in claims of mistreatment and bias in the workplace (Sharma 2016). The fourth theme is the universal equality model, which acknowledges human diversity. Thus, the management of a diverse workforce requires a change in organisational culture and a keen managerial team that supports minorities by introducing appropriate surroundings for them. Organisations that introduce cultural, societal, individual and organisational values, supported by their management, will improve working conditions and attract diverse people, including women and minorities (Sharma 2016).

Two primary values have kept immigrants on American shores: freedom and opportunity—freedom to follow one's own lifestyle and religion, and opportunity to establish a decent standard of living. Therefore, since the melting-pot approach failed to provide equal opportunities for people of colour and women, the government introduced a legal approach in the 1960s, which has been more effective. Businesses with more than 15 employees were subject to EEO, which was essential for people of colour and women, who could complain to their employers about any discrimination on the basis of EEOC guidelines. While the advantage of EEO is that it enables employees to deal with discrimination, the disadvantage is the difficulty of proving discrimination (Carr-Ruffino 2005).

The Practice of Strategic Management of Diversity in Canada

The cohabitation of new settlers from around the world for centuries shaped Canada's history, culture and values, making the country a unique place for traditions and customs. Thus, Canada developed into one of the most tolerant and diverse countries in the world. Additionally, Canada leads the world in the ethnic diversity of its immigrants, and ranks fifth in the number of foreign-born residents (Rotundo 2012). Although there has been no history of investment and inclusion in Canada, approximately half (49%) of Canada's organisations invested in diversity during the last five years. This investment was based on three primary reasons. First, to enhance employee engagement, which is in the top list (34%). Second, to build the organisation's brand externally, which placed third in the list (32%). Third, to enhance the organisation's ability to acquire new talent, which placed second in the list (32%) (Garr, Shellenback and Scales 2014). To 'serve customers better' and 'increase innovation and agility' were placed fifth and seventh on the list, respectively. It is surprising that these two factors were not placed in the top three reasons for Canadian organisations to invest in diversity, since they are key indicators noted by leaders in diversity and inclusion issues in the US. Therefore, organisations must invest in diversity and inclusion by creating a diversity and inclusion function (Garr, Shellenback and Scales 2014).

In the Canadian context, diversity management is a voluntary corporate approach, and is considered an alternative to employment equity and AA, which enables organisations to benefit from workforce diversity. A diverse workforce can benefit from talent that increases profits and leads to a positive public image. In Canada, government agencies are leaders in promoting public awareness of diversity matters, since diversity represents workplaces consisting of people of various backgrounds, sexes and styles of behaviour (Hiranandani 2012). Further, there are several powerful reasons for increasing diversity in Canadian organisations. The first reason is to foster creativity and innovation, given that the business environment is changing rapidly. Canadian organisations must change, learn and develop a diverse workforce in the competitive market to better reflect the various perspectives, experiences and insights that businesses need to achieve success. Diversity in the

Canadian workplace is imperative to reach talented people (Hiranandani 2012). The second reason is to tap new global markets, as global business is no longer restricted to exports and imports. As such, Canadian organisations now rely on vendors, service businesses and alliances worldwide. Promoting workforce diversity enables Canadian organisations to access global markets and subsequently increase corporate success. Foreign-born visible minorities residing in Canada have knowledge of and connections to other countries, which can be helpful to gain access to overseas markets (Hiranandani 2012). The final reason for increasing diversity in Canadian organisations is to enter ethnic markets. It is commonly agreed that an organisation with a workforce that resembles its customer base is more competitive to enter ethnic markets. For example, the Bank of Montreal focused on Chinese Canadians, opened new branches across the country, and hired Chinese-speaking employees who knew the community's culture. The result was an increase in business by 400% over a five-year period (Hiranandani 2012).

TD Canada, one of the top-ten financial services companies in North America, has also been successful in implementing a culture that supports diversity and inclusion that derives from its hierarchy. The CEO decided to establish diversity and inclusion 10 years ago because of its importance in business, as well as being a compliance and social issue. Today, diversity and inclusion at TD Canada consists of six areas of interest of which two relate to our topic. The first category is the diversity agenda, which serves diverse communities. The second category supports the bank's employees who are affiliated to diverse groups to encompass a more inclusive environment. The bank's approach to diversity and inclusion is effective and helps the bank achieve its business goals. As a result of the executive-level commitment to diversity and inclusion, employee resource groups serve as the 'eyes and ears' of the community. By so doing, they underpin talent and markets that the bank should pursue and create awareness in the public domain of its inclusive culture. The bank's culture of inclusion has been acknowledged because of its effect on employers and communities. Thus, the bank has won Canada's Best Diversity Employer Award three times. It was also named by the Human Rights Campaign Foundation a '2012 Best Place to Work for LGBT Equality', with a score of 100% on the foundation's corporate equality index for four consecutive years (Garr, Shellenback and Scales 2014).

The adoption and implementation of diversity, as well as management strategies, are viewed as helpful for Canadian organisations to achieve their goals by providing services to the diverse public. Hence, public and private sector organisations in Canada promote their diversity management strategies. The implementation of diversity management programs in the Canadian public sector dates back to the era of adoption of both AA and EEO policies (Ohemeng and McGrandle 2015).

The state of Ontario, which is the second-largest public sector employer in Canada, and the first to establish a diversity office to supervise diversity and inclusion programs in 2008, is an interesting case with regard to diversity management in the Canadian public sector. Examination of the workforce of the Ontario Public Service (OPS) indicates that the organisation does not reflect diversity that is present in the population from which it could benefit (Ohemeng and McGrandle 2015). While the government has made some progress in diversifying the population, it realised that it had to do more. To address the labour needs of the OPS and social demands, it introduced an OPS strategy as part of the 2008 Framework for Action (FA) to modernise the public service. However, managing diversity in Ontario did not commence with the 2008 FA—a series of Acts were passed by the government with administrative directives to the OPS to promote a diverse population in Ontario. There are two major Acts in Ontario related to diversity—the *Accessibility for Ontarians with Disability Act 2005* and the *Employment Standard Acts 2000* (Ohemeng and McGrandle 2015). In 2008, the Ontario government formed the OPS Diversity Office (OPSDO) and appointed the first Chief Diversity Officer. The importance of diversity management is reflected in the status given to the Diversity Officer position—a position of excellence and expertise that equals membership to the Deputy Minister's Council. The Diversity Office is endeavouring to transform the OPS into a global leader. The OPSDO is helping the OPS become more diverse, with different values respected, thereby becoming a champion of the OPS diversity management strategy (Ohemeng and McGrandle 2015).

The OPSDO initiated a three-year plan for diversity management that started in 2008 to 2009, as a guide. Further, the government then associated the FA on diversity with the OPS human resource plan, which was designed for the workforce of the whole public service. It was also joined to the *Public Service of Ontario Act* and public servants' behavioural expectations (Ohemeng and McGrandle 2015). Not everyone was expected to accept diversity management, as it required cultural change in the organisation. Another proposal in the OPS is the formation of OPS employee networks— voluntary associations based on common bonds or backgrounds, where members of underrepresented groups would feel supported and included in the workplace. Another program called Inclusion Lens is an online tool designed to help OPS employees gain knowledge about diversity, inclusion and identifying barriers in the diversity policy. The lens enables employees to ask questions on this issue and obtain the right information and reveals the OPS values of diversity and efficiency, as well as the OPS programs and services. Thus, the OPS has achieved notable progress in implementing diversity as a major factor of its program (Ohemeng and McGrandle 2015).

In the Canadian public sector at the federal level, the Royal Bank of Canada (RBC) is one of the most prominent organisations in the area of diversity management. The RBC is strongly committed to building a culture of inclusion as a federal public institution. The organisation intends not only to increase the numbers of minority group members, but also to create an environment of inclusion where every member has the opportunity to reach his or her potential (Rotundo 2012). In its diversity management strategy, the RBC has special emphasis on newcomers to Canada. As a result of the strong commitment of the leadership team, the RBC implemented programs and initiatives aimed at improving the representation of minorities through education, training, employment and economic independence to serve the interests of minority groups in the community (Rotundo 2012). In 2009, ethnic groups represented 27% of the RBC's employees, with 25% in management positions. In 1998, these figures were 12% and 13%, respectively, which indicates that significant progress is possible and would have a positive effect on the advancement of minority group members (Rotundo 2012).

In relation to the impact of diversity and inclusion on organisations, almost all Canadian organisations surveyed (87%) in a recent study (Garr, Shellenback and Scales 2014) employed three or fewer dedicated diversity and inclusion staff. In considering the areas in which diversity and inclusion affect organisations—such as 'talent acquisition, external brand, suppliers, business operations, customer service, community relations, etc.') (Garr, Shellenback and Scales 2014, 20)—leaders of organisations need to question the benefits of employing such a small number of diversity staff. However, it is noted that a large number of organisations' key business function areas employ more than three people.

Further, an annual survey is conducted by the RBC to measure and analyse progress through the Diversity Leadership Council, which was established in 2006. The RBC is so committed to diversity that it earned the 2010 Catalyst Diversity Award for advancing women and minorities, as well as being Canada's Best Diversity Employer for its diversity and inclusiveness programs (Rotundo 2012). The RBC continues its diversity policy by providing opportunities to advance, reward and retain the best employees to meet the needs of Canada's pluralistic society. Moreover, it is extending its aim far beyond the workplace to protect the natural resources that attracted newcomers to Canada in the first place (Rotundo 2012).

The Practice of Strategic Management of Diversity in the UK

Diversity management in the UK has acquired different meanings and perspectives, as managers have to deal with the challenges and differences that are considered problematic in the workplace if diversity is treated with antagonism (Ozbilgin and Syed 2015). Nevertheless, the treatment of diversity in British organisations along the axes of 'diversity as problem' and 'diversity as resource' has been challenged, and organisations tend to deal with both the negative and positive outcomes. The negative consequences include disharmony in the workplace, industrial conflict and problems of communication. The positive outcomes encompass the benefits deriving from using diversity as a resource to enhance performance, innovation and problem solving at work (Ozbilgin and Syed 2015).

In previous research on UK employers and equality, it was noted that public service organisations that develop equality policies tend to implement them before private sector employers, and thus are unlikely to have an 'empty shell' (Greene and Kirton 2009). It was intended to have a mixed workplace in terms of gender and race. There was an awareness of cultural diversity, manifested in the promotion of a few members of ethnic minorities, which proved to be moving in the right direction. Additionally, there was a common view agreed by line managers and trade union representatives in the UK that women were promoted to senior jobs. BME employees lacked promotion due to the fact that the way to progress was to 'bow down to management' (Greene and Kirton 2009).

However, there is an academic debate among UK scholars regarding diversity and equality, and the advocates and critics of managing diversity reveal diversity management and equal opportunities as opposing philosophies. Further, the findings of case study research on private sector organisations in the UK revealed a shift from equal opportunities to diversity management, as diversity management policies and programs place the organisation in an advantageous and competitive position that enables them to enter new markets and reach new customers and talented people (Tatli 2010).

Diversity managers in the public sector emphasise the benefits of workforce diversity by enhancing both the social and relational structure of their organisation. This is in contrast to their colleagues in the private sector, who seem to capitalise on the effect of diversity on the bottom line (Tatli 2010). As for the definition of diversity in the organisation, respondents in the public sector in the UK confined it to inequality covered by anti-discrimination legislation:

> We've got sexual orientation, age, social class, race, religion, marital status, gender, disability. It is about the service users and employers, disability, gender, race and age, and obviously sexual orientation, religion, everything. As more legislation comes on line, we amend it.
>
> (Tatli 2010, 291)

The National Health Service (NHS), the publicly funded healthcare system in the UK, constitutes a good example of legislation-based diversity management in the UK public sector. As a public body, the NHS is bound by the *Equality Act 2010* and Public Sector Equality Duty to reduce inequalities in employment. Further, NHS organisations are required to consider individual differences and provide fair treatment to all, irrespective of their backgrounds. The NHS comprises 500 organisations; therefore, it seems difficult to attain consistency in the management of diversity. The head of equality, diversity and human rights at the NHS revealed a political shift in diversity and its effect on the NHS (Powell and Johns 2015).

Diversity was introduced into UK workplaces to overcome deficiencies and as a partial recognition that, while legislation is essential, it is insufficient to counter what Kochan et al. (2003, 4) called 'entrenched organisational cultures', which do not accept underrepresented groups. Diversity calls for different groups not to assimilate, but to have their differences nurtured and rewarded. In the UK, most organisations associate the success of their diversity management with the inclusion of women and BME staff (Tatli 2010). Focusing on these categories reveals the gap between managing diversity as an approach of inclusion and encompassing all differences, and the practice of diversity management as a framework built around legal compliance (Tatli 2010).

There is heated debate regarding the effect of immigration in the UK, which is contributing significantly to the economy. In terms of progress made, there has been an increase in BME representation in Parliament, and the appearance of successful BME entrepreneurs who make great contributions to the UK economy. Further success has been noted in education, where positions of power and influence have been attained, yet there is little hope when looking at senior levels of organisations in the UK (Ozbilgin and Syed 2015). A case study on diversity management in UK law firms confirmed this claim by indicating that, in practice, even when there is an objective to benefit from a diverse workforce, diversity management has not been successful in UK law firms (Ashley 2010), with non-traditional candidates (people with non-Anglo backgrounds) still expected to assimilate into the organisation's processes. In addition, individuals in the legal profession tend to be less inclined to promote a more advanced system that recognises and rewards difference based on social class because the inclusion of working-class lawyers could threaten the firm's brand and affect its profits. It is further suggested that the way to assess diversity strategies is based on an acknowledged pragmatism (Ozbilgin and Syed 2015).

In their comparative case study research on the involvement of line managers in diversity management in the UK, Greene and Kirton (2009) focused on two case study organisations: ServiceCo, a multi-divisional private sector organisation, and PSO, a public sector organisation. Similar to the failure of diversity management in the UK private sector, as detailed earlier, Greene and Kirton concluded that the implementation of diversity management policy in the UK public sector was driven by adherence to legislative compliance. Again, in terms of whether the equality and diversity policy had any benefits for employees, there appeared to be some scepticism and cynicism regarding its influence and it was likened to 'a lollipop in the desert' that may stop one's thirst for a few minutes, but is useless in the long term (Greene and Kirton 2009, 181).

The Practice of Strategic Management of Diversity in Australia

There is currently no law in Australia that requires workplaces to promote diversity, rather than assimilation. However, there has been a shift from a policy of assimilation. While assimilation demanded and encouraged a 'oneness' that implied 'sameness' and involved 'exclusive policies', multiculturalism recognises the diversity of cultures in Australia and embraces many languages, traditions, heritages and customs, and thus creates 'inclusiveness' as a policy for 'all Australians' (Cattalini 1995). Multiculturalism became an official policy in Australia in 1973, and eased the restrictions of the assimilation policies of the 1940s and 1950s. Since then, Australia has developed into a multicultural society. An influx of migrants has increased migrant participation in the workforce, leading to the current Australian policy and legislative framework.

Multiculturalism in Australia has affected the workplace, where people of different cultural backgrounds are employed, and has brought benefits to organisations. Certain ethnic groups tend to maintain their cultural traditions and values to the extent that they practice them in the workplace and in Australian society in general. The study of multiculturalism in Australia has two strands. While some scholars examine Australian multiculturalism in the context of the 'war on terror', with a special emphasis on Islamophobia (Cherney 2015; Dryzek and Kanra 2014), other scholars deal with the issue as everyday multiculturalism (Anita 2013; Ho and Jakubowicz 2014), with the claim that, at an everyday level, the dominant type of multiculturalism is banal multiculturalism. This book argues that these two strands of multiculturalism exist at the same time in Australian organisations. Recent case studies revealed examples of how the political discourse associated with the war on terror has affected Australian multiculturalism, and how multiculturalism is regarded by managers not as a political issue, but as an everyday issue, with an emphasis on engaging with people of diverse backgrounds (Chidiac 2015). The findings of case studies also indicated that some organisations view diversity as being more akin to assimilation than acculturation, given that they expect their staff to forget their cultural differences to work as a group (Chidiac 2015). However, such an understanding of diversity may result in recruitment practices through which managers can select individuals who are like themselves.

In Australia, government policies seem to provide equality, fairness and harmony in the workplace, yet lack awareness and understanding of ethnic and cultural differences. Therefore, organisations should implement a diversity policy dealing directly with the cultural backgrounds of employees to create a higher level of awareness among both management and the workforce. This would provide a clear framework along with equity and justice. It is clear that diversity is here to stay in the Australian context; thus, proper policies regarding its management in the workplace are imperative to maintain harmony, increase productivity and provide benefits from the skills and experiences of people from different cultural backgrounds. Given the trends in migration, diversity is on the increase in the Australian workplace, and must be managed in accordance with work-related government policies to cope with the challenges offered by diverse workforces.

The effects of multiculturalism in the workplace in Australia appear to derive from three factors (Collins 2008):

- permanent immigration in recent years, which has recovered from its previously low level;
- a high level of immigration because of the reduction in employment rates and high demand for labour;
- temporary immigration, which has increased with globalisation.

These three concurrent processes highlight the current dynamics of the Australian labour market. They also emphasise the increasing importance of strategically managing diversity to reap the benefits and address the challenges associated with increasing levels of ethnic and cultural diversity in the workplace. In this context, there is a strong relationship between communication and diversity management in Australia. Communication skills open up global opportunities and subsequently make Australia a melting pot of ideas, hopes and aspirations. The hidden skills of staff are being recognised, and organisations wish to develop and harness these skills. Therefore, the focus should be on taking full advantage of employees' skills and abilities in the organisation. A diverse workforce provides better communication with customers from different cultural backgrounds. In this sense, diversity management offers benefits to both employers and employees. In relation to experience gained prior to employment, a diverse workforce brings advantages to the organisation, such as language skills, communication styles, country-specific knowledge and life experience. In addition, enhancing communication skills and productivity can increase a team's effectiveness. Further, in their research on employment perceptions of diversity management in the APS, Soldan and Nankervis (2014) examined a large federal government agency selected based on its reputation for being a genuine leader in and committed to diversity management. However, the findings indicated a lack of communication between management and staff. It was reported that some employees claimed that 'in general, the policies are fair, but the implementation of them is not always fair', leading to a perception that management 'does not practice what it preaches' (Soldan and Nankervis 2014, 549).

In a recent case study (Chidiac 2015), the interviewed managers recognised and appreciated the benefits of diversity in the way they recruited, trained and retained employees of CALD backgrounds because of their skills and languages. Organisations benefit from diverse workforces that serve their clients in Australia and overseas. These benefits include the increased ability to serve customers who speak languages other than English, thereby presenting a good corporate image by valuing diversity in the workplace, and enabling organisations to gain access to new markets. Interestingly, in recruitment practices, language seems to not be an overriding criterion for employment, largely because employees are not recruited for their various languages because they have to perform other duties in the workplace. Although each employee is required to understand English well enough to be able to communicate with other employees and customers, ethnic languages are a desirable, though not essential, criterion for employment (Chidiac 2015).

In relation to the benefits of a diverse workforce, the literature provides rich insight into various relevant aspects, such as acknowledgement of the costs associated with a diverse workforce, and the fact that diversity offers mutual benefits to employees and employers (Gordon 2007; Hollwell 2007; Romanenko 2012; Stone 2008). In this regard, intelligent and creative management of diversity not only results in social, economic, artistic and political progress, but also increases the productivity of the contemporary workplace. In addition, a diverse workforce can work in unison to solve problems for all groups in the organisation by creating and enhancing a 'we' mentality, rather than an 'us versus them' mentality. In Australian business circles, there is a growing realisation that a diverse workforce brings skills, languages and benefits to organisations and customers, which enhances business and promotes the corporate image in Australia and overseas. The benefits of a diverse workforce are the key issue that enables organisations to serve their customers with diverse ethnic backgrounds in multicultural Australia, and enter new markets with the help of such skills, languages and values. Thus, a diverse workforce offers valuable hidden talents through employees who are waiting to be given the opportunity by management to contribute to the organisation (Chidiac 2015).

Community language skills are also considered valuable assets to Australian organisations. When employees communicate skilfully with customers from various backgrounds, customer service improves. People of different cultures and backgrounds have a lot to contribute to Australian society in general and to the workplace in particular. A diverse workforce brings skills and values, and enhances the work environment by introducing different cultures through language, attitude, values, behaviour, food and traditions. However, the use of language can also be a source of conflict associated with communication and the ability to understand and speak English. Language-related issues constitute a major source of conflict in organisations (Chidiac 2015) because of misunderstandings between management and staff and between staff. The major sources of such misunderstandings are the ways that employees with CALD backgrounds converse in English, or a lack of understanding of certain terms and expressions. Different cultures use different means and forms of communication, and what may be acceptable in Anglo-Saxon culture may not be acceptable in other cultures. Although English is the same language in Australia, it is different from English-speaking countries in style, form and nuance.

A culture-related challenge is the colloquial use of language in the Australian workplace. To prevent or manage conflicts arising from the colloquial use of language in the workplace, management should play an important role in explaining the real meaning of colloquial terms for non-English-speaking employees and English-speaking employees who are unfamiliar with such terms. Colloquial language used in the workplace can be problematic and cause misunderstanding and lack of communication with employees of CALD backgrounds. In Australian workplaces, the use of slang is very common. Australian employees frequently express themselves in grammatically incorrect phrases, such as 'I wanna go' or 'I ain't coming'. In addition, terms such as 'pull your socks up' or 'you gotta be joking' may be confusing, unless employees are familiar with these terms or have them explained by someone in the workplace. They can be taken literally by employees of non-English backgrounds and the real meaning can be lost in the translation. It seems that colloquial language is particularly used by workers performing manual work, while, in a professional work environment, formal English is used by employees who have some formal education that enables them to use more grammatically correct English in their conversations (Chidiac 2015).

As the official language in Australia, English plays a central role in communication, and the ability of employees to speak and understand English is one of the most critical aspects of diversity management in the workplace. Employees are given instructions in English and are expected to communicate with their supervisors and their colleagues in the same language. Although English is the unifying language in India and the second language in China, as explained previously, people of different cultures can still find it difficult to comprehend the meaning of some Australian terms. Therefore, previous research indicates that employees of CALD backgrounds cannot communicate if they fail to understand certain terms used by their Australian supervisors. Language is the means of communication in the workplace that enables employees to comprehend instructions given by management, including changes to policies. Communication between management and employees and between employees must be in clear and simple language. This is particularly essential for CALD employees so they understand the information correctly. Thus, clarity, simplicity and consistency should be regarded as the three essential elements in communication when addressing people of different cultures (Dozier, Grunig and Grunig 2010; Huo, Binning and Begeny 2015; Mazzei 2010). Organisations should include these elements and emphasise their importance in training practices.

One of the prominent aspects of diversity management in Australia is the belief that diversity in the workplace presents a good corporate image in multicultural Australia. Further, there is some emerging research into CSR, corporate transparency and corporate legislation for work-related policies. It has been reported that perceived benefits arise from cultural diversity as a result of working in a multicultural work environment. The first emerging benefit is increased creativity. 'There are opportunities to learn from one another about different cultures. Different employees contribute to different ideas to get the job done easily' and 'diverse employees make the workplace interesting, like a real community' (D'Netto et al. 2014, 1252). The second benefit incorporates employee commitment and a strong work ethic. Ethnic employees are frequently very committed and cherish employment opportunities via a strong work ethic. They often cannot afford to lose their jobs because their families and relatives in their countries of origin depend on their income and support. The third benefit involves aiming to improve capabilities to handle international markets. The majority of ethnic employees felt that their organisation could access new overseas markets through their multicultural employees. Another issue deals with language difficulties, as the groups of ethnic employees felt that lack of fluency in English influenced their ability to perform their duties effectively. Organisations should help migrant employees from non-English-speaking backgrounds by providing them with English classes to help them improve their language skills. In addition, diversity should be embraced as an advantage, rather than viewed as a legal obligation (D'Netto et al. 2014). A recent study by Chidiac (2015) revealed the benefits of a diverse workforce, as shown in Table 5.2.

Some of these benefits can be seen as confirmation of the results of other studies conducted in the field of strategic management. For example, Stone (2008) suggested that recognition of cultural diversity in management generates benefits and aids in the development and marketing of products. Similarly, Prasad et al. (1997) viewed diversity management as a long-term strategy from which organisations will attain economic benefits. These thoughts align with the research finding that organisations can economically benefit from diversity as a business expansion tool. From a business perspective, it was interesting to note that certain participants in Chidiac's (2015) case study stated that diversity in the workplace provides a good corporate image in multicultural Australia. Further, another interesting point raised

Table 5.2 Benefits of Diversity Management in Australia

Benefits for organisations	Benefits for employees	Benefits for customers
A tool for business expansion	More flexible working practices	Better communication with customers from different cultural backgrounds
A tool for conflict prevention	Opportunity to learn about other cultures	
A tool for qualitative improvement of the employee base		
An enabling device for recruiting, training and retaining employees of non-English-speaking backgrounds		
A way of using community language skills		

Source: (Chidiac 2015)

was to regard diversity as a tool for business expansion. Having a diverse workforce with different skills and languages enhances customer services by satisfying the needs and requirements of a diverse customer base.

Another interesting practice of diversity management adopted by an Australian organisation is to use a local offsider, who is familiar with cultural and religious practices, to enable managers to communicate efficiently and effectively with clients (Chidiac 2015). Asking employees with ethnic backgrounds to explain cultural issues and clarify matters that create conflict would avoid possible and unnecessary conflicts resulting from different cultures. Therefore, it is evident that the managers not only recognised and appreciated the benefits of diversity in the workplace, but also used such differences as opportunities. Another key benefit for organisations is to use diversity policy to achieve qualitative improvements of the employee base. This helps organisations have more effective tools for communication between staff with different backgrounds and hire skilled employees. Organisations also benefit from a diverse workforce when designing and implementing their recruitment, training and retaining policies. Diverse employees understand the needs of diverse customers. For example, Telstra Corporation Limited employed individuals who could speak up to seven different languages to join its multilingual customer service centres. It is estimated that these multilingual sales consultants take about 2,700 calls a month, with positive feedback from customers who are happy to communicate in their native language (Mor Barak 2017).

In addition to the benefits discussed, diversity poses serious challenges to both Australian organisations and employees. Attitude enables people to scrutinise their values and beliefs about cultural differences and understand their origin. This is evident when employees of different cultural backgrounds hold a variety of values, work ethics and ethnically and culturally rooted behaviours. A study of organisational policies in Australia indicated that many organisations do not develop equity programs, and merely operate on the basis of legislative compliance (Strachan, French and Burgess 2010). In this context, cultural differences can lead to conflicts in the workplace because employees have different perceptions, fears, norms and beliefs that constitute the sources of most conflict in the workplace. Cox (1993) claimed that conflicts between diverse groups may occur because of misunderstandings and misperceptions related to differences in their worldviews. This was confirmed by the findings of research on diversity management in the Australian manufacturing sector, in which D'Netto et al. (2014) showed that a diverse workforce can cause many problems, such as communication breakdown, low cohesion and high turnover. Moreover, they found that another important barrier in the workforce is English literacy as a communication issue. Thus, multiculturalism in Australia creates many benefits and challenges in the workplace. However, potential benefits can be realised through effective diversity management, while human resource practices can lead to the creation of a workforce with the necessary skills to convert diversity into an advantage and achieve positive performance results (D'Netto et al. 2014).

The findings of a recent study (Soldan and Nankervis 2014) on the effectiveness of diversity management in the APS have important implications for management and human resource policy makers in the APS. The findings included a lack of line-management training, lack of line-management involvement in developing diversity management, and lack of managerial accountability for diversity efforts. Additionally, an internal culture that blunts diversity-oriented change was reported as a serious issue, together with widening the entry for specific target groups just to satisfy legal requirements, yet not acknowledging or addressing these groups' needs once they are employed (Soldan and Nankervis 2014).

The government regulations in Australia deal with issues after events occur, yet a diversity policy would provide awareness and understanding of cultural differences, and offer mechanisms to prevent the rise of such problems. However, in Australian practice, there have been two pieces of legislation with a proactive approach to diversity management: gender-related EEO and *WGEA* legislations. However, this proactive approach does not exist in the Australian legislations dealing with other aspects of diversity, such as ethnic and cultural dimensions. Following the development of equal opportunity initiatives in Australia, diversity management has become a second-generation EEO after the legislation of anti-discrimination and AA during the 1970s and 1980s. Diversity management is still in its infancy. While Australian managers are aware of diversity issues, they do not prioritise the management of a diverse workforce. In a recent study on diversity management in the Australian energy industry by Dalton, D'Netto and Bhanugopan (2015), the findings indicated that, while managers in the industry need more ability to manage diverse people, organisations have not yet concentrated on developing diversity competencies. In this study aimed at measuring managers' diversity management competencies in the workplace, the authors formulated a Diversity Management Competency Model, which consisted of four quadrants: (i) understanding self, (ii) understanding others, (iii) workplace analysis and (iv) workplace application (Dalton, D'Netto and Bhanugopan 2015). The results indicated that, when the level of diversity competencies in Quadrant (i) was 'moderate', the remaining three quadrants were all 'low' (Dalton, D'Netto and Bhanugopan 2015), which indicated that the managers had a moderate level of competencies in relation to 'understanding self', yet low levels for all the other quadrants. The authors suggested that organisations should include these competencies in reward systems to encourage managers to improve diversity management in the workplace. However, there is more to be undertaken, as the challenge of managing diversity in the workplace will continue to develop and grow (Dalton, D'Netto and Bhanugopan 2015).

The emphasis on managing diversity in Australia has shifted from treating everyone the same—which was the approach used in the context of a predominantly white male workforce—to managing people as individuals (Teicher and Spearitt 1996). This shift is a direct outcome of EEO and AA policies introduced by Australian governments. However, commitment to diversity appears to be lacking in many Australian companies. For example, Sinclair (2006) argued that there is resistance by companies to enhancing and expanding diversity training, despite various 'awareness-raising' activities being conducted. Organisations that rely exclusively on government legislation to manage diversity in the workplace do not have ongoing training programs, but deal with issues and conflicts associated with cultural differences as they occur. Thus, institutionalised diversity policy leads to minimising, if not eliminating, the occurrence of such problems or conflicts through the use of diversity training programs.

Examining the Australian policy and legislation on diversity indicates that the policies introduced in the workplace include AA (which is no longer applicable), EEO and anti-harassment policies. As Australia is a multicultural society and continuously accepts migrants from various countries, the diversity of the workforce will increase. Multiculturalism has been an official policy in Australia since 1973, and policies such as AA and EEO were introduced in that context. This book argues that relying exclusively on the existing government policies to manage a diverse workforce can lead to ineffective practices in organisations. Therefore, for companies that do not introduce diversity policies, their success will ultimately be limited by the issues covered under EEO and anti-harassment legislation. Therefore, this book argues that the anti-discrimination legislation in Australia does not produce the desired outcomes. The findings of D'Netto et al.'s (2014) study on diversity management in the Australian manufacturing sector supports this argument. The authors highlighted that organisations in Australia do not acknowledge the benefits of workforce diversity. Organisations can benefit from 'the increased creativity, innovation and strong work ethic of migrant employees' (D'Netto et al. 2014, 1258). Further, there should be government policies designed for people from non-traditional backgrounds to integrate into the mainstream community. The findings also indicated that 'organisations in Australia are not managing their diverse workforce in a way that effectiveness, efficiency and competitiveness could be created and maintained' (D'Netto et al. 2014, 1259).

The current literature identifies a clear gap concerning the implementation and monitoring of diversity policies in Australian settings. The *WGEA* (formerly known as *EOWWA*) has a voluntary reporting system, and not all organisations report their practices. In addition, the *WGEA's* main focus is on women in the workplace. Current practices that consider or actively seek to include cultural diversity appear absent in many cases, and are certainly hidden from external consideration. The case studies research in Australia (Chidiac 2015) indicated that Australian organisations are mainly operating only to comply with the various state and national laws on anti-discrimination, rather than proactively seeking to manage diversity. Further, the legislation offers 'management by exception', whereby only organisations that have reported a breach of the various Acts and do not settle at conciliation must report for the public to see. There are various issues associated with the strategic management of diversity in the workplace based on gender, culture, habits, traditions, age and language. Various policies dealing with equal employment and fair treatment to all employees have been adopted, but there exists no diversity policy to address cultural and ethnic differences (Chidiac 2015).

Under the title 'A Place for Everyone, on How Inclusion and Diversity Benefit All Australians', Stan Grant—an Australian journalist and advisor on Indigenous constitutional recognition to the Australian Prime Minister, Malcolm Turnbull—claimed that it is insufficient to have diversity just for the sake of having it, and stated that some organisations are achieving progress in this area. He has lent his name to an Australian Human Resources Institute award for 2017 called the Stan Grant Indigenous Employment Award, which recognises excellence in Indigenous initiatives and programs in the workplace. He further stated that leaders must act to ensure that diversity and inclusion succeed. He added that:

> Through us, Australia finds a belonging and legitimacy that flows to all. Through us and a final reconciliation, a final settlement of those issues, we will find a sense of belonging.
>
> (Grant 2017, 14)

It is evident that diversity management is an enabling tool for productivity, profitability and employee effectiveness. This book argues that a diverse workforce also leads to qualitative improvement of the employee base. This implies that, in a multicultural setting, organisations could convert their diverse workforce into an asset through which they can serve the diverse needs and demands associated with the services they provide, and to their ethnically and culturally diverse client base.

In Australia, policies dealing with the management of diverse workforces aim to create a workplace that is fair and flexible and covers groups that include women in senior leadership roles; Aboriginal and Torres Strait Islander peoples; gay, lesbian, bisexual, transgender and intersex people; people from CALD backgrounds; and people with disabilities. Diversity policy provides more tools and opportunities to organisations than do government policies on issues such as EEO, AA and anti-harassment. As Ezeanu (2011) reported, under diversity policies, organisations are committed to implementing plans, programs and initiatives aimed at recognising, respecting and promoting workforce diversity. This includes the recognition of skills, prior learning and experience. The policy ensures that employees are selected for positions on merit, without unlawful discrimination and harassment.

Further, diversity policy recognises the benefits of workforce diversity, as well as the skills, life experience, educational level, socio-economic status, marital status, political affiliation, sexual orientation, gender, age, creed, religion, language, nationality, origin, disability and members of minority groups. Therefore, implementing workplace diversity policies in line with industry-led codes of practice is imperative in organisations to promote equity, fairness and inclusion for the diverse workforce. This is done because EEO is not a substitute for a diversity policy that specifically deals with cultural and ethnic differences, including equality by breaking down barriers, eliminating discrimination and providing equal opportunities and access to all employees in the workplace. A diversity policy incorporates the acceptance of individuals with cultural differences, and the valuation of their contributions and skills. There can be no equality of opportunity if cultural differences are not valued and considered by employers. Thus, understanding the benefits of diversity in the workplace and ensuring diversity management through an adequate policy framework are the key issues at stake (Chidiac 2015).

While EEO deals with providing equal employment opportunities to all people, without discrimination, diversity policies clarify cultural differences and create awareness and comprehension of various cultural issues. Following Hubbard's (2004) four types of diversity—workforce, behavioural, structural, and business and global diversity—the implementation of diversity policy has clear advantages over EEO and AA.

The second important aspect of organisational practice relates to recruitment and training. Sinclair (2006) elaborated that commitment to diversity in many Australian companies is still lacking. Although 'awareness-raising' activities are conducted, some significant resistance exists with respect to further diversity training. The training programs implemented in Australian organisations are also of a diverse nature, and commonly include introductory training provided at the commencement of employment as an induction program that incorporates team leadership and management, information systems, new technologies, product training, product presentation and custom-made tailoring. Newly recruited employees must undergo these training procedures to prepare and equip them with enough information at the initial stage of employment. However, ongoing diversity training is not part of the training practices of Australian organisations relying only on government regulations (Chidiac 2015).

This book argues that there is a need for legislation forcing organisations to introduce, implement and monitor diversity policies in the Australian workplace. As discussed earlier, diversity policy offers a more extensive list of tools and benefits to organisations than adopting government policies only. Supplementing the already existing compulsory policies with diversity policy would help minimise, if not eliminate, the potential risks posed by the emerging new racism in Australia targeting certain cultural groups, such as Asian-Australians and Australians of Middle Eastern backgrounds. Cultural racism indeed occurs in the Australian workplace; thus, there is a pressing need for diversity-related legislation dealing with cultural diversity in the workplace. Therefore, this book highlights the need for the introduction of industry-led codes of practice that outline a framework for best practice in relation to diversity management, beyond the existing anti-discrimination legislation. The issue of industry-led diversity standards has been subject to intense discussion in the recent literature; however, further studies are required to investigate how industry-led initiatives can be designed to address the existing problems and challenges. Organisations and human resources professionals would see the value of such a code of practice. Unions and industry associations should also support a best-practice view because it increases the chances of managing cultural and ethnic differences before conflict-provoking events occur.

The introduction of diversity policy may face objections and resistance from members of management and some segments of the workforce. However, management must understand the importance of change, the reasons for change and how the change will benefit both the employees and organisation. The onus is on management to introduce change for the benefit of all in the workplace, and to help employees cope with the change by convincing them that the change is imperative to keep abreast of contemporary society. Employees must be informed that change is necessary to improve the working conditions by introducing a new policy that ensures employees' rights and equality. Making it compulsory for employers to implement diversity policies would also help manage the problems associated with so-called uncertainty avoidance.

Summary

This chapter discusses the rise of diversity management in the US, and the economy needs for skilled individuals. It highlights the immigrants' attraction to the US and the implementation of diversity management in both the public and private sectors by welcoming workers from different backgrounds and providing equal opportunities. The benefits of a diverse workforce are explained together with the positive influence of diversity upon the performance of organisations through the greatest asset of their people. Diversity enables organisations to expand globally and gain competitive advantage in foreign markets. Examples of how diversity helps organisations to meet business challenges are illustrated through the various views of senior executives.

In addition, commitment to diversity and inclusion by organisations in the US enable employees to enjoy equal treatment and be valued for their differences. The development of diversity management policies in public and private organisations is addressed in this chapter, including challenges and the significant impact of immigrants on the US economy. Additionally, the changes in the workplace caused by globalisation are highlighted in this chapter, including the values that keep immigrants in the US and the failure of the melting-pot approach.

This chapter outlines the development of Canada into becoming a leading country in ethnic diversity and how diversity management superseded employment equity and AA. There is a discussion about the common belief that Canadian organisations have a competitive advantage to have access to ethnic markets through matching their customer base with a diverse workforce. Furthermore, there is an explanation of how diversity management is viewed by organisations in fulfilling their goals, and how diversity is promoted by both the public and private sector organisations. The legislation of Acts by Ontario in relation to diversity and the promotion of a diverse population indicate commitment by the Ontario government in dealing with the OPS labour needs and social demands. The commitment to diversity in Canada is emphasised by prominent organisations such as the RBC which implemented programs to ensure adequate representation of minorities.

The challenges and differences in the workplace faced by managers of diversity management in the UK, and how British organisations treat diversity to reap the benefits are discussed. There has been a shift from equal opportunities to diversity management in the UK to enable organisations to acquire a competitive advantage in new markets. Whilst the benefits of diversity management have been emphasised by management in the public sector, the situation differs in the private sector where the emphasis is on the financial outcome and adherence to legislative compliance. The continuing debate about the significant impact of immigration in the UK indicates its importance and the contributions made to the economy by BME entrepreneurs.

In the absence of laws to enhance diversity in Australia, there has been a shift to multiculturalism which embraced various cultures leading to the introduction of multiculturalism policy which has been in existence since 1973. Multiculturalism has, undoubtedly, affected the workplace in Australian organisations with an emphasis on individuals from different ethnic and cultural backgrounds. However, lack of awareness by management of ethnic and cultural differences remains an issue in the workplace.

The effect of multiculturalism in Australia and its derivation are outlined in this chapter, due to the important role of immigration which affected employment and globalisation. There has been an emphasis on strategic management of diversity which addresses the challenges in the workplace and reaps the benefits of diversity. Having a diverse workforce proved to be beneficial to both employees and organisations by managing diversity well and recognising people's skills and experiences. Employees of CALD backgrounds have made significant contributions to organisations and their customers through communication skills which enabled organisations to gain access to new markets. Communication has proved to be essential in the workplace to overcome problems and create awareness and understanding of different cultures.

Various studies conducted on diversity management in Australia reveal that organisations do not operate in accordance with equity programs, but rather adhere to legislative compliance. This chapter discusses how misunderstandings and misperceptions of other people's differences pose a challenge in the workplace. However, the aspects of diversity are dealt with in relation to legislation, and how to treat and manage a diverse workforce well in order to reap ultimate benefits. Additionally, it is essential for management in Australian organisations to recognise the importance of change in the workplace in respect of diversity. Thus, it is the responsibility of management to effect such a change for the benefit of employees, employers and the corporate image.

References

Anita, Harris. 2013. 'Everyday Multiculturalism in Australia'. *Peace and Culture 5* (1): 31–7.

Asari, Eva-Maria, Daphne Halikiopoulou and Steven Mock. 2008. 'British National Identity and the Dilemmas of Multiculturalism'. *Nationalism and Ethnic Politics* 14 (1): 1–28.

Ashley, Louise. 2010. 'Making a Difference. The Use (and Abuse) of Diversity Management at the UK's Elite Law Firms'. *Work Employment Society* 24: 711.

Bawaba, Al. 2014. 'Dell Applauds White House's Executive Order Promoting Diversity and Inclusion in the Workplace'. *MENA Report*, 24 July.

Burns, Crosby, Kimberly Barton and Sophia Kerby. 2012. *The State of Diversity in Today's Workforce: As Our Nation Becomes More Diverse So Too Does Our Workforce*. Washington, DC: Center for American Progress.

Canas, Kathryn. 2014. 'Exemplary Diversity Leaders and Organizations'. In *Opportunities and Challenges of Workplace Diversity: Theory, Cases and Exercises*, edited by Kathryn Canas and Harris Sondak, 65–72. Boston: Pearson Education.

Carr-Ruffino, Norma. 2005. *Making Diversity Work*. Upper Saddle River, NJ: Pearson/Prentice Hall.

Carter, Harry. 2017. 'Command Post: Diversity is a Must, Not an Option'. *Firehouse*. August 2017.

Cattalini, H. 1995. 'Australian Immigration'. Proceedings of the 1995 Global Cultural Diversity Conference, Sydney, Australia. 26–28 April 1995.

Cherney, Adrian. 2015. 'Being a "Suspect Community" in a Post 9/11 World—the Impact of the War on Terror on Muslim Communities in Australia'. *Australian and New Zealand Journal of Criminology* 49 (4): 480–96.

Chidiac, Emile. 2015. 'A Study of the Strategic Management of Ethnic and Cultural Diversity in Australian Settings: A Multiple Case Study' (PhD thesis, Southern Cross University).

Collins, J. 2008. 'Globalisation, Immigration and the Second Long Post-War Boom in Australia'. *Journal of Australian Political Economy* 61: 244–66.

Cox, T. 1993. *Cultural Diversity in Organisations*. San Francisco: Berrett-Koehler.

Dalton, Linda, Brian D'Netto and Ramudu Bhanugopan. 2015. 'Cultural Diversity Competencies of Managers in the Australian Energy Industry'. *The Journal of Developing Areas* 49 (6): 387–94.

DiversityInc. 2017. 'The 2017 DiversityInc Top 50 Companies for Diversity'. Accessed 14 December 2017. www.diversityinc.com/the-diversityinc-top-50-companies-for-diversity-2017/.

DiversityInc Staff. 2010. '3 Case Studies: Why Companies Decline on the Diversity Inc Top 50'. Accessed 14 December 2017. www.diversityinc.com/diversity-management/3-case-studies-why-companies-decline-on-the-diversityinc-top-50/.

D'Netto, Brian, Jie Shen, John Chelliah and Manjit Monga. 2014. 'Human Resource Diversity Management Practices in the Australian Manufacturing Sector'. *The International Journal of Human Resource Management* 25 (9): 1243–66.

Douglas, C., G. R. Ferris, M. R. Buckley and M. J. Gundlach. 2003. 'Organizational and Social Influences on Leader—Member Exchange Processes: Implications for the Management of Diversity'. In *Dealing with Diversity*, edited by George B. Graen, 59–90. Greenwich, CT: Information Age Publishing.

Dozier, David M., L. A. Grunig, and J. E. Grunig. 2010. *Manager's Guide to Excellence in Public Relations and Communication Management*. Mahwah: Lawrance Erlbaum Associates.

Dryzek, J. S. and B. Kanra. 2014. 'Muslims and the Mainstream in Australia: Polarisation or Engagement?'. *Journal of Ethnic and Migration Studies* 40 (8): 1236–53.

Ezeanu, E. 2011. 'Fostering Diversity: Recognizing All the Benefits'. Accessed 14 February 2013. www.brighthub.com/office/human-resources/articles/90910.aspx.

Farnsworth Riche, Martha and Michàlle E. Mor Barak. 2005. 'Global Demographic Trends: Impact on Workforce Diversity by 2005'. In *Managing Diversity: Toward a Globally Inclusive Workplace*, edited by Michàlle E. Mor-Barak, 107–21. Thousand Oaks, CA: SAGE Publications.

Garr, S. S., K. Shellenback and J. Scales. 2014. *Diversity and Inclusion in Canada: The Current State*. Stamford, CT: Deloitte Development LLC.

Gordon, Christopher. 2007. 'Managing Diversity in the Garda Siochana'. *An Garda Siochana Management Journal*: 10–15.

Grant, Stan. 2017. 'A Place for Everyone'. *HRM: The Magazine of Australian HR Institute*, 12–14. October 2017.

Greene, A. M. and G. Kirton. 2009. *Diversity Management in the UK: Organisational and Stakeholder Experiences*. New York: Routledge.

Henderson, George. 1994. *Cultural Diversity in the Workplace: Issues and Strategies*. Westport, CT: Praeger Publishers.

Hiranandani, V. 2012. 'Diversity Management in the Canadian Workplace: Towards an Antiracism Approach'. *Urban Studies Research* 2012: 1–13.

Ho, C. and A. Jakubowicz. 2014. 'The Realities of Australian Multiculturalism'. In *For Those Who've come across the Seas: Australian Multicultural Theory, Policy and Practice*, edited by A. Jakubowicz and C. Ho, 3–14. North Melbourne: Australian Scholarly Publishing.

Hollwell, B. J. 2007. 'Examining the Relationship Between Diversity and Firm Performance'. *Journal of Diversity Management* 2 (2): 51–60.

Hubbard, E. E. 2004. *The Diversity Scorecard: Evaluating the Impact of Diversity on Organizational Performance*. Burlington: Elsevier Butterworth-Heinemann.

Huo, Y. J., K. R. Binning and C. T. Begeny. 2015. 'Respect and the Viability of Ethnically Diverse Institutions'. In *Towards Inclusive Organisations: Determinants of Successful Diversity Management at Work*, edited by S. Otten, Karen I. Van Der Zee and Marilynn B. Brewer, 49–66. East Sussex: Psychology Press.

Kim, Sungchan and Soyoung Park. 2017. 'Diversity Management and Fairness in Public Organizations'. *A Global Journal* 17 (2): 179–93.

Kochan, T., K. Berzrukova, R. Ely, S. Jackson, A. Joshi, K. John, J. Leonard, D. Levine and D. Thomas. 2003. 'The Effects of Diversity on Business Performance:

Report of the Diversity Research Network'. *Human Resource Management Journal* 42 (1): 3–21.

Maltbia, T. E. and A. T. Powe. 2009. *A Leader's Guide to Leveraging Diversity: Strategic Learning Capabilities for Breakthrough Performance*. Burlington: Elsevier.

Mazzei, A. 2010. 'Promoting Active Communication Behaviours Through Internal Communication'. *Corporate Communications: An International Journal* 15 (3): 221–34.

Mor Barak, Michàlle E. 2017. *Managing Diversity: Toward a Globally Inclusive Workplace*. 4th ed. Los Angeles: SAGE Publications.

Ohemeng, Frank and Jocelyn McGrandle. 2015. 'The Prospects for Managing Diversity in the Public Sector: The Case of the Ontario Public Service'. *A Global Journal* 15 (4): 487–507.

Ozbilgin, M. F. and J. Syed. 2015. 'Conclusion: Future of Diversity Management'. In *Managing Diversity and Inclusion: An International Perspective*, edited by J. Syed and M. F. Ozbilgin, 336–48. London: SAGE Publications.

Powell, Martin and Nick Johns. 2015. 'Realising the Business Case for Diversity: A Realist Perspective on the British National Health Service'. *Social Policy and Society* 14 (2): 161–73.

Prasad, P., A. Mills, M. Elmes and A. Prasad. 1997. *Managing the Organisational Melting Pot: Dilemmas of Workplace Diversity*. Thousand Oaks, CA: SAGE Publications.

Price, H. B. 1992. 'Multiculturalism: Myths or Realities'. *The Phi Delta Kappan* 74 (3): 208–13.

Reed, Susan E. 2011. *The Diversity Index: The Alarming Truth about Diversity in Corporate America . . . and What Can Be Done about It*. Saranac Lake: Amacom Books.

Romanenko, A. 2012. *Cultural Diversity Management in Organisations: The Role of Psychological Variables in Diversity Initiatives*. Hamburg: Diplomica Verlag.

Rotundo, Maria. 2012. 'Building a Culture of Inclusion at the Royal Bank of Canada: Strategies for Aboriginal Peoples and Newcomers to Canada'. In *Global Human Resource Management Casebook*, edited by James C. Hayton, Michal Biron, Castro Christiansen and Bard Kuvaas, 331–42. New York: Routledge.

Sharma, Angel. 2016. 'Managing Diversity and Equality in the Workplace'. *Cogent Business & Management* 3 (1): 1–14.

Sinclair, A. 2006. 'Critical Diversity Management Practice in Australia: Romanced or Co-opted'. In *Handbook of Workplace Diversity*, edited by A. M. Konrad, P. Prasad and J. K. Pringle, 511–53. Thousand Oaks, CA: SAGE Publications.

Soldan, Zhanna and Alan Nankervis. 2014. 'Employee Perceptions of the Effectiveness of Diversity Management in the Australian Public Service'. *Public Personnel Management* 43 (4): 543–64.

Stone, J. R. 2008. *Managing Human Resources*. Milton: John Wiley & Sons.

Strachan, G., E. French and J. Burgess. 2010. 'Equity and Diversity within Organisations: Putting Policy into Practice'. In *Managing Diversity in Australia: Theory and Practice*, edited by G. Strachan, E. French and J. Burgess, 57–74. Sydney: McGraw-Hill Australia.

Tatli, A. 2010. 'Discourses and Practices of Diversity Management in the UK'. In *International Handbook on Diversity Management at Work: Country Perspectives on Diversity and Equal Treatment*, edited by A. Klarsfeld, 283–303. Cheltenham: Edward Elgar.

Teicher, J. and K. Spearitt. 1996. 'From Employment Opportunity to Diversity Management: The Australian Experience'. *International Journal of Manpower* 17 (4/5): 109.

Walmart. 2015. 2015 *Diversity & Inclusion Report*. Accessed 14 April 2017. https://cdn.corporate.walmart.com/01/8b/4e0af18a45f3a043fc85196c2cbe/2015-diversity-and-inclusion-report.pdf.

Conclusion

Globalisation has produced a new world that has increased the number of nation-states in the global political system and altered the porous borders between them. The new world has created a space for millions of migrants (Davidson 2007). The global migrant of today is described as 'in between' or 'in transition' (Davidson 2007, 22). Migration is likened to the airport transit lounge, but with about 10% of travellers leaving their country of origin permanently. However, if they are refugees, they do not know where the forces of globalisation will cast them in their pursuit for survival. Thus, they become members of the mobile workforce, with either many places to reside or none (Davidson 2007).

In those many places, the meaning and influence of multiculturalism is limited without underpinning the role it plays in everyday life. Comprehending the reality of multiculturalism requires close examination of the daily practices and interactions between people of different ethnic and religious backgrounds (Hardy 2017). The term 'multiculturalism' first appeared in the 1960s and 1970s from within Canada and Australia. While multiculturalism in Canada dealt with the constitutional rights and land ownership of indigenous peoples, multiculturalism in Australia focused on the assimilation of new migrants, before including indigenous peoples. In both countries, multiculturalism was extended to encompass individual freedoms and equal citizenship. In Britain, multiculturalism was first discussed in the 1960s as a result of the increasing number of immigrants from the West Indies, India, Pakistan and Bangladesh following the enactment of the *Nationality Act 1948*. Additionally, successive British governments introduced multicultural policies that stipulated equal treatment for minority ethnic and religious groups, and the right to maintain their cultural identities (Hardy 2017). Under the *British Nationality Act 1948*, anybody who was a British subject was allowed to settle in Britain, regardless of race and colour, which transformed the UK into a multiracial society. In 2001, the UK officially became a multi-ethnic, multicultural society, and multiculturalism worked effectively in the UK, successfully replacing assimilation and integration. Today, the UK still supports multiculturalism, irrespective of challenges and criticisms. The term 'Multiculturalism' became popular in the 1980s in the US, which acknowledged the changing demographic and cultural structure. By the 1990s, multiculturalism in the US was interpreted by some social workers as a means to promote the needs of racial and ethnic groups, which led social workers to believe that multiculturalism would ignore 'the internal variations in traditional culture' (Reisch 2008, p. 798). Recent efforts made to bond the conceptual gaps that exist between social justice and multiculturalism have failed. Whilst the efforts of minorities shaped the mainstream practices to distinct conditions, there were some constraints caused by insufficient economic resources and political power. However, there remains the challenge today of reconciling the needs of specific groups within a framework of equitable policy in the US (Reisch 2008).

The lack of a specific definition for multiculturalism means multiculturalism can change with differing attitudes in different countries. In Australia and Canada, multiculturalism does not include indigenous peoples, and indigenous groups refuse to be encompassed by multiculturalism because of legitimacy issues. In contrast, in other countries, indigenous peoples use the term 'multiculturalism' to be distinguished from immigrant groups. Despite the differences in the definitions of multiculturalism in Australia, Canada, the UK and the US, these countries share the common factor of having an increasing foreign-born population. There has been a shift in multiculturalism by focusing on a globalised migration culture, where organisations in countries with secular democracies enable immigrants from various backgrounds to thrive. However, multiculturalism has caused hostility when immigrants have maintained their differences, rather than being encouraged to integrate into one society, as is the case in the UK.

The four countries examined in this book are destinations for immigrants from various countries around the world. As a result, while most people in Australia, Canada, the UK and the US speak English, all these countries are linguistically diverse. Canada has developed an official language education policy with programs that enable students to retain their mother tongue. The Canadian Constitution guarantees the country's official bilingual policy, which requires all official documents to be provided in both English and French (Banks 2010). Despite the fact that some states have unofficial bilingualism, the US has not adopted an official policy on language diversity. Although politicians defend spoken English, a close analysis in the US indicated greater acceptance of language diversity, such as through printing signs and brochures in Florida in Spanish, and providing services in Hawaii in Asian languages (Banks 2010).

There is an interesting connection between language and identity, especially in the UK. According to Sir Keith Ajegbo (quoted in Asari, Halikiopoulou and Mock 2008, 1), a former school headmaster and Home Office Advisor, the investigation discovered that British identity is not included in the curriculum, and there is more to be done to provide the 'essential glue that binds people together'. This is one of the main problems experienced by British society—failing to have a discussion that integrates different ethnic groups under the auspices of a common British identity (Asari, Halikiopoulou and Mock 2008). The Education Minister declared that a review was conducted as a result of the terrorist attacks of 7 July 2005, and the assumption that it was the lack of a unifying British identity that led some people to consider ethnic and religious signifiers. The 7 July London bombings were caused because of the lack of a civic British identity. The London bombings were undertaken by British citizens whose loyalties were to their ethnic and religious identities, unlike the terrorist attacks of 11 September 2001 in the US (Asari, Halikiopoulou and Mock 2008).

The global migrant of today is one of the essential elements of multicultural societies around the world. As discussed in the earlier chapters, multiculturalism has been strongest in Canada, while multiculturalism is fluctuating in many other countries, and the influx of immigrants who were expected to assimilate into the mainstream culture meant that governments deemed multiculturalism policies unnecessary. Multiculturalism was well received in Australia, the UK and the US until the terrorist attacks of 11 September 2001, with different cultural groups and their experiences and contributions encouraged by multiculturalist ideologies. However, a shift in the global and economic structures occurred after the attacks on 11 September, where the focus was on immigration in Western Europe, apart from the US. Having received many immigrants, liberal states must tolerate multiculturalism and recognise cultural differences. Immigration has caused both majority and minority populations to become multicultural, and the 11 September attack led to the creation of a new period of diversity management, known as the 'post—9/11' era. As a result, multiculturalism is known as 'anti- and/or post-multiculturalism discourse', used initially in the UK to promote cohesion, assimilation and a common identity. In Australia, multiculturalism has been responsible for 'hollowing out' the significance of being an Australian citizen. Additionally, the former British Prime Minister David Cameron attributed the weakening of collective British identity and the rise of Islamist extremism to multiculturalism (Crowder 2013).

While multiculturalism is an asset, diversity of itself does not yield benefits; thus, to benefit from multiculturalism, the shortcomings of a specific group must be recognised so they can be managed well. Thus, organisational management is responsible for identifying the cultural differences and backgrounds of a group, and for valuing and supporting employees. Canada adopted its *Multiculturalism Act* in 1988—becoming the first country in the world to adopt a multicultural policy—to help immigrants maintain their cultures, instead of assimilating into the mainstream. As a result of the retirement of baby boomers and labour shortages, Canada must rely on its immigrants to fill this shortage in the workforce. Canadian multiculturalism experienced success in Canada because of the refugee policy introduced by the Canadian government under Prime Minister Justin Trudeau. Canada presented the most ethnically diverse government and accepted government-sponsored refugees from Iraq and Syria as a way of demonstrating its support of multiculturalism. Evidence of Canada's support of multiculturalism was articulated in Trudeau's address, titled 'Diversity is Canada's Strength', delivered at Canada House in November 2015. Canada is considered second only to Australia in terms of the increasing diversity of the population. Moreover, diversity is now part of Canadian organisations, which have strong commitment to diversity by adopting an inclusive approach to diversity management and embracing diversity while endeavouring to increase the benefits in organisations. Only one-fourth of organisations have to comply with culture which they view as a problem. This is in contrast to the findings in the US, which indicate that 11% of US organisations have a 'compliance' culture. This is an indication that, while Canadian organisations are still adhering to compliance laws, about half of them have begun to implement inclusion (Garr, Shellenback and Scales 2014).

In the UK, although the labour force has become diverse because of the involvement of minorities, equality has not yet been achieved. Ethnic and religious minorities still face segregation and pay gaps, especially women and black graduates. Public sector organisations enforce equality legislation more firmly, while private sector organisations have a more voluntary approach in implementing the *Equity Act*. BAME tend to be underrepresented at management levels in the workplace, and, although they are ambitious and enjoy work, their white colleagues have more opportunities to advance. While organisations in the UK are endeavouring to emphasise diversity, it is important for organisations to consider the impact of diversity on customers, suppliers, employers, shareholders and the public. All these considerations will take some time to ensure that ethnic minorities are fairly represented in both the public and private sectors.

Australia has always been a multicultural society, as a nation that has received waves of immigration since 1788; however, multiculturalism became an official policy in 1973, replacing the White Australia policy. Multiculturalism is so valued in Australia that former Prime Minister Bob Hawke (Foster and Stockley 1988) stated the developing process of a multicultural society for 200 years. However, diversity in Australia poses challenges at all levels of organisations, and must be managed both internally (because of changes in the workforce) and externally (because of changes in customer populations and global markets). It is important to examine the effect of these changes on the national economy, and the way such changes are managed in organisations as a result of the increased diversity in the workplace. Diversity management is a result of globalisation; thus, diversity is necessary to ensure strategic success in major organisations to enable them to gain access to global markets. Globalisation affects immigrants from various cultural backgrounds who enter the Australian workforce. However, the government is also seeking to impose national barriers to limit the free movement of people. In addition, both the Australian workforce and global marketplace have significantly changed, and diversity management depends on valuing employees' differences and skills.

Globalisation, worker migration, family reunification, forced migration and environmental disasters have contributed to the growth of demographic multiculturalism in many countries. This growth in demographic diversity has occurred in the traditional countries of immigration, including Australia, Canada and the US, as well as new immigration countries, ranging from Denmark to South Korea (Ng and Bloemraad 2015). Diversity improves equal opportunities in the workplace and society, since differences in people can bring experiences and innovative solutions to problems. Diversity helps business grow both internationally because of intercultural knowledge, and domestically in regard to trade—especially when approaching special target groups, such as women or customers with a background of migration. A diversified workforce facilitates successful entry to new markets. Multicultural employees originating from various countries are useful for international organisations because of their many abilities and skills, which can be important for solving problems. Thus, international organisations should focus on the potential benefits of diversity (Urbancová, Čermáková and Vostrovská 2016).

Organisations that go beyond compliance often adopt an identity conscious approach to diversity, and believe that different employees bring different knowledge to the workplace. These organisations subsequently gain a competitive advantage, and employees know what is expected of them at work, which enables them to use their skills and experience. Strategic management of diversity enables employees to contribute to organisations, and recognition of employees' differences in the workplace constitutes a potential strength in the organisation that can advance businesses. Moreover, multicultural organisations attract and retain employees from various diverse cultural backgrounds, which gives organisations a competitive advantage. Diversity appeals to the best employees and can benefit the organisation, if managed well. Employing a diverse workforce enables organisations to reach improved markets and understand the employees' countries of origin. Communication is another benefit for the organisation, as knowing more than one language is an added economic bonus and a valued skill that employees must have in certain types of employment. This knowledge also protects individuals' jobs during dire economic situations.

A diverse workforce is beneficial to organisations and brings useful skills—such as languages, experience and ideas—which generate growth in opportunities for individuals and challenges for diversity managers. It is critical for management to turn these challenges into opportunities and a source of productivity through successful strategic management of diversity. Productive diversity is of benefit to organisations, as it promotes the corporate image, advances creativity and builds a bridge of better communication and relationships between management and employees in the workplace.

In the US and Australia, the workforce was dominated by white males in the twentieth century. However, today, women and cultural groups are becoming more visible in the workplace; thus, communication skills are essential in the workplace to avoid misunderstandings. In addition, feedback is considered an effective form of communication and an important aspect of diversity management in the workplace. Diversity training is also an essential element in diversity programs to maximise employee effectiveness and increase the attractiveness of the organisation as a place to work. Diversity training enables employees to value their differences and overcome stereotypes, and leads to competitive advantage. In addition, it has been found that organisations search for talented employees, such as students and women on maternity leave, who are offered temporary employment, which can develop into permanent jobs.

There is ample evidence that equal opportunities make good business sense, and organisations that do not employ diverse people lose opportunities to attract various types of customers (Chidiac 2015). In addition, many scholars believe that organisations that reject diversity management miss out on competitive advantage. Diversity is perceived to promote competitive advantage by giving organisations a better corporate image and enhancing both group and organisational performance to entice and retain employees (Ohemeng and McGrandle 2015). Diversity management can increase organisational efficiency, effectiveness, productivity and profitability, and directly relates to job satisfaction, with satisfied employees reporting diversity management as being strong (Ohemeng and McGrandle 2015). Organisations that introduce diversity in the workplace tend to increase productivity and profits; attract highly skilled and professional people (a major advantage of diversity management); and reduce job turnover and absenteeism, which leads to employee retention. These factors are particularly important in the public service, given the competition between the public and private sectors to recruit the most desirable employees (Ohemeng and McGrandle 2015).

However, some critics of diversity management have raised criticisms, as discussed in detail by Ohemeng and McGrandle (2015). Some critics have claimed that diversity management is AA in disguise to avert any negative response similar to the situation that occurred when AA was introduced some decades ago. Additionally, critics argue that diversity management upholds stereotypes in organisations and strengthens the status quo. Diversity management policies do not have quotas for hiring employees, yet many qualified minority employees can still gain the impression that they were recruited because of their minority status, thereby creating resentment. Tokenism causes further problems in diversity management when only one representative of a minority group in the organisation is expected to join many committees and attend numerous meetings, as the token representative of the minority group, which can lead to serious detraction from job performance (Ohemeng and McGrandle 2015). Thus, problems accumulate for senior managers in organisations, which make them reluctant to introduce diversity policies in the workplace.

Today, managers seem to appreciate the benefits of diversity in the workplace and acknowledge that a diverse workforce improves productivity and maximises effectiveness in the organisation. Diversity management has become a reality in contemporary organisations, and it has been found that, when employees face conflicts in the workplace, dissatisfaction arises and employees can resign. Other reasons leading to resignation include low wages and lack of opportunities.

When examining the legal and political aspects of diversity, it is possible to see a number of similarities and differences in the diverse workforce. In Canada, diversity management focuses on the 'business imperative' and the need to fill shortages in the skilled labour force and compensate for the declining population. In the UK, diversity practitioners focus more on corporate reputation, rather than equality, social justice and employee rights. Unions have played a significant role in the growth of workplace culture, but maintain their suspicion of organisations addressing discrimination and inequalities. In addition, trade union presence varies largely between the public and private sectors, and unions favour equalities legislation in the workplace. Equal opportunities policies exist in the majority of UK private sector workplaces. However, while large organisations have policies, the implementation of these policies is not monitored in most UK workplaces. Moreover, discrimination exists in the UK labour market against ethnic and racial minorities and the ageing population, while sexual and gender identity minorities are not supported in the workplace.

Australia adheres to a few methods of diversity management, such as the 'colour-blind' approach, the 'melting-pot' method and the 'multicultural' method. However, the 'equal footing' managers are considered the most effective in managing diversity in Australia. It is believed that Australia will remain dependent on immigration to meet skill shortages, while Australian organisations are still coping with the waves of skilled and unskilled immigrants, especially in terms of their English language skills. The lack of diversity management policies in Australian organisations is due to the fact that diversity is considered a legal obligation, rather than being a source of benefits to the organisation. Further, the passing of some Acts and some amendments to the Australian Constitution in 1996 guaranteed fairness and justice in both society and the workplace. In the meantime, there is no evidence of diversity management being implemented in private sector organisations, hence the lack of legislation and absence of compulsory policies to be enforced in the private sector. The current Australian legal frameworks in the workplace are considered ineffective in the absence of any recognition of the disadvantages faced by different groups of women, indigenous people and low-paid migrants. This necessitates legislation to ensure equity and fairness to all employees, irrespective of gender and backgrounds (Chidiac 2015).

In the US, AA has increased diversity and led to changes in the public sector and military, while organisations in the private sector have their own policies and are subject to prosecution in the absence of fair treatment. In addition, diverse groups have gained representation as a result of a diverse workforce and the implementation of AA. Despite the diverse US workforce, the underrepresentation of minorities and women still prevails, irrespective of the efforts made by the federal government to rectify the situation. The US is described as a 'melting pot' for races and ethnic groups, but most immigrants wished to become Americans, leaving behind difficult pasts to assimilate into a better society. Religion is the major reason for immigrants to flee war and religious persecution, sometimes leading to illegal migration. However, terrorism has led to rejection of Muslims and opposition to constructing mosques. Over 200 years of migration complicated the class formation in the US, with each immigrant group bringing its own culture and competing with other cultures, which led to the formation of the contemporary working-class culture. Undoubtedly, the waves of immigrants seeking better economic opportunities and personal freedom have changed the American people and identity.

The US has mixed feelings regarding its relationship with immigrants. Federal legislation has dealt with the control of immigration through quotas and other laws. The *Chinese Exclusion Act of 1882* prevented Chinese immigration to the US, and legislation in the 1920s restricted immigration from Catholic, Eastern Orthodox and Jewish regions of Europe. Only white Protestants from Northern and Western Europe were welcome as immigrants by Congress. The *Chinese Exclusion Act* repeal in 1943 was a shift in view because of China being an ally in World War II. Further, the *Immigration and Nationality Act of 1965* removed the discriminatory nationality quotas, thereby allowing family unification and skill preferences, and welcoming more immigrants from Asia (Bayor 2016). Today, the contemporary attitude targets Arab Muslim and Hispanic people (Bayor 2016). The election of Barack Obama as President revealed a trend of acceptance, and laws changed to allow refugees, war brides and family members of people living in the US to enter the country. Additionally, citizenship was extended to members serving in the US Armed Forces. A significant change in politics and assimilation for immigrants is the easier communication that is possible with their home countries, supported through emails, video calls, social media and so forth, in contrast to the previous reliance on letters as a means to decide acculturation, assimilation and dual identities. Internet-based forms of communication—such as chat rooms, websites and Skype—have also made it possible to monitor communication and identify terrorism suspects, which was non-existent in earlier times (Bayor 2016).

During the period 1945 to 1970 (see Table C.1), labelled the 'age of inequality', no legislations were passed in Canada, the UK or Australia. The US was the pioneer in introducing legislation dealing with civil rights, immigration, pay equality and age discrimination in employment, which led to Title VII of the *Civil Rights Act of 1946*, the *Immigration and Nationality Act of 1952*, the *Equality Pay Act of 1963* and the *ADEA of 1967*.

During the period 1970 to 1999, known as the 'age of equality', the US introduced three pieces of legislation dealing with immigration reform,

Table C.1 Major Legislative Responses to the Changing Identifications of Diversity in the US, Canada, the UK and Australia

1945–1970 *Age of inequality*	1970–1999 *Age of equality*	2000 + *Age of equity*
US		
Title VII of the Civil Rights Act of 1946 *Immigration and Nationality Act of 1952* *Equality Pay Act of 1963* *ADEA of 1967*	*Immigration Reform and Control Act of 1986* *(also known as Simpson-Mazzoli Act)* *ADA of 1990* *Civil Rights Act of 1991*	*ADA of 1990 and ADAAA of 2008*
Canada		

No legislation	*Canadian Human Rights Act 1985*
	Canadian Multiculturalism Act 1988
	EEA 1995
		Human Resources Management Standards,
		  Standard 4.3, 2008
		Human Resources Management Standards,
		  Standard 4.4, 2008

UK		

No legislation	*Equal Pay Act 1970*
	Sex Discrimination Act 1975
	Race Relations Act 1976
	Disability Discrimination Act 1995
	Gender Reassignment Regulations 1999
		Employment Equality (Religion or Belief)
		  Regulations 2003
		Employment Equality (Sexual Orientation)
		  Regulations 2003
		Employment Equality (Age) Regulations
		  2006
		Equality Act 2010

Australia		
No legislation	*Racial Discrimination Act 1975* *Australian Human Rights and Equal* *Opportunity Commission Act 1986 (amended)* *AAA 1986 (amended)* *Disability Discrimination Act 1992* *Racial Hatred Act 1995* *Public Service Act 1999* *EOWWA 1999 (amended)*	*Age Discrimination Act 2004* *Sex Discrimination Act 2004* *WorkChoices Act 2005 (repealed)* *Fair Work Act 2009* *WGEA 2012*

Source: Based on Silk et al. (2000).

disability and civil rights. In Canada, the major unions, Canadian Labour Congress, Canadian Union of Public Employees, Public Service Alliance of Canada and others focused on workplace equality through AA in the mid-1970s. In 1978, the federal government introduced a voluntary AA program targeting private industry. In 1983, the federal government introduced an AA program aimed at increasing the 'representation of women, Aboriginal and persons with disabilities in the federal public sector' (Public Service Alliance of Canada 2017). In 1985, visible minorities were included in the AA program and the *Human Rights Act* came into force. In 1995, the Canadian Parliament adopted the revised federal *EEA*, which affected the federal public service.

In the UK, diversity-related legislation goes back to the early days of the age of equality, with the enactment of the *Equal Pay Act 1970*, indicating the ineffectiveness of legislation to deal with embedded inequalities (Burns 2009). The 1970s constituted a difficult period, and the *Sex Discrimination Act 1975* was initiated, together with the more comprehensive *Race Relations Act 1976*, which provided similar types of protection to that passed in the other three countries. These three Acts of Parliament (regarding pay, sex and race), together with other regulations, covered all aspects of equality for two decades from the 1970s. In 1972, the UK joined the then European Community (which became known as the EU in 1992) by signing the Maastricht Treaty, which encompassed provisions that lay the foundations for anti-discrimination law. Although the Conservative Party (Tories) passed the *Disability Discrimination Act 1995*, it was not until Tony Blair's 'New Labour' government won office in 1997 that the UK followed the social provisions of EU law (Burns 2009).

In Australia, during the age of equality, the Commonwealth Government and the state and territory governments passed and introduced laws providing protection to people from discrimination and harassment, based on race and disability, thereby following the pattern of the other three countries. Gender equality was also a prime focus, as evidenced by the enactment of the *AAA 1986* and *EOWWA 1999*.

During the period that began with the new millennium, labelled the 'age of equity', the focus in the US has been on disability, marked by the enactments of the *ADA of 1990* and *ADAAA of 2008*. Meanwhile, Canada enacted two HRM standards in the age of equity. Standard 4.3 aimed to ensure a harassment-free work environment for employees, with clear confidentiality rules in complaint processes. Standard 4.4 aimed to provide and promote equity-based business practices at the workplace, including recruitment and selection.

In the age of equity, the UK first enacted Employment Equality (Religion or Belief) Regulations in 2003, which were designed to protect people from discrimination on the grounds of religion or belief or absence of religion or belief. These regulations were introduced to adhere to the EU Directive 2000/78/EC, which was similar to legislation introduced in the US. The aim of the EU Directive was to protect people with a specific sexual orientation, religion, belief and age, and to update the protection against disability, race and gender discrimination. These two regulations in the UK were later superseded by the *Equality Act 2010*, which was introduced on 1 October 2010, including more than 116 separate pieces of legislation to protect the rights of people, promote equality of opportunity for all and protect people from unfair treatment (Equality and Human Rights Commission 2017).

The early days of the age of equity in Australia were dominated by discussions regarding the pay gap between men and women employees. The pay gap in Australia between men and women led to the legislation of the federal *WGEA 2012*, which replaced the *EOWWA 1999*. Employers with 100 or more employees were obliged to report annually to the Workplace Gender Equality Agency.

When examining the practice of diversity management in the US, Canada, the UK and Australia, it is possible to see the transition from the age of inequality to the age of equality and then to the age equity. In the US public sector, EEO or AA policies are implemented, while diversity is used in the private sector. Organisations need management strategies and policies to attract skilled employees and compete. Further, promoting diversity and employing a diverse workforce improves productivity, increases profits and captures more markets. There is a need to value employees as the greatest asset and to include more women and minorities. Organisations realise the benefits of changing their strategies to address the differences in their customer base, and a culturally aware management can influence a business as a global organisation. The US workforce is becoming increasingly diverse with the passage of time, and the labour market has attracted both skilled and unskilled immigrants. The US economy has also been affected by the influx of immigrants, who reduced production costs in factories. Immigrants were attracted to the US based on the political freedom and economic opportunities.

Significant changes occurred in organisations, which affected the workplace as a result of globalisation of markets. Commitment to diversity and inclusion ensures equal and fair treatment in the workplace and reveals a diverse global marketplace. The adoption of US management diversity was based on fairness, equality and inclusive workforce. In the US public sector, diversity management deals with fairness in the federal workplace, while, in the private sector, it is implemented by EEO or AA. The US focus in diversity management is on differences and inclusion of employees of various social groups, not on discrimination. Additionally, the importance of diversity management is that it results in competitive advantages; thus, managers value the benefits of a diverse workforce.

New settlers from various countries have shaped Canada's history, culture and values, and caused Canada to become unique in terms of traditions and customs. Canada is considered the leading nation in accepting immigrants of ethnic diversity backgrounds. Diversity management in Canada is voluntary and replaced employment equity and AA. A diverse workforce in Canada can benefit from talent, since diversity includes people from various ethnic and cultural backgrounds. Similarly, diversity in the workplace helps organisations gain and compete in global markets, as well as gain access to ethnic markets and improve corporate image. The implementation of diversity helps Canadian organisations fulfil their goals and serve their diverse public. Prominent organisations in the Canadian public sector are committed to culture and inclusion, with emphasis on newcomers and ethnic group representation. Their diversity policy provides opportunities to promote, reward and retain the best employees, and attracts newcomers to join the diverse workforce.

Diversity management in British organisations deals with negative and positive outcomes in the workplace, such as the disharmony and challenges caused by diversity, as well as the benefits caused by diversity. Cultural diversity has helped some young ethnic minority groups and women gain promotions to senior jobs, yet has not helped BME employees. Further, there has been a shift from equal opportunities to diversity management in private sector organisations in the UK. Moreover, the benefits of workforce diversity are emphasised by diversity managers in the public sector, unlike their colleagues in the private sector, who focus on the influence of diversity on the bottom-line. Immigration in the UK has had a positive effect on the economy, yet diversity management has been unsuccessful in law firms for people with non-Anglo backgrounds. Although diversity management has failed in the UK private sector, the implementation of diversity management in the public sector has been prompted by adherence to legislative compliance.

Similar to the other three countries, waves of immigration have increased the number of immigrants in the Australian workforce, which has led to the rise of the Australian policy. Although Australian multiculturalism recognises the diversity of cultures, the country has no laws to promote diversity in the workplace, rather than assimilation. Australia is a multicultural society and the workplace has subsequently been affected by multiculturalism, embracing people from various ethnic and cultural backgrounds. Equality, fairness and harmony are provided in the workplace in Australia, yet ethnic and cultural differences are not understood. Thus, workplaces lack the awareness that would enable management to benefit from the skills and experiences of migrants with various ethnic backgrounds.

Languages are considered valuable assets that enable employees to communicate with customers and various cultures. Meanwhile, lack of communication can lead to misunderstanding and conflict, and the use of colloquial English in the Australian workplace can create communication issues in the workplace, especially among employees of CALD backgrounds. It is believed that, in diversity management, diversity enhances the corporate image of organisations in Australia, yielding benefits from multicultural environments at work. While cultural differences can cause conflicts in the workplace because of misunderstandings, benefits can be achieved through the skills and effectiveness of diversity management.

Australian legislation lacks a proactive approach, a commitment to diversity, ongoing training programs and diversity policies to manage ethnic and cultural differences. Diversity is increasing because of Australia's multiculturalism and continuous influx of immigrants. However, there is an absence of diversity policy legislation and lack of recognition of the workforce diversity and cultural differences. Mere adherence to national laws, without proactively managing diversity, is insufficient to address the differences that exist in the Australian workplace. Further, implementation of diversity policies in Australian organisations is overdue, and must be made compulsory, with the onus on management to emphasise the need for a change.

References

Asari, Eva-Maria, Daphne Halikiopoulou and Steven Mock. 2008. 'British National Identity and the Dilemmas of Multiculturalism'. *Nationalism and Ethnic Politics* 14 (1): 1–28.

Banks, James A. 2010. 'Multicultural Education: Characteristics and Goals'. In *Multicultural Education: Issues and Perspectives*, edited by James. A Banks and Cherry A. McGee Banks, 3–26. Wilton: John Wiley & Sons.

Bayor, Ronald H. 2016. 'The Making of America'. In *The Oxford Handbook of American Immigration and Ethnicity*, edited by Ronald H. Bayor, 1–13. New York: Oxford University Press.

Burns, Christine. 2009. 'A Brief History of Equalities Law in the UK'. Accessed 27 November 2017. http://blog.plain-sense.co.uk/2009/02/brief-history-of-equalities-law-in-uk.html.

Chidiac, Emile. 2015. 'A Study of the Strategic Management of Ethnic and Cultural Diversity in Australian Settings: A Multiple Case Study' (PhD thesis, Southern Cross University).

Crowder, George. 2013. *Theories of Multiculturalism: An Introduction*. Cambridge: Polity Press.

Davidson, Alastair. 2007. 'National Identity and Global Migration: Listening to the "Pariahs"'. In *Managing Diversity: Practices of Citizenship*, edited by Nicholas Brown and Linda Cardinal, 17–35. Ottawa: The University of Ottawa Press.

Equality and Human Rights Commission. 2017. 'What is the Equality Act?'. Accessed 28 November 2017. www.equalityhumanrights.com/en/equality-act-2010/what-equality-act.

Foster, L. and D. Stockley. 1988. *Australian Multiculturalism: A Documentary History and Critique*. Avon: Multilingual Matters.

Garr, S. S., K. Shellenback and J. Scales. 2014. 'Diversity and Inclusion in Canada: The Current State'. Deloitte Development LLC. Accessed 18 September 2017. https://www2.deloitte.com/content/dam/Deloitte/ca/Documents/human-capital/ca-en-human-capital-diversity-and-Inclusion-in-canada.pdf

Hardy, Stevie-Jade. 2017. *Everyday Multiculturalism and 'Hidden' Hate*. London: Palgrave Macmillan UK.

Ng, Eddy S. and Irene Bloemraad. 2015. 'A SWOT Analysis of Multiculturalism in Canada, Europe, Mauritius, and South Korea'. *American Behavioral Scientist* 59 (6): 619–36.

Ohemeng, Frank and Jocelyn McGrandle. 2015. 'The Prospects for Managing Diversity in the Public Sector: The Case of the Ontario Public Service'. *A Global Journal* 15 (4): 487–507.

Public Service Alliance of Canada. 2017. 'A Brief History of Employment Equity in Canada'. Accessed 28 November 2017. http://psacunion.ca/brief-history-employment-equity-canada.

Reisch, Michael. 2008. 'From Melting Pot to Multiculturalism: The Impact of Racial and Ethnic Diversity on Social Work and Social Justice in the USA'. *The British Journal of Social Work* 38 (4): 788–804.

Silk, C., R. Boyle, A. Bright, M. Bassett and N. Roach. 2000. *The Case for Cultural Diversity in Defence*. Canberra: Australian Defence Organisation.

Urbancová, Hana, Helena Čermáková and Hana Vostrovská. 2016. 'Diversity Management in the Workplace'. *Acta Universitatis Agriculturae et Silviculturae Mendelianae Brunensis* 64 (3): 1083–92.

Index

Note: Page numbers in *italics* and **bold** denote references to Figures and Tables, respectively.

11 September 2001 3–5, 22, 23, 34, 130, 155; *see also* post-9/11 era
Abbott, Tony 28, 30
Accessibility for Ontarians with Disability Act 2005 133
Act to Encourage Immigration *see* Immigration Act of 1864 (US)
ADA Amendments Act (ADAAA) 1990 (US) **86, 161, 162**
advocacy, definition of 31
AFC Enterprises 127–8
Affirmative Action (AA): criticism for 90; diversity management program 73; as driving force in diversity 40; employer response to 89–90; employment quotas 112; federal contractors and 81; linking to workplace diversity 60–1; managing diversity vs. 56; success of 90; training programs 144; US requirements in 90–1, 112, 159–60
Affirmative Action Act (AAA) 1986 (Australia) 107, **108,** 112, **161**
African Americans, in labour force 42
age, diversity openness and 72
Age Discrimination Act 2004 (Australia) **109, 161**
Age Discrimination in Employment Act (ADEA) of 1967 (US) 85, 160, **161**
age of equality **29,** 160–2, **161**
age of equity **29, 161,** 162–3
age of inequality **29,** 160, **161**
Ajegbo, Keith 154
Aluko, Y.A. 71
Amendments Act of 2008 (US) **88**

American Indians 7
American schools, teaching patriotism in 10
Americans with Disabilities Act (ADA) of 1990 (US) **86, 161**
America On Line 125
Anarchist Exclusion Act *see* Immigration Act of 1903 (US)
anti-communist projects 8
anti-discrimination laws 89–90
anti-harassment policies 144
anti-multiculturalism discourse 5
anti-racism policies 99
Appelbaum, Steven H. 6
Asari, Eva-Maria 126
Asian Exclusion Act *see* Immigration Act of 1875 (US)
Asian immigration 4–5
Asianisation 33
Asian population, in United States 8, 40
Asiatic Barred Zone Act *see* Immigration Act of 1917 (US)
Asiatic Exclusion policy (US) 8
assimilation: immigrant 16, 21, 23, 24, 28; workplace 105
assimilation, immigrant 136–7
attitude 142
attraction, retention and promotion 105
Australia: assimilation policy 107, 136–7; benefits of diversity management in **141;** changing identifications of diversity in 29; changing nature of diversity 28–30; community language skills 139;

Community Relations Commission for Multicultural New South Wales (Australia) 50; core social values 32–3; corporate social responsibility in 106; cultural and linguistic statistics **26**; diversity policies 144–6, 165; male dominated workforce in 69; migrant influx 25; as multicultural society 24, 28, 137; organisations complying with legislative requirements 107; population statistics 25–26, **25**; social consensus of 33; women employees 107; *see also* legislation, Australian diversity-related; multiculturalism, Australian
Australian Council of Social Service 30
Australian Defence Organisation 114
Australian Human Rights Commission 110–11, 112
Australian Labor Government 24
Australian Public Service (APS) 111, 143
Australian Social Inclusion Board 30
Australian workforce: colour-blind managers 105, 159; communication between management and employees 140–2; demographic changes in 110; melting pot managers 105, 159; *see also* legislation, Australian diversity-related
Automatic Data Processing 125
awareness-raising activities 144, 145

Bank of Montreal 132
Bayor, Ronald H. 9
Berry, John W. 12
Betts, Jim 128
Bhadury, J. 68
Bhanugopan, Ramudu 143
black, Asian and minority ethnic (BAME) groups 48
Blair, Tony 22
Blake, S. 56
Bleijenberg, I. 60–1
blind approach to diversity management 59–60
Bliss, Michael 11
Bloemraad, Irene 4
Blunkett, David 22
Bowen, Chris 31
Bracero Agreement of 1942 (US) **83**
British identity 5, 23, 155

British Nationality Act 1948 (UK) 18
British Nationality Act 1981 (UK) 21
broad definitions of diversity 63–4
Bush, George W. 5
business expansion, diversity as tool of 141–2
business imperative 97–8, 159
Butler, M. 62

CALD (Culturally and Linguistically Diverse) backgrounds, benefits of 138–9
Cameron, David 5, 23, 155
Canada: business imperative 97–8; Department of Canadian Heritage 44; dependence on immigrants 46; diversity and inclusion staff size **47**; diversity management model in 95; employment/unemployment rates **45**; immigrant population by place of birth **14**; labour force gap 46, 155–6; labour market growth **47**; negative legislation 95; official language education policy 154; population by ethnic origin in **14**; population growth 45–6; positive legislation 95; public sector 132–4; racial discrimination in 99; skilled labour shortage 46, 98; visible minorities 13–15, **15**, 98–9, 132, 162; voluntary corporate approach to diversity management 131; workforce diversity 44–7; workforce participation rates **45**; workplace compliance culture 46–7; *see also* laws, Canadian diversity management; multiculturalism, Canadian
Canadian Charter of Rights and Freedoms (CCRF) 94
Canadian Human Rights Act 1985 94, 95–7, **96**, **161**
Canadian Human Rights Commission 97, 99
Canadian Multiculturalism Act 1988 11–18, 94, **96**, 99–100, 155, **161**
case studies, Canada: Bank of Montreal 132; Royal Bank of Canada (RBC) 133–4; state of Ontario 132–3; TD Canada 132
case studies, UK 134–6
case studies, US: AFC Enterprises 127–8; America On Line 125;

Automatic Data Processing 125;
Choice Hotels 128; Dell 128;
Denny's 128; DiversityInc 129;
Domino's Pizza 128; Hanes and
Boone 125; Kodak 127; Minneapolis
Fire Department 124; PepsiCo
124–5; public sector 124; Verizon
127; Walmart Stores Inc. 126
categorisation-elaboration model 57
Cattalini, H. 31
Chidiac, Emile 141
Chinese Canadians 132
Chinese Exclusion Act of 1882 (US) 81,
82, 160
Chinese Exclusion Repeal Act of 1943
see Magnuson Act of 1943 (US)
Chinese labourers 80–1
Choice Hotels 128
Civil Rights Act of 1866 (US) 7
Civil Rights Act of 1991 (US) 87, **161**
Clancy, G. 32–3
Collins, J. 27, 32
colloquial language 139–40
colour-blind managers 105, 159
Commonwealth Immigrants Act 1962
(UK) 18, 20
Commonwealth Immigration
Restriction Act 1901 (Australia) 24
communication: to achieve goals and
control destinies 65–6; colloquial
language 139–40; English literacy
and 142; feedback 71, 157–8;
hearable difference 72; knowledge
of people's backgrounds to increase
71; leading to misunderstandings and
conflicts 164; slang 139–40; weak
68; *see also* language
communication skills 66, 70–1, 138,
157–8
communitarian multiculturalism 3
community language skills 139
Community Relations Commission
for Multicultural New South Wales
(Australia) 50
Conference Board of Canada 46,
93, 98
Convention 100 (Australia) 106
Convention 111 (Australia) 106
Corporate Equality Index 128–9, 132
corporate multiculturalism 5
corporate reputation 159
corporate social responsibility
(CSR) 106

cosmopolitan citizenship 21–2
cost savings by managing diversity
66–7
Cox, T. 56, 142
creativity/innovation 66, 140–1
criticisms of diversity management 158
cross-national diversity management
64–5
cultural diversity: Australia embracing
26; democracy and 54; effectively
managing 59; management for 61;
management of 61; success factors
of 61
cultural plurality/pluralism 1–2, 11
cultural racism 144–5

Dalton, Linda 143
Damar, H. 68
D'Amico, C. 42–4
Deane, William 32
De Cieri, H. 63
Declaration of Human Rights 1948
(United Nations) 55
Deferred Action for Childhood Arrivals
(DACA) Program Expanded of 2014
(US) **88**
Deferred for Parents of American and
Lawful Permanent Residents (DAPA)
of 2014 (US) **88**
deism 4
Dell 128
democracies: managing cultural
diversity 54; rule of law and 54;
variations in 54; voting, as a duty
54; voting, as a right 54
Denny's 128
Department of Canadian Heritage 44
Disability Discrimination Act 1992
(Australia) **109, 161**
Disability Discrimination Act 1995
(UK) **103, 161, 162**
discrimination: direct indicator of
70; indirect indicators of 70; racial
and ethnic 62, 69–70; reluctance to
acknowledge 70; *see also* workplace
discrimination
DiTomaso, N. 63
diversity: broad definitions of 63–4;
difference vs. 91–2; intrinsic value
of 125; referring to demographic
cultural differences 13; as tool of
business expansion 141–2
diversity awareness 126

Diversity Council Australia 114
DiversityInc 129
diversity management, definition of
  60–1
Diversity Management Competency
  Model 143
diversity management programs,
  implementation of 72–4
diversity openness, age and 72
diversity training *see* training programs
D'Netto, Brian 107, 142, 143, 144
Domino's Pizza 128

Economist Intelligence Unit 92
Edewor, P.A. 71
Eisenhower, Dwight David 81
El Sherif, F. 72
Emergency Quota Act of 1921 (US) 83
employee commitment 141
employee relations, improving 64
employers of choice 93
Employment Equality (Age)
  Regulations 2006 (UK) **104, 161**
Employment Equality (Religion or
  Belief) Regulations 2003 (UK)
  104, 161
Employment Equality (Sexual
  Orientation) Regulations 2003 (UK)
  104, 161
Employment Equity Act (EEA) 1995
  (Canada) 95, **96**, 97, **161**
Employment Standards Act 2000
  (Ontario, Canada) 133
England *see* United Kingdom (UK)
English literacy 142
English nationalism 18–19
Enhanced Border Security and Visa
  Entry Reform Act of 2002 (US) **87**
Equal Employment Opportunity
  (Commonwealth Authorities) Act
  1987 (Australia) **108**
Equal Employment Opportunity
  (EEO): diversity management vs.
  111; diversity policies vs. 145;
  employer response to 89–90; federal
  enforcement of 82; managing
  diversity vs. 61, **61**; training
  programs 144
Equal Employment Opportunity
  Commission (EEOC) 82
equal footing 105
equal footing managers 105
Equality Act 2010 (UK) 135, 163

Equality Pay Act of 1963 (US)
  160, **161**
equal opportunity 56
Equal Opportunity for Women in the
  Workplace Act (EOWWA) 112,
  161, 162
Equal Opportunity for Women in the
  Workplace Agency 112
Equal Pay Act 1970 (UK) **103,
  161, 162**
Equal Pay Act of 1963 (US) **84**
ethnic discrimination *see*
  discrimination
ethnic diversity: in Canadian
  population 13, 99, 131, 148, 163–4;
  in organisations 59; in United
  Kingdom 18; in United States 7, 40
ethnicity multiculturalism 12–13
ethnic penalties 70
ethnic/religious minorities in United
  Kingdom 48
ethnocentrism 129–30
ethno-cultural diversity 16
European multiculturalism 2
Evans, A.J. 69
Executive Order No. 8802 of 1941
  (US) **83**
Executive Order No. 10925 of 1961
  (US) 81–2
Executive Order No. 11246 in 1965
  (US) 81–2, 85
Executive Order No. 11375 in 1967
  (US) 81, 85
Executive Order No. 11478 of 1969
  (US) 85
Executive Order No. 12138 of 1979
  (US) 86
Executive Order No. 13087 in 1998
  (US) 87
Executive Order No. 13152 of 2000
  (US) 87
Executive Order No. 13279 of 2002
  (US) 87
Executive Order No. 13672 of 2014
  (US) 88
Ezeanu, E. 145

fairness, organisational 123–4, 159
Fair Work Act 2009 (Australia) **161**
fear, effect on diversity 62–3
feedback 71, 157–8; *see also*
  communication
Finn, Chester 10

foreign-born populations 2, 3, 13, 83, 154
Foster, L. 91
Fraser, J.M. 28
Fraser, Malcolm 28
Freeman, Gary 20
Fullerton, J. 65

Gandz, J. 68
gender neutrality 113
gender participation in workplace 68–9
Gender Reassignment Regulations 1999 (UK) 103, 161
global importance of diversity management 125
globalisation: of Australian economy 106, 156–7; demographic diversity and 41, 112; diversity management as natural outcome of 50; effecting migration 50–1; increasing number of nation-states 153
global markets 49, 50, 128, 132, 156, 163–4
global migrant 153, 155
Gordon, Tiane Mitchel 125
Grant, Stan 145
Grassby, Al 31
Great Britain *see* United Kingdom (UK)
Greene, A.M. 136
Guiora, Amos N. 5

Halikiopoulou, Daphne 126
Hanes and Boone 125
Hanson, Pauline 4, 33
Hart-Celler Act (US) 1965 amendments 85
Hart-Celler Act of 1964 (US) 81, 84
Hartman, Ellen 127–8
Hawke, Bob 28, 156
Hawkins, Robert 91
hearable difference 72
Henry, O. 69
Hiranandani, V. 13–15, 99
Hispanics 8, 40, 42
Hodge, B. 33
Holland, P. 111
home-grown terrorism 5
homophobia 3
Hood-Phillips, Rachelle 128
Howard, John 30, 112
Hsu, Madeleine Y. 8
Hubbard, E.E. 145
Hudson Institute 92

human mobility 2
human resources, attracting and retaining 65
Human Resources Management Standards Standard 4.3 2008 (Canada) 96, 161
Human Resources Management Standards Standard 4.4 2008 (Canada) 96, 161
Human Rights and Equal Opportunity Act 1991 (Australia) 108
Human Rights and Equal Opportunity Commission Act 1986 (Australia) 108, 161
Human Rights Campaign 128–9
Human Rights Campaign Foundation 132

identity blind option to diversity management 59–60
identity conscious approach to diversity 60, 157
Illegal Immigration Reform and Immigrant Responsibility Act of 1996 (US) 87
immigrants, forming self-segregating parallel societies 5–6
Immigration Act 1971 (UK) 20–1
Immigration Act of 1864 (US) 82
Immigration Act of 1875 (US) 80, 82
Immigration Act of 1891 (US) 82
Immigration Act of 1903 (US) 83
Immigration Act of 1917 (US) 83
Immigration Act of 1952 (US) 81
Immigration Act of 1965 (US) 81
Immigration Act of 1990 (US) 86
Immigration and Nationality Act of 1952 (US) 81, 84, 160, 161
Immigration and Nationality Act of 1965 (US) 85, 160
Immigration and Refugee Protection Act (Canada) 98
Immigration Reform and Control Act of 1986 (US) 86, 161
inclusion and exclusion duality 69
inclusion lens program 133
inclusion paradigm 30–2
Indian Citizenship Act of 1924 (US) 7
Indigenous Australians 110, 114–15
indigenous peoples 2, 13, 153, 154, 159
Industrial Task force on Leadership and Management Skills 114

industrial union movement 7
innovation and creativity 66
international diversity management 64
international language management 72
international markets 141
Islamist extremism 5, 155

Jamieson, D. 68–9
Janssens, M. 72
Jawor, Anna 3
Johnson, Lyndon 81
Judy, Richard W. 42–4

Kalisch, David W. 25
Kandola, R. 65
Kennedy, John F. 81–2
Kirton, G. 136
Kochan, T. 136
Kodak 127
Kramar, R. 63, 106–7, 111, 114
Krautil, Fiona 107
Kuga, L. 66, 71
Ku Klux Klan movement 8

language: economic value of 65–6;
    identity and 154–5; as means of
    communication 72; in recruitment
    practices 138–9; role in diversity
    management 64; as valuable
    assets to employers 164; *see also*
    communication
language diversity policy 154
laws, Canadian diversity management:
    ban on Sunday shopping 94–5;
    Canadian Human Rights Act 1985
    94, 95–7, **96**, **161**; Canadian
    Multiculturalism Act 1988 11–18,
    94, **96**, **161**; Employment Equity
    Act 95; Employment Equity Act
    (EEA) 1995 95, **96**, 97, **161**; Equity
    Act 1995 97; Human Resources
    Management Standards Standard
    4.3 2008 (Canada) **96**, **161**; Human
    Resources Management Standards
    Standard 4.4 2008 (Canada) **96**,
    161; negative legislation 95; positive
    legislation 95
laws, UK diversity management 100–5,
    103–4, **161**
laws, US diversity management: ADA
    Amendments Act 1990 (ADAAA) **86**;
    Age Discrimination in Employment
    Act (ADEA) of 1967 **85**, 160,
    161; Amendments Act of 2008 **88**;
    Americans with Disabilities Act
    (ADA) of 1990 **86**, **161**; Bracero
    Agreement of 1942 **83**; Chinese
    Exclusion Act of 1882 **81**, **82**, 160;
    Civil Rights Act of 1991 **87**, **161**;
    Deferred Action for Childhood
    Arrivals (DACA) Program Expanded
    of 2014 **88**; Deferred for Parents of
    American and Lawful Permanent
    Residents (DAPA) **88**; Emergency
    Quota Act of 1921 **83**; Enhanced
    Border Security and Visa Entry
    Reform Act of 2002 **87**; Equality Pay
    Act of 1963 160, **161**; Equal Pay Act
    of 1963 **84**; Executive Order No.
    8802 of 1941 **83**; Executive Order
    No. 10925 of 1961 81–2; Executive
    Order No. 11246 in 1965 81–2, **85**;
    Executive Order No. 11375 in 1967
    81, **85**; Executive Order No. 11478
    of 1969 **85**; Executive Order No.
    12138 of 1979 **86**; Executive Order
    No. 13087 in 1998 **87**; Executive
    Order No. 13152 of 2000 **87**;
    Executive Order No. 13279 of 2002
    (US) **87**; Executive Order No. 13672
    of 2014 **88**; Hart-Celler Act of 1964
    81, **84**; Illegal Immigration Reform
    and Immigrant Responsibility
    Act of 1996 **87**; Immigration Act
    of 1864 **82**; Immigration Act of
    1875 80, **82**; Immigration Act
    of 1891 **82**; Immigration Act
    of 1903 **83**; Immigration Act of
    1917 **83**; Immigration Act of 1952
    81; Immigration Act of 1965
    81; Immigration Act of 1990 **86**;
    Immigration and Nationality Act
    of 1952 **84**, 160, **161**; Immigration
    and Nationality Act of 1965 **85**,
    160; Immigration and Refugee
    Protection Act 98; Immigration
    Reform and Control Act of 1986
    86, **161**; Magnuson Act of 1943
    83; Pregnancy Discrimination Act
    of 1978 **86**; quotas and mandated
    targets 109–110; Refugee Act of
    1953 81; Secure Fence Act of 2006
    87; Simpson-Mazzoli Act **86**, **161**;
    Title VII of Civil Rights Act of 1946
    84, **161**; Title VII of Civil Rights Act
    of 1964 **82**, **85**, 88–9, 160

legislation, Australian diversity-related: Affirmative Action Act (AAA) 1986 107, **108**, 112, **161**, 162; Age Discrimination Act 2004 109, **161**; Convention 100 106; Convention 111 106; Disability Discrimination Act 1992 109, **161**; Equal Employment Opportunity (Commonwealth Authorities) Act 1987 **108**; Equal Opportunity for Women in the Workplace Act (EOWWA) 112, **161**, 162; Fair Work Act 2009 **161**; Human Rights and Equal Opportunity Act 1991 **108**; Human Rights and Equal Opportunity Commission Act 1986 **108**, **161**; Human Rights Commission Act 1986 110–111; Public Service Act 1999 111, **161**; Racial Discrimination Act 1975 **108**, 110, **161**; Racial Hatred Act 1995 **161**; Sex Discrimination Act 1984 **108**; Sex Discrimination Act 2004 **161**; WorkChoices Act 2005 **161**; Workplace Gender Equality Act 2012 **109**, 112–13, **161**
legitimisation, issue of 3
Leonard, J. 91
level playing field managers 105
liberal multiculturalism 3–4
limited democracy 18
London bombings 23, 155

Magnuson Act of 1943 (US) **83**
managing diversity, definition of 58; *see also* strategic diversity management
managing for diversity program 73
market share, increasing 65
McGrandle, Jocelyn 158
McLauren, David 64
McMillon, Dough 126
melting-pot belief system 6, 7, 93–4, 129
melting pot managers 105, 159
Merkel, Angela 4–5
Mighty, E.J. 68
Mills, A. 63
Minneapolis Fire Department 124
Mock, Steven 126
Modood, Tariq 4
monolithic organisations 54
Mor Barak, Michàlle E. 127

multiculturalism: advance of 1; in Australia 24–34, 153; in bilingual framework 11–12; in Canada 11–18, 153; core dimensions of 2; definition of 1–2, 154; empirical concept of 1; European approaches to 2; factors effecting 138; failure of 5; features of 12–13; first appearance of 153; logics of 3–4; normative concept of 1–2; paving way to fragmentation and divisions 23; social cohesion shift 16; SWOT analysis of 4, *4*; in United Kingdom 18–24, 153; in United States 6–11, 153–4; war on terror and 137
multiculturalism, Australian: Asianisation and 33; assimilation emphasis 28; Commonwealth Immigration Restriction Act 1901 24; definition of 24; diversity vs. inclusion 30; economic benefits 27; immigrant challenges 27; immigration policies 28; inclusiveness in workplace 26; leading free and equal society 32; oneness, concept of 31; political opposition to 33; political support for 31–2; social inclusion 30–2; social opposition to 32–3; success of 32; White Australia policy 24; *see also* multiculturalism
multiculturalism, Canadian: assimilationist approach to immigration 16; generation status of visible minority populations 15; government policies 13–15; Multiculturalism Act 1988 12; multiculturalism in 11–18; national unity 12; refugee intake 16–17; visible minorities 13–15, *15*; *see also* multiculturalism
multiculturalism, United Kingdom (UK): assimilating immigrants 21; British Nationality Act 1948 18; British Nationality Act 1981 21; Commonwealth Immigrants Act 1962 18, 20; Commonwealth immigration 19–20; cosmopolitan citizenship 21–2; English nationalism 18–19; Immigration Act 1971 20–1; London bombings 23; multiculturalism not succeeding in 23; multiraciality in 21; patrial clause 20–1; postcolonial influx

of immigrants 23–4; race riots 18; shift from race to faith 22; *see also* multiculturalism
multiculturalism, United States (US): Asian communities in 8; Civil Rights Act of 1866 7; ethnic diversity in 7; Indian Citizenship Act of 1924 7; industrial union movement 7; Ku Klux Klan movement 8; as melting pot 6; religion-based discrimination 8; working-class population 7; *see also* multiculturalism
Multiculturalism Act 1988 (Canada) 12, 155
multicultural managers 105
multiraciality 21
Muslims 2, 5, 9–10, 22, 48, 160

Nairn, Tom 18
Nalliah, Daniel 33
Nankervis, A. 111, 138
National Health Service (NHS) 135
Nationality Act 1948 (UK) 153
national origin quotas 81
negative views of diversity management 124
Ng, Eddy S. 4
Noonuccal, Oodgeroo 33

Obama, Barack 41, 160
O'Carroll, J. 33
Ohemeng, Frank 158
Oliver, D. 98–9
O'Mara, J. 68–9
One Nation Party (Australia) 33
oneness 31
Ontario Public Service (OPS) 133
OPS Diversity Office (OPSDO) 133
organisational diversity, benefits of 124
organisational efficiency 158
organisational fairness 123–4, 159
organisations: accommodating reasonable adjustments 72; altering strategies 126; anti-racism policies 99; corporate social responsibility (CSR) 106; diversity management effects on 68; improving productivity 124; increasing profits 124; productivity in 158; voluntary corporate approach to diversity management 131
Orlopp, Sharon 126
the other 2–3
outsiders 91

Page Act of 1875 *see* Immigration Act of 1875 (US)
Palmer, Howard 16
Palmisano, Sam 125
Patterson, A. 33
pay gaps 48, 163
people of color 42
PepsiCo 124–5
perceptions of diversity management 124
Pérez, Antonio 127
performance appraisals 130
persons with disabilities **96**, 97, 162
Peters, P. 60–1
Philippines 8
pluralistic organisations 54–5
plurality 57–8
positive discrimination 90
post-9/11 era 5, 155
post-multiculturalism discourse 5
Poutsma, E. 60–1
Powell, Enoch 22
practical benefits of diversity management 64
Prasad, P. 63, 141
Pregnancy Discrimination Act of 1978 (US) **86**
Price, H.B. 129
private-sector organisations: fairness and 123; in UK 101–2; workplace diversity in 91–2
productivity, organisation 56, 61, 66–7, 74, 93, 97, 116, 124, 137–138, 145, 157–8, 163
protective multiculturalism 3
PSO 136
public sector: state of Ontario 132–3; in UK 101–2; in United Kingdom 134–5; *see also* laws, US diversity management
Public Sector Equality Duty 135
Public Service Act 1999 (Australia) 111, **161**
Public Service of Ontario Act 133

Querling, L. 62

'Race at Work' report 48
Race Relations Act 1976 (UK) **103**, **161**, 162
racial bias 130
Racial Discrimination Act 1975 (Australia) 108, 110, **161**
racial diversity 59, 62, 65, 144–5

racial/ethnic discrimination *see*
  discrimination
Racial Hatred Act 1995 (Australia)
  110, **161**
Racism-Free Workplace Strategy 99
Reagan, Ronald 89
Refugee Act of 1953 (US) 81
Reinemund, Steve 124–5
relationship conflicts 70
religion, as driving force of
  immigrants 9
religion-based discrimination 8
respect for diversity, schools
  teaching 10
Riccucci, N.M. 50, 60–1, 72
Rise Up Australia Party 33
Rising, Jay C. 125
Robbins, S.P. 73–4
Romanenko, A. 74
Royal Bank of Canada (RBC) 133–4
Rudd, Kevin 30
rule of law 54
Ryan, P. 17

sales income 65
Secure Fence Act of 2006 (US) 87
Seidenberg, Ivan 127
Sex Discrimination Act 1975 (UK) **103,
  161**, 162
Sex Discrimination Act 1984
  (Australia) **108**
Sex Discrimination Act 2004
  (Australia) **161**
Shore, Lynn M. 30
Simlin, J. 72
Simpson-Mazzoli Act (US) **86, 161**
Sinclair, A. 144
slang 139–40
social group identity 60, 62
Society for Human Resource
  Management 67, 93
Soldan, Z. 111, 138
Stan Grant Indigenous Employment
  Award 145
stereotypes 6, 58, 62, 73–4, **109**, 158
Stone, J.R. 141
St-Onge, Sylvie 6
strategic diversity management:
  benefits of 63–8; challenges of
  68–72; definition of 56; features
  organisations must implement 58;
  gaining momentum 55; rise of 55–6;
  shift from equal opportunity to 56;
  as voluntary measure 55
Stuart, F. 71

Stuart, M. 62
Syed, J. 114
Syrian refugees 17, 155–6

talent, securing new sources of 64
talent war 67
task conflicts 70
Taylor-Gooby, Peter 23
TD Canada 132
Telstra Corporation Limited 142
terrorism: as driving force of
  immigrants 9; home-grown 5
Thomas, R.R., Jr. 112
Thornton, Margaret 113
Title VII of Civil Rights Act of 1946
  (US) **84, 161**
Title VII of Civil Rights Act of 1964
  (US) 82, **85**, 88–9, 160
tokenism 158
trade unions 101, 159
training programs: awareness-raising
  activities 144; on bullying 68; focus
  of 58; for frontline managers 74;
  maximising employee effectiveness
  158; WE CAN diversity training
  processes 128
Trudeau, Justin 17, 99–100, 155–6
Trudeau, Pierre Elliott 11
Truman, Harry S. 81

United Kingdom (UK): black, Asian
  and minority ethnic (BAME)
  groups 48; British identity 5, 23,
  155; corporate reputation 159;
  Disability Discrimination Act
  1995 **103, 161**, 162; diversity-
  related legislation 100–5, **161**, 162;
  economy 136; Employment Equality
  (Age) Regulations 2006 **104, 161**;
  Employment Equality (Religion
  or Belief) Regulations 2003 **104,
  161**; Employment Equality (Sexual
  Orientation) Regulations 2003 **104,
  161**; employment equity legislation
  48; employment regulation program
  objectives 104; Equality Act 2010
  163; Equal Pay Act 1970 **103, 161**,
  162; ethnic and religious minorities
  in 156; ethnicity of non-UK-born
  population 20; extensive employment
  laws 102; Gender Reassignment
  Regulations 1999 **103, 161**; law
  firms 136; London bombings
  23, 155; population statistics **19**;
  private-sector organizations 101–2;

public sector 101–2, 134–5; Race Relations Act 1976 103, 161, 162; racial harassment and bullying 45–9; Sex Discrimination Act 1975 103, 161, 162; trade unions 101, 159; workforce diversity 48–9; workplace discrimination legislation 103–104; *see also* multiculturalism, United Kingdom (UK)

United Nations, Declaration of Human Rights 1948 55

United Nations Educational, Scientific and Cultural Organization (UNESCO) 1

United States (US): employment status by age and race 43; foreign workers as threat to jobs of US workers 129–30; immigration sources 9; language diversity policy 154; as melting pot 160; occupation distribution of recently arrived immigrants in 41; population 40; population by race and ethnicity 7; protected classes 89; public sector 123; teaching patriotism in schools 10; top 50 companies for diversity 129; white racism in 81; workforce diversity 40–4; workplace demographics 88–9; see *also* laws, US diversity management; multiculturalism, United States (US)

universal equality model 130

US Supreme Court 80

'us versus them' mentality 139

valuing diversity program 73

Verizon 127

visible minorities 13–15, 15, 98–9, 132, 162

voluntary nature of diversity management 63

voting, variations in 54

wage gap 46

wage inequality 92

Waite, Edmund 23

Walmart Stores Inc. 126

war on terror 137

WE CAN diversity training 128

'we' mentality 139

White, R.D. 65

White Australia policy 24, 107, 156

white job segregation 41

white racism 81

women: in Australian private sector 110; joining labour force 89; in the workforce 69

WorkChoices Act 2005 (Australia) 161

work ethic 141

Workforce 2000 report 92

Workforce 2020 (Judy) 42–4

workforce diversity: attraction, retention and promotion 67; in Australia 49–51; benefit of 58–9; in Canada 44–7; as competitive advantage 91; English literacy as barrier in 142–3; male domination in 69; as social justice 91; in United Kingdom 48–9; in United States 40–4, 47, 90–2; women and 69; see *also* laws, US diversity management

workplace culture audit 93

workplace discrimination: Australian legislation related to 108–9; Canadian legislation related to 96; performance appraisals 130; racial bias 130; UK legislation related to 103–4; US legislation related to 82–8

workplace diversity: accepting social identities 62; cultural racism and 144–5; definition of 57; demographic changes in 91; federal legislation 82–4; gender participation in 68–9; in global context 92–3; inclusion and 30–2; inclusion-exclusion in 69; integrating diversity approach 57; introducing specific strategies for 71; leveraging variety approach 57; linking to EEO and AA initiatives 60–1; as natural reflection of diverse populations 57; relationships of management and employees 67; as voluntary measure 163–4

Workplace Gender Equality Act 2012 (Australia) 109, 112–13, 144, 161

Workplace Gender Equality Agency 163

Wrench, J. 69–70

xenophobia 3, 21

Young, Nareen 26

Zanoni, P. 72

Zepeda, Jose 26

Zubrzycki, George 31

Printed in the United States
by Baker & Taylor Publisher Services